Planning to Care

Regulation, procedure and practice under t

Roger Grimshaw and Ruth Sinclair

C000141499

The National Children's Bureau was established as a registered charity in 1963. Our purpose is to identify and promote the interests of all children and young people and to improve their status in a diverse society.

We work closely with professionals and policy makers to improve the lives of all children but especially young children, those affected by family instability, children with special needs or disabilities and those suffering the effects of poverty and deprivation.

We collect and disseminate information about children and promote good practice in children's services through research, policy and practice development, publications, seminars, training and an extensive library and information service.

The Bureau works in partnership with Children in Scotland and Children in Wales.

© National Children's Bureau, 1997

All rights reserved. No part of this publication may be reproduced, stored in a retrieval system or transmitted in any form by any person without the written permission of the publisher.

ISBN 1 874579 94 6

Published by National Children's Bureau Enterprises, 8 Wakley Street, London EC1V 7QE. Telephone 0171 843 6000

National Children's Bureau Enterprises is the trading company for the National Children's Bureau (Registered Charity number 258825).

Typeset by Books Unlimited (Nottm), NG21 9BF

Printed and bound in the United Kingdom by Redwood Books

Contents

List of tables

List of figures

Author's note

For the sake of clarity a number of Figures show percentages rather than actual numbers. Details about the data in the Figures were given in Sinclair and Grimshaw (1996). In the present book the numerical size of the samples is indicated in the text as well as in the Tables.

In creating the bar charts the conversion of numbers into percentages occasionally posed technical problems. Where necessary, the largest percentage has therefore been adjusted by a single percentage point, so as to ensure that the bar reaches exactly 100 per cent.

Acknowledgements

The research discussed in this book was sponsored by the Department of Health and we wish to express our thanks for its sustained support, including a project extension in order to disseminate the findings and consult with local authority representatives.

Research projects of this kind cannot function well in isolation. Our work on plans and reviews has benefited enormously from expert consultation and advice.

We are especially grateful to members of both our advisory groups, at the Bureau and at the Department of Health, for their consistent support and for their insightful comments on drafts of the project report. Harriet Ward, of the University of Leicester, has always given generously of her time as a member of both groups. The advisory group brought together by the Bureau has also included Jane Aldgate, David Bottomley, Neil Grant, David Hodgson and Martin Stephenson. Members of the Department of Health advisory group included Carolyn Davies, Valerie Brasse, Hilary Corrick, Nola Ishmael, Debbie Jones, Helen Jones, Felicity Leenders, David Matthews and John Rowlands.

In carrying out the second phase we were greatly assisted by Christine Chin, who joined us on a student placement from the University of North London. She played a very significant part in facilitating the focus group sessions with young people, as well as helping with the survey of social workers.

We owe a particular debt of gratitude to the many authorities who contributed documents to our surveys and answered our questions. The fieldwork took place in three local authorities which here are called Midshire, Northborough and Westside. Their cooperation and interest helped to make this phase fruitful. Many individuals donated their time to aspects of the research, not least the children who are its focus and, of course, their parents.

A particular vote of thanks should go to those who have collaborated with us at various conferences featuring the research, especially Juliet Coke, Cath Daly, Jane Scott and Hilary Corrick.

Matthew Batchelor, Sabina Collier, Janine Gregory and Kay Rufai have greatly assisted in the production of the book.

To all these people, we offer our appreciation and thanks for their support. Any errors remain, of course, our responsibility.

Roger Grimshaw and Ruth Sinclair
January 1997

Introduction

Child care planning has increasingly been recognised as central to effective social work intervention with children and young people (Howe, 1983; DHSS, 1985; Mallucio, Fein and Olmstead, 1986; Department of Health, 1991a). In recognition of this, care planning has now become a statutory duty in many countries, including those in the United Kingdom. For instance, in England and Wales, the Children Act 1989 requires that every young person who is 'looked after' by a local authority should have an individual Care Plan and that this should be reviewed regularly. Similarly, the importance of reviewing the cases of children in public care is acknowledged within the UN Convention on the Rights of the Child. Article 25 of the Convention calls on signatories 'to recognise the right of a child who has been placed by the competent authorities . . . to a periodic review of the treatment provided to the child and all other circumstances relevant to his or her placement' (see Newell, 1993).

As well as establishing a legal duty to plan for children in public care, the Guidance and Regulations that accompany the Children Act 1989 prescribe, in significant detail, the manner in which this planning and review duty should be fulfilled. To what extent do these Guidance and Regulations facilitate and enhance the quality of child care planning and hence promote the welfare of children and young people being looked after by the local authority? Are local authority social services departments meeting the requirements of the Act and doing so in a way which furthers the principles of the Act? Do the current standards of child care practice enable children, young people and their families to have a clear and active voice in decisions that are made about them? Are plans sufficiently comprehensive, based on adequate assessment of the child's current and future needs?

These are some of the questions addressed by the research reported in this book.

The research study

Contained within the Children Act is a duty for Government to monitor its implementation and to assess the impact on children and families.

That commitment is being fulfilled in a variety of ways, including the commission by the Department of Health of a substantial body of research which will examine the implementation of particular sections of the Act (Department of Health, 1994). The study reported here is part of that programme of research.

The thinking behind this study can only be understood in the context of the Children Act, which represented a decisive landmark in the field of child care. The Act sought to achieve a new coherence in law by enunciating basic principles designed to show how specific provisions should be interpreted. For example, the importance accorded to the child's 'ascertainable wishes and feelings' is the foundation for a series of specific children's rights in decision making; new concepts of parental responsibility, and of a partnership with parents, were placed at the heart of the Act. Its scope was comprehensive. The Act was seen as an opportunity, not simply to reform court procedure but to create an up-to-date framework regulating services for children in the community and in public care. New statutory provisions were applied to the welfare of children 'in need', as well as those being 'looked after' by local authorities. In these ways the Act spanned a broad field of children's welfare.

The oversight of service provision was to be achieved by issuing Guidance and Regulations attached to the statute itself. These were meant not simply to explain legal language but to issue powerful signals about 'good practice' in service provision. These definitions of good practice were informed by three influences: the basic principles underpinning the Act; a perceived need for administrative clarity; and key messages from research that had been absorbed during the Act's long gestation.

Major themes of the Act, such as consultation with children or partnership with parents are echoed again and again in the paragraphs of Guidance. This translation of legal principles into practical prescriptions is a striking feature of the Regulations and Guidance as a whole. In particular sections, the 'good practice' themes were reinforced by administrative standards: the obligations to record consultations and agreements; to make arrangements within timescales; and so on. In this respect there was a positive attempt to embed the principles of the Act inside a well organised system of welfare administration.

The net effect was to outline standards for procedure and practice which reflected a solid consensus about how children's welfare should be safeguarded and promoted. This concept of a standard is not only central to understanding the Act, it is also crucial in defining what this study is about. Standards are intended to provide benchmarks against which a service can be evaluated. They indicate outcomes which should result from a service: they establish clearly what the service should offer to the user and function as a guide both to providers and users about these expectations.

However, standards are not a guarantee that each user will receive the best possible service; they are more like a promise of specific action, attention and consideration. This is an important distinction, which has influenced the nature of this research. Like other studies commissioned by the Department of Health, this research was designed to focus on the standards set by the Guidance and Regulations and to ascertain the extent to which they have been realised. This task is not to be confused with a full evaluation of planning and reviewing in terms of its capacity to meet all the needs of each individual child. That would have required a differently designed study. Instead the evaluation of planning and reviewing in this study has concentrated on relating the standards set by the Guidance and Regulations to procedure and practice in working with all children and young people.

Yet it is important to ask how relevant is all this detailed regulation to practice in individual cases. The standards rest on the assumption that while individual children may have different and even unique needs, potentially they all have a common range of needs that can be identified. While the standards focus on general needs, practitioners are expected to consider particular needs. A question running throughout this study therefore, has been whether the implementation of the standards facilitates the delivery of specific help to individual children: whether for example the local authorities have translated the Guidance and Regulations on planning and reviewing into systems that are likely to affect practice appropriately; whether the practice of planning and reviewing has given an appropriate level of attention to a range of children in different circumstances, being neither scanty nor officious.

The statutory framework

So how has this legal duty towards child care planning and review been framed in England and Wales? Undoubtedly the statutory framework is both detailed and complex. The Children Act 1989 is best viewed as a package: in addition to the actual statute there are several Regulations in the form of Statutory Instruments and eight volumes of Guidance.

The key parts of the Act which relate specifically to planning and reviewing are Section 20 on the provision of accommodation and Section 26 which provides for statutory regulation on reviewing cases. Some of the duties imposed by the Children Act apply only to local authorities, others apply to the 'responsible authority' which may be a local authority or a voluntary organisation or those running a private children's home. Duties in respect of voluntary organisations are contained in Section 61 and in respect of those running a registered children's home in Section 64.

Further detailed requirements on planning and reviewing are contained in two sets of Regulations, the *Arrangements for Placement of*

Children Regulations and the *Review of Children's Cases Regulations*. Appended to these Regulations are several important Schedules which incorporate further matters of detail about the expected content of care plans and matters to be considered at a review.

Good practice in implementing these Regulations is described in Chapters 2 and 8 of Volume 3 of the Guidance and Regulations, *Family Placements* (Department of Health, 1991b) and is repeated in Chapters 2 and 3 of Volume 4 of the Guidance and Regulations, *Residential Care* (Department of Health, 1991c). As this Guidance recognises, the term 'arrangements for placement' is more often referred to as a 'plan' and hence adopts that terminology (Volume 3, Chapter 2, 43); similarly we refer to the planning and review regulations.

Implementation of these statutory duties relating to planning and reviewing must also be guided by the key principles of the Children Act: working in partnership; involving children, young people and their families in decision making; and taking account of all the child's needs, including their racial and cultural background.

It is these statutory duties and Guidance which provide the framework for this research on planning and reviewing.

The research aims

The general purpose of this research study has been to show how far those particular sections of the Act and accompanying Guidance and Regulations relating to the planning and reviewing of the care of children looked after, have had an impact on local authority procedure and practice. The more specific aims of the project were originally identified as:

- to map the way in which local authorities have translated the *Arrangements for Placement of Children* and the *Review of Children's Cases* Regulations into local codes of practice and procedural guides;
- to examine the extent to which the operation of local planning and review systems complies with the Regulations and furthers the underlying principles of the Children Act;
- to consider the contribution of the planning and review process to the total intervention with the child and his or her family;
- to identify ways in which the planning of individual cases can be aggregated to provide useful management information, including information on outcomes.

The first of these aims was fulfilled by carrying out a national survey of the documentation produced by local authorities in England and Wales in order to comply with their statutory obligations. This survey formed the first stage of the research. It was conducted as a discrete piece of work and the detailed results have already been published (Sinclair and Grimshaw, 1995). The second research aim was fulfilled by undertaking an extensive examination, in three local authorities, of the actual practice of care planning and reviewing of children's cases.

The contribution of planning and reviewing to social work intervention was specifically addressed by following up data on the outcomes of decisions and in particular the effectiveness of plans. A survey of the attitudes of social workers and managers on the purpose of planning and reviewing added a further perspective.

The final aim – looking at ways of aggregating individual planning data into management information – was largely overtaken by the development of the Looking After Children (LAC) Project which has adopted this as a major broad objective (Ward, 1995). In order to take account of such a key development, one of the local authorities involved in the fieldwork was selected because it was piloting the first generation of LAC forms. The LAC system represents one way of organising recorded information that may enable local authorities to find ways of converting such data into indicators that can inform the wider policy and service developments.

In addition to those four original aims, it was subsequently decided to undertake a supplementary research study that would examine the arrangements for the chairing of reviews within local authorities. The findings from that additional piece of work are reported here, and their implications are integrated with those of the main study.

As the research progressed, it was possible to draw out some of the emerging themes and feed these back to the community of practitioners via conferences and regional consultative seminars. This helped inform the development of the concluding chapter.

Also as the research progressed, the lack of specific attention to promoting young people's participation became very apparent. This prompted the development of two practice initiatives for young people: the first took the form of a lively training day for young people; the second was the publication of a training guide entitled *It's Your Meeting*. This was specifically aimed at young people and was designed to enable them to get the most from the planning and review process (Wheal and Sinclair, 1995).

The scheme of the book

As the research reported here is primarily an evaluation of the implementation of the Children Act, it is appropriate to begin this book by considering the foundations of that Act: the research messages which informed it and the adoption of a regulatory strategy as the mechanism for ensuring the translation of those messages into new standards for child care practice.

Even Guidance and Regulations as detailed as those relating to planning and reviewing need to be translated into local policies and procedures. The manner in which local authorities in England and Wales went about this task is the subject of Chapter 2. Chapter 3 moves us on from consideration of regulation to an examination of practice. Fieldwork was undertaken in three local authorities, called here Midshire, Northborough and Westside. These three local authorities represent distinctive geographical locations; a Midlands rural district, an inner-city area in the North and a similarly situated area in London. The 'looked after' populations of these three areas contain children from a wide range of different backgrounds and circumstances, yet all subject to the planning and review requirements of the Children Act. This chapter provides some necessary contextual information about the research areas and the relevant characteristics of the children included within the sample.

The next six chapters report the main findings in respect of particular aspects of child care planning and review practice. Chapter 4 presents data about three key components of the planning process, namely inquiry, consultation and assessment. The fifth and sixth chapters take a close look at review meetings, showing how these were organised and conducted. The extent of participation by children and parents is discussed on the basis of research observations as well as on the views of children and their families. Chapter 7 explores some of the issues raised by the variety of arrangements that have emerged for the chairing of planning and review meetings. The eighth chapter evaluates the plans recorded at the review meetings and considers the ways in which children and parents were involved at this stage. Chapter 9 brings together evidence about planning and reviewing as a process. After describing the range of meetings held in respect of each child, it examines the outcomes of the decisions, showing how often decisions were implemented, whether this was done within set timescales and how many unplanned changes occurred.

In the final chapter we return again to discuss the fundamentals of plans and reviews and consider how far the introduction of the Children Act has facilitated the creation of planning and review systems that encourage high standards of practice, furthering the principles of the Act and thereby increasing the chances of good outcomes for children in public care.

1. Plans and reviews under the Children Act 1989

Introduction

Fundamentally, child care planning is about bringing together information from children and young people, their families, carers and professionals in order to plan for the care of the young person and to review that plan on a regular basis. For children in public care or who are 'looked after', this not only requires an understanding of the importance of child care planning, it also requires a recognised procedural framework. Corporate parenting means shared parenting and hence a framework for the sharing of information and tasks, one that helps ensure children and their families are treated with openness and honesty and understand decisions that affect them; it means a structure that provides for accountability by social services staff in exercising their powers and duties.

Turning this understanding of the purposes of planning into a workable system is a task which has preoccupied social services departments in England and Wales since the implementation of the Children Act. Given the bureaucratic tendencies of local authorities and the detailed regulatory framework of the Act, the potential exists for planning and reviewing to be regarded as a fairly mechanistic process, for staff to see this solely as an administrative task, unrelated to their social work skills. Such a tendency may be avoided by going back to first principles, to reconsider the purposes and the benefits of child care planning; to rehearse again the answers to such questions as: 'What are plans and reviews actually for?', 'How can decisions be made in a way that actively involves the child?', 'How can we ensure that planning and review systems do achieve what is best for each young person looked after?', 'How do they help us work in partnership with parents?'

The research study reported here seeks to answer these questions. We begin, in this first chapter, to look back to some of the influences that have informed those parts of the Children Act which relate to planning and reviewing. We trace how these have emerged as a statutory framework and explore the role of a regulatory strategy as a mechanism for changing practice and improving outcomes for children.

The foundations of the Children Act

The Children Act 1989 was a well considered piece of legislation. Its architects drew upon research findings and evaluations of current practice as well as the many reports from child abuse inquiries. By building upon this substantial body of widely disseminated knowledge the Act was able to formalise what was known to be good practice, while at the same time regulating out poor practice. When we examine the Guidance and Regulations on plans and reviews the research base on which these were built is very clearly distinguishable.

The functions of reviews

While the duty to draw up written care plans for each 'looked after' child is a new one, the statutory requirement to conduct reviews of cases has been around since 1955 when it was first introduced into the Boarding Out Regulations and subsequently extended to all children in care by the Children and Young Persons Act 1969. However the way in which this statutory duty was to be carried out was never defined, although the Children Act 1975 gave the power to make such regulation. So there is substantial experience of conducting reviews and a body of research on their operation, effective or otherwise (McDonnell and Aldgate, 1984c; Sinclair, 1984; Gardner, 1985).

During this development of the statutory review its functions emerged rather than being explicit. When the review was first introduced in the Boarding Out Regulations it was primarily for managerial purposes – to monitor the standards of care that were being offered to children by the foster parents who cared for them on a day to day basis on behalf of the local authority. Over time this managerial or monitoring function was extended to social work practice, so reviews became a mechanism for senior staff to re-examine the casework of front line workers.

By the 1980s, following a decade of continuous growth in the numbers of children in care, the issue of planning gained much more prominence. The very influential research, *Children Who Wait*, highlighted the large numbers of children, then resident in children's homes, who were waiting, and had been waiting for a long time, for a foster home placement (Rowe and Lambert, 1973). Subsequently, this study was replicated in-house in many local authorities and the findings invariably demonstrated the lack of any purposeful long-term planning for children within the care system and the consequent damaging drift that characterised so many children's time in care.

This discovery brought the issue of child care planning more clearly onto the agenda and the statutory review meeting was seen as the most suitable forum for fulfilling this planning function. This was clearly the conclusion of the House of Commons Select Committee on Children in Care which reported in 1984 (House of Commons, 1984):

If drift and indecision are to be prevented and if the concept of planning a child's future with some degree of permanence is to have any meaning, the review process must be tightened up.

Reflecting the growing strength of the broader consumer movement, the 1980s saw an increased emphasis on the involvement of young people in decision-making processes. This was another strand in the development of the functions of review. Originally this became articulated as a demand that the revised regulations on reviews, as promised in the 1975 Act, should require that all young people be invited to attend their review meetings (Stein and Ellis, 1983a; Children's Legal Centre, 1984).

So prior to the Children Act 1989 reviews were being asked to perform a range of functions; to monitor the care provided, the social work undertaken and the decision-making processes; to act as a forum for making decisions and for long-term planning; and to provide a mechanism for the involvement of young people and their families. The limited articulation of these functions did cause some confusion. However, as we shall discuss in more detail in Chapter 10, the Children Act acknowledges that the review process must serve a range of purposes and each of these are recognised within the detailed Guidance and Regulations. How well are these different purposes understood; how compatible are they; how can systems best be designed to accommodate them?

The practice of planning

Whatever was seen as the primary function or purpose of the review, the collation by the Department of Health of a substantial body of research in *Social Work Decisions in Child Care* (the 'Pink Book') pointed to significant failings in *all* these aspects of review practice (DHSS, 1985). The active dissemination of these research findings, which resonated with the day to day experiences of staff, increased awareness of the need for new policies and procedures to improve the quality of planning for children.

That body of research presented a set of consistent research messages which identified ways in which the effectiveness of planning could be improved, all of which are specifically addressed by the Children Act (Packman, Randall and Jacques, 1986; Vernon and Fruin, 1986; Fisher and others, 1986; Sinclair, 1984; Ahmed, Cheetham and Small, 1986; Jackson, 1987; Bamford and Wolkind, 1988; Millham and others, 1986; Stein and Carey, 1986). These can be summarised in the following way:

- the need for *structured, open planning*, with managers accepting responsibility for decisions and their implementation;
- the importance of *purposeful planning* which established and communicated coherent long-term and short-term objectives; and *early*

planning to avoid drift and enable children to remain with their families;

- decisions which were *specific*, and which recorded clearly what needed to be done, by whom and when;
- the significance of understanding and taking full account of a child's background, especially in respect of their *race and culture*;
- the importance of assessing and addressing *all the needs of a child*, in particular an increase in the priority to be given to health and education;
- to actively make plans to ensure that children remain in *contact* with their families;
- early and purposeful planning for *leaving care and aftercare support*.

For each identified message it is possible to find a corresponding legislative duty within the Children Act or its Guidance and Regulations. These linkages have been detailed in an earlier report (Sinclair and Grimshaw, 1995).

Young people's views

A growing component in research studies was the perspectives or views of young people on the relevance and effectiveness of planning and reviews. The arguments for involving children in decisions from a children's rights perspective were supported by studies which pointed to the contribution that young people could make to effective planning (Stein and Ellis, 1983a and b; Children's Legal Centre, 1984; Hodgson, 1988; Gardner, 1985). However, these and other studies made it clear that genuine participation by young people required significant changes in the culture and practice of child care planning (Fletcher, 1993; Dolphin Project, 1993). The following quotations from young people (Dolphin Project, 1993) pinpoint neatly aspects of practice that were problematic to them and therefore unlikely to be effective.

They talk about you as if you are not there, so you just shut up – and listen without saying a word.

I never have the courage to talk because I am alone in a room with about five types of social worker. When I do speak everyone doesn't listen.

Because I got angry at a planning meeting I was not allowed to my last meeting and things were decided without me.

. . . many young people thought reviews were unhelpful, and others did not attend . . . . Most young people wanted a quiet discussion before their review with their social worker/key worker. They felt intimidated by large meetings. Sometimes they would have preferred not to have certain people there but felt unable to say so. It was important that planning meetings and reviews were held at times convenient to families and the young person. (Dolphin Project, 1993)

The Guidance states that 'the attendance of the child and his parents at meetings to review the child's case will be the norm rather than the exception' (Volume 4, para. 3.15). It also specifies that children and young people should be consulted about who should attend their review meetings and about the timing and venue for these. The standards which social work practice has achieved in this respect since the Children Act will be discussed in Chapter 6.

Planning and reviewing as a process

In an effort to address some of the concerns expressed by these evaluations, the later half of the 1980s saw the development, in many authorities, of local child care policies and procedures. A survey undertaken in 1987/88 demonstrated the centrality of child care planning to many of these policies, which led to a range of new organisational arrangements for making decisions on individual child care cases.

> The documents demonstrate a clear, general commitment to the concept of planning, both as a technique for avoiding care, and as a way of ensuring that social work intervention in cases of family breakdown is positive, and as limited as is consistent with the interests of the child. (Robbins, 1990, p.23)

As these new policies and procedures derived from local initiatives rather than any statutory directive they were, inevitably, somewhat variable – and bypassed some authorities altogether. When, in 1991, the Department of Health came to publish a second volume of research findings on child care practice, it was possible to report some significant changes, although overall the standard of planning and reviewing was still patchy.

> Considerable progress has been made in establishing the importance of planning for children, and some success achieved in putting it into practice, although disturbing instances of lack of plans are also mentioned in a number of SSI and other reports. (Department of Health, 1991a)

Whereas this new body of research was able to point to a much higher priority accorded to planning for children, it did raise significant concerns about the *evidence* on which plans were being based.

> Sound assessment of the problems and strengths of individual children and families must be based on clear, sufficient and well recorded evidence about past and present functioning. Decisions can only be as good as the evidence on which they are based and if evidence is distorted, ignored or not weighed up carefully, the decisions will be flawed. (Department of Health, 1991a)

Such concerns were an important influence on the evolution of the Assessment and Action Records, the central component of the *Looking After Children* materials. This set of paperwork tools, which were developed contemporaneously with the implementation of the Children Act, is designed to gather evidence, in a consultative way, about the needs of children and young people over seven key developmental dimensions and to link these to the mechanisms for decision making, planning and review (Department of Health, 1991a, 1995a; Ward, 1995).

The importance of a strong evidential base to child care planning is reflected in the Guidance where planning is defined as a four-stage process consisting of inquiry, consultation, assessment and decision making (see 2.43 to 2.59, Volume 3 of Guidance, Department of Health, 1991b).

Here the Guidance clearly perceives planning as an process. How then is this linked to the review, especially to the review meeting, which is more often seen as an event? What is the relationship between planning and reviewing; how is this understood by practitioners? Earlier research studies demonstrated much confusion in conceptual interpretations of the review as either an event or a process (Sinclair, 1984). The Children Act Guidance sought to dispel any such confusions. This study will test how successfully that has been achieved.

Regulatory strategy

In looking at the foundations of the Children Act thus far we have pointed to the translation of individual research findings into specific Guidance or Regulations. This body of research also presented a strong overarching message – that unless standards of good practice are contained within regulations they are unlikely to become the norm across all authorities. It is apparent from the comprehensive package that is the Children Act that this message has been heard – perhaps exemplified by the complex Guidance and Regulations in respect of planning and reviewing.

The regulatory approach of the Children Act can be seen as part of a growing trend whereby central government departments use procedural guidelines as a way of establishing minimum standards. Perhaps the most striking example has been in the field of child protection, where even prior to the Children Act, initiatives from the centre have had a marked impact on local systems (*Working Together*, DHSS/WO, 1988). It can be argued that a broad regulatory movement – what has been called the bureaucratisation of social work – has occurred right across the field of child care, encompassing measures of different legal status, from departmental advice (for example, 'Dear Director' letters) to statutory regulations and there are those who feel the trend has gone too far, that a procedural approach inhibits rather than enhances good social work practice (Howe, 1992; Parton, 1991; Frost and Stein, 1989; Valentine, 1994). Several reasons can be advanced for this growth of the regulatory framework in which child care is delivered.

Past omissions: Many of the weaknesses in child care practice that have been identified through research and public inquires have been due to failures to act as much as ill-conceived or poor practice – what could be deemed to be sins of omission rather than commission (DHSS, 1985; Department of Health, 1991a; Parker and others, 1991). This suggests that a regulatory framework is necessary to ensure that the process whereby social work is delivered leads to high quality services.

Procedural failures: A common thread to the many child abuse enquiries in the 1980s was the failure of the systems to facilitate communication, especially in inter-agency cooperation, leading directly to the *Working Together* guidance (DHSS/WO, 1988; Department of Health, 1991a). Similarly, there was growing awareness of the detrimental consequences of not communicating openly with users of services, including young people (Gardner, 1987b; Lewis, 1992).

A desire for consistency: Where there is limited documentary guidance and hence greater autonomy in following policies and practices, then there may be inconsistency in the services that are offered to children and their families, both within and between local authorities. The drive for greater consistency and predictability in the handling of child care cases was emphasised by the Social Services Inspectorate's reflections on planning (SSI, 1989).

Managerial control: Since the publication of the 'Pink Book' (DHSS, 1985) there has been greater involvement by managers in the decisions taken in individual child care cases. A changing climate towards greater accountability in public services has resulted in more managerial controls, designed to uphold regulatory standards.

Increasing centralised influence: Throughout the past decade and a half there have been complex shifts in the balance of power between central and local government and between headquarters and local units. The autonomy of local authorities has been greatly reduced, for example, in determining their total spending budgets and through the imposition of many more statutory duties. At the same time there has been an increase in decision making by localised units through devolution of budgets and delegation of powers.

Perhaps this is seen most clearly in relation to schools. The 1988 Education Reform Act instituted local management of schools, together with local financial management. However, this Act also brought the National Curriculum. So, while individual schools had been given more autonomy, in practice their freedom of action was greatly constrained by the details of statutory requirements.

Similar trends are apparent in the provision of social services; here an important mechanism of central government in improving quality of service delivery has been the establishment of common statutory standards. Undoubtedly, in comparison to previous child care legislation, the Children Act and accompanying Guidance and Regulations represents a significant increase in the degree of prescription in the execution of statutory duties. Indeed this prescriptiveness was part and parcel of a specific *regulatory strategy*, a strategy whereby the Guidance and Regulations were seen as the key mechanism for changing practice and improving outcomes for children and young people. It can best be depicted as a series of steps, as sketched in Figure 1.1.

Figure 1.1   The regulatory strategy

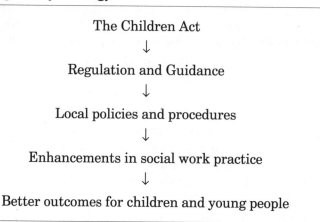

The Children Act
↓
Regulation and Guidance
↓
Local policies and procedures
↓
Enhancements in social work practice
↓
Better outcomes for children and young people

Legislation – here in the form of the Children Act – provides the necessary framework for local authority activity and establishes the standards that such activity is intended to achieve. Yet, by its very nature, legislation, even with accompanying Guidance and Regulations, can never prescribe in every detail the way in which a local authority discharges the responsibilities imposed upon it by statute. Moreover, child care services can only be delivered in the context of the structure and working practices developed within the organisation and that requires coherent local policies and procedures.

So a necessary step for local authorities in fulfilling their statutory duties is to develop local policies and procedures. The creation of these local systems and standards should in turn enhance social work practice and ultimately improve the outcomes for children and young people looked after by the local authorities.

Monitoring the implementation of the Children Act

The research study reported here follows a similar pattern to that of the regulatory strategy. The overall purpose of the research was to examine how far the Children Act and its accompanying Guidance and Regulations in respect of child care planning promotes better practice and facilitates good outcomes for children. The more specific aims of the research relate to different stages of the regulatory strategy.

The first phase – the national survey of local authority policies and procedures – examines the manner in which local authorities across England and Wales have translated the Guidance and Regulations into local frameworks for practice. Did the Guidance and Regulations expedite the development of coherent planning and reviewing systems? Did these meet statutory requirements? Did they promote continuity in care planning? Were they shared and understood by staff from a range of agencies; by parents; by children? Detailed responses to these and other similar questions were reported in an earlier publication (Sinclair and Grimshaw, 1995). An overall evaluation of this step in implementing the Children Act follows in the next chapter.

The second phase of the research addresses a further stage in the regulatory strategy – namely the quality of social work practice in respect of planning and reviewing. Detailed fieldwork in three authorities examined, from a range of perspectives, planning and reviewing practice in almost 180 child care cases. This explored the outcomes from the decision-making process. It went some way, but only some way, to follow the final stage in the regulatory strategy. However, the research was not designed to be a full evaluation of planning and reviewing in terms of its capacity to meet all the needs of each individual child. Such a fundamental evaluation would seek to establish indicators of need, in order to evaluate the relevance of assessments and plans to the needs of individual children. It would take direct measures of the quality and quantity of service delivery, following from care plans. It would also entail close attention to a whole range of child- and family-centred outcomes, including satisfaction and changes in behaviour as well as changes in status (reunification with parents, adoption and so on). Such a study would require a longitudinal methodology, collecting initial baseline data and then detailed information about subsequent services and outcomes. It would, in one sense, be a great deal more than a study of planning and reviewing (Cullen and Hills, 1996; Courtney, 1993).

Rather, the evaluation of planning and reviewing in this study has concentrated on relating the standards set nationally, by the Children Act, its principles and Guidance and Regulations, to local procedures and practice in working with all categories of children and young people looked after.

2. From regulation to procedure

Introduction

In the first two sections of this chapter we bring together the findings from a national survey of local policies, procedures and information concerning plans and reviews. An extended presentation can be found in our earlier publication (Sinclair and Grimshaw, 1995). In further sections, the issues following on from the survey are explored, particularly the possible tensions between establishing administrative consistency and making good judgements in the interests of individual children.

In March 1993, letters were dispatched to all local authority Social Services Departments in England and Wales, asking for copies of any current local documentation concerned with plans and reviews, including:

- policies
- procedures
- forms
- information leaflets for children and for parents.

Respondents were also asked for further details about the origins, purpose and significance of individual documents. With the help of a follow-up letter, there was an excellent response rate, with 80 authorities (from 116 approached) sending material in some form.

Creating and distributing local planning and review documentation

First of all, we report how this documentation was produced, what consultations had taken place, who authorised them and who was intended to receive and read them. We consider these matters in relation to each of the four types of documents, starting with policies and procedures.

Documents on policy and procedure

In all, we received just 42 policies and no less than 72 procedures. Table 2.1 compares the data on each type. Most had come into operation as a response to the Children Act. They were also documents of some significance: the median numbers of copies distributed was at least 200 in each case.

Preparation of the documents had been undertaken by an officers' working party in almost half the cases. In only one authority did a joint officer/member group prepare a policy document. The pattern of authorship for policy documents was similar to that discovered by Robbins in her broad review of child care policies (1990).

Given the emphasis in the Children Act on partnership and interdisciplinary working it was important to find out whether significant groups had been consulted. Health and education authorities and other local authority departments had been consulted in less than a third of cases. Furthermore, consultations with child or parent advocacy groups or with representatives of minority ethnic groups took place in less than one case in ten. The pattern of consultation for both procedure and policy documents was therefore depressingly similar. On policy, only a quarter of authorities consulted other voluntary groups, some of which may be looking after children under the Regulations.

The authorisation of policy and procedure documents was most often undertaken by a social services management group. Social services committees were the next most frequent authorisers of policy documents. (This contrasted with the Robbins' survey of policy in the 1980s, where the social services committee was the most frequent agent of authorisation.) Approval by a management group of the local authority or by the full council occurred much less frequently.

The main perceived objective of the policy and procedure documents was to communicate with social services staff. Policy documents were more often intended for outside audiences than were procedures: for example, two thirds of policy documents were also meant to address other professionals, compared with only four ninths of procedure documents. The availability of copies mirrored this list of priorities. Not surprisingly, they had very frequently been given to senior managers, team leaders and unit managers. Though three quarters of authorities gave procedure documents to social workers, they were reported to have received copies of policies in just less than two thirds of cases; disappointingly, care staff received documents in no more than half the cases. Given that communication with social services staff was a widely recognised objective, higher circulation figures might have been expected for these categories.

The proportions of education and health authorities which received copies of either policy or procedure documents ranged from one fifth to just two fifths. Copies for parent or child advocacy groups or representatives of minority ethnic groups were mentioned by very few authorities; indeed, less than a fifth of respondents mentioned giving a copy of their policy to other voluntary groups, while hardly any had shared their procedures with such groups.

Only one third of the sample authorities had definitely published policy documents but these had not been widely publicised; very few of the procedural documents were in the public domain. In general, the circulation of documents appeared focused on internal audiences and even in this respect was hierarchically organised, with some key operational groups dependent on other sources for their information about policy and procedure.

Table 2.1   The policy and procedure documents compared: a summary of the evidence

	Policy	Procedure
Sample size	N=42	N=72
Copies distributed (median)	250–300	200–250
	per cent	*per cent*
Preparation by officers' working party	48	49
Consultation with: health	31	29
education	26	25
minority ethnic group representatives	7	1
child or parent advocacy group	7	6
other voluntary groups	26	7
Authorisation by social services management	62	74
Copies for: social workers	62	75
care staff	45	49
health	31	22
education	38	28
minority ethnic group representatives	5	1
child or parent advocacy group	5	1
other voluntary groups	17	7
Published	33	6

Plan and review forms

The forms used locally represent another key dimension of the implementation of the Guidance and Regulations. How were they produced and who received copies? To answer these questions we sampled one form from each package of documentation and looked at the further information about it supplied by the local authority. The great majority of responses contained such additional information. Information about 72 *individual* forms – the same number as for procedures – was thus available, dealing with various aspects of planning and reviewing. This is summarised in Table 2.2. Virtually all had come into effect between 1991 and 1993. The median number of these forms distributed by local authorities lay between 305 and 325.

Like policies and procedures, the responsibility for preparing the forms lay most commonly with an officers' working party (50 per cent), followed by an individual author consulting with others (40 per cent). Consultation with other agencies was reported to have taken place in only 29 per cent of authorities, other local authority departments being mentioned by only one in ten. Table 2.2 reaffirms the pattern of low rates of consultation with significant agencies and groups with an advocacy role and shows that significant external agencies and groups were less frequently recipients of the forms. The forms had a low public profile, only ten per cent having been definitely published.

Table 2.2   Sample forms (one per authority)

Sample size	N=72	
Copies distributed (median)	N=305–325	
	Consulted	*Receiving copies*
	per cent	*per cent*
Health	19	22
Education	15	26
Child or parent advocacy group	6	2
Minority ethnic group representatives	1	1
Other voluntary groups	8	6

The content and language of forms

Further evidence was derived from closely examining the whole *group* of forms contained in 77 local authority packages. The major issue to be explored was the range of functions associated with the forms – especially inquiry, assessment, consultation and decision making in relation to plans and reviews (Department of Health, 1991b, Volume 3 of Guidance). What were the sets of forms supposed to do?

Inquiry and assessment was a widely represented function of the forms, identifiable in over two thirds of cases. As Table 2.3 demonstrates, consultation with children and parents was slightly less prevalent as a function, but only a minority contained forms for consulting education, health and other groups. Under one third included a form outlining the agenda. The most frequent functions, however, were to record a plan for a child, and to record a meeting. But following up the meeting was not such a common function. Some means of notifying the result of a meeting was identified in less than half the packages, and only a third showed a form with a monitoring function.

Table 2.3   Functions of forms

Sample size	N=77
	per cent
Inquiry and assessment	69
Consultation with: child	56
parent	53
education	23
health	18
other	27
Planning	91
Agenda for meeting	29
Recording a meeting	84
Notifying the result of a meeting	46
Monitoring plans and reviews	30

Clearly, the planning function was a predominant feature of the forms, but there are several issues to be addressed in the planning process. As Table 2.4 indicates, provision for signed agreements was very frequent. Given the requirement to promote partnership, this was an encouraging sign. However, while most contained a space for long-term plans to be recorded, less than half had room for an overview of changes in the child's life.

Table 2.4   Planning issues dealt with by the forms

	per cent
Space for signing agreements	84
Space for long-term plans	64
Space for overview of changes	47

The focus of planning on an individual placement was apparent where it was made very clear that the 'placement plan and agreement' constituted the plan for the child, apparently requiring a new form to be completed if circumstances changed. For example:

> This form constitutes the plan for the child/young person while accommodation is being provided. It must be regularly reviewed *and* redrawn when there are *any significant changes* eg change of carer/placement, change in legal status. (emphases added)

Care plans, however, have to be more than 'arrangements for place-ment' in the narrow sense. The use of a separate form for each place-ment, found in the majority of cases, highlighted the significance of this distinction between *plans* and *placements*, which is also reflected in the recent revisions of the *Looking After Children* forms.

Forms were typically fairly detailed, very few offering merely a list of headings. The goal of more detailed and comprehensive information led to an expansion of the number of pages. There was a very large range here, from one authority with a bare two pages to one submitting 132 pages! The median number of pages was 27. The size of the task under-taken by the designers of local authority forms became obvious. It is not surprising that the series of forms designed by the *Looking After Children* (LAC) project created considerable interest. In fact, even at this early date in 1993, 14 per cent of authorities included forms based on the Assessment and Action Record or stipulated its use. The same propor-tion had adopted the LAC Review form. It was to be expected therefore that there were demands for the LAC forms to take on further tasks; the subsequent development of the LAC forms into a comprehensive pack-age has at the time of writing attracted the support of most authorities.

The language used in forms is of particular importance when they are intended for use by children or their parents; we felt the language used in the consultation forms did occasionally present problems. For exam-ple, one form addressed 'other participants' views' with the injunction:

> As appropriate to your involvement with user, state any issue you wish to be discussed at the meeting.

In another example the child was termed 'the User' and given a blank sheet headed '*YOUR VIEWS*'. In the same fashion, there were four instances where the language used was considered likely to raise any doubts in someone from a minority culture, religious persuasion or eth-nic origin. In one example, keeping 'in touch' was the only issue cited in relation to 'race', yet it might be asked whether racism was not also an appropriate topic.

Information about plans and reviews

The survey identified 29 authorities with items of explanatory informa-tion about plans and reviews – just over a third of the total sample. In cases where the data was available, all but one had come into effect between 1991 and 1993. The median value for the distribution of these information items was between 300 and 450.

Some of the information was purchased from outside sources and in these cases the process of preparation was not relevant. Nonetheless, unlike the other types of documents, the information items were most frequently reported to have been prepared by an individual author (52 per cent) rather than an officers' working party (28 per cent). Consultation with other agencies apparently took place in one out of three instances. Reports of specific consultations were consistently low, numbering less than ten for all the specific agencies and groups considered in Table 2.5. No instance of consultation with representatives of a minority ethnic group was mentioned.

Table 2.5   Information about plans and reviews

Sample size		N=29
Copies distributed (median)		N=300–450
	Consulted (numbers)	*Receiving copies (numbers)*
Health	4	5
Education	3	7
Parent advocacy group	2	0
Child advocacy group	3	0
Minority ethnic group representatives	0	0
Other voluntary group	0	3
Published	12 (41 %)	

Authorisation of the information was most often given by a social services management group. The overwhelming purpose was communication with parents (69 per cent), children (52 per cent) and other relatives (48 per cent), while professionals and other agencies were the intended recipients in a minority of cases.

Issuing copies of information was a different process from deciding the target audiences. Social services staff were reported to be the leading recipients, with care staff again left trailing behind (38 per cent). Parents and children were recipients in 45 per cent and 28 per cent of cases, respectively, and foster carers in only 17 per cent of cases. It appeared that a major responsibility for the distribution of the information was given to practitioners. However, the possible role of care staff and foster carers in this respect did not appear to be well recognised. Other agencies and groups with an advocacy role might also be expected to perform such a role but there was very little evidence of them receiving copies.

There seemed to be an even split between those available to the general public and those not so available. However, levels of publicity were not reported to be high. Thus, 24 per cent were publicised through libraries, 7 per cent through the local press, 14 per cent through public meetings and 17 per cent through other means.

There was limited information provided specifically for children and parents. Table 2.6 reveals that, on key topics, outline or fairly detailed information was available in little more than a dozen cases. It is significant that, from a total sample of 80 local authorities, the number offering simple outline information on a range of important questions was remarkably low. The general clarity and style of the information also on occasions left something to be desired: only 13 cases were rated as positive or good.

Table 2.6   Information presented in outline or some detail

Topic	For Children	For Parents
Consultation	10	14
Comprehensive planning	7	8
Issues of ethnicity, culture, religion and language	7	7

Minority languages and translation

In view of the significance of language and cultural issues within the Guidance and the Act as a whole, it was important to ask whether the various documents were available in minority languages, including those for people with special needs. As shown in Table 2.7, the responses to these questions indicated that the availability of documents of all kinds was very limited. The least translated documents were *procedures*: only one response confirmed the availability of procedures in minority group languages (Bengali, Arabic and Cantonese). In two cases, procedures were reported to be available in special languages such as Braille or tapes. The picture was only marginally different for *policy documents*: only three positive responses giving rise to four examples – Bengali (2), Arabic (1) and Cantonese (1). Just three authorities made policies available in languages for people with special needs.

Table 2.7   Availability of documents in minority and special languages

Documents	Minority Language	Special Language
Policies	3	3
Procedures	1	2
Forms	5	6
Information	3	2

Policies and procedures may be of somewhat less practical relevance than information leaflets and forms. But even for forms the picture was little different. Only five authorities stated that their *forms* were available in other languages, such as Welsh, Bengali, Hindi and other Asian languages. Forms were apparently available in languages for people with special needs in six cases – one of the highest results for any language or type of document.

It was indeed surprising to find that *information items* were not available more frequently in minority languages. Only three of the authorities indicated that this was the case, the distribution appearing very similar to that for forms. In two cases, information was available in languages for people with special needs.

Looking across the responses, it appeared that in no more than five cases was there a clear indication that at least one document was available in a language other than English (six, if we also include special needs). The most consistently mentioned minority languages were Bengali, Arabic and Cantonese; translation into Welsh occurred only for forms and leaflets.

Unfortunately it appears a matter for speculation exactly how far there is a need for child care services to communicate in languages other than English (Shah, 1995; Fitches, 1994). At the same time there are various ways of meeting language needs – employing interpreters, asking for informal help and so on – which are used as alternatives or in addition to formal translation of documents.

A recent project in Birmingham (Birmingham City Council, 1994) has identified the importance of translating 'key terms' in order to facilitate accurate and consistent interpreting. It is well known that Asian children are under-represented among those looked after by local authorities and issues of communication may play a part in this. Children with disabilities also feature significantly among those in short-term or 'shared care' arrangements. Much more needs to be known about the role of language in the handling of such cases. The availability of translated documents in a handful of authorities should prompt further discussion about how all authorities can meet those needs in consultation with users.

Openness and the sharing of documentation

The question of language has continued our discussion of a key theme of this chapter – how far were the documents part of a process of sharing ideas and information with significant participants in planning and reviewing? We asked if a range of agencies and groups with an advocacy role had been involved, whether care staff and foster carers had received copies and so on. The evidence shows that some progress had been made to bring these groups and agencies positively into the process but only in a minority of cases. It is interesting that one of the most significant achievements was the production of forms which enabled consultation with children and parents. Yet in general it was evident that the promotion of involvement and empowerment of children and families required fresh impetus. These are central issues to which we shall return in later chapters.

This section has described the range of documentation produced by local authorities to guide them in implementing their planning and review duties under the Children Act 1989. In the next section we report on the next step of our analysis, namely an evaluation of the *content* of the documentation.

Evaluating planning and review documentation

This section presents our evaluation of the content of the documentation on plans and reviews from 80 different local authorities. It focuses, first, on a series of organisational topics, second, on messages about partnership and co-working, and, finally, on substantive themes, such as family links, culture, health and education.

The method of evaluation

These documents on plans and reviews represent the guidance that local authorities have given to their staff to enable them to fulfil their duties under the Children Act. The evaluation exercise was designed to find out whether the procedural guidelines were in fact in accordance with Children Act Guidance and Regulations and how helpful they were in enabling staff to work in a way that furthered the principles of the Act. On some questions, especially procedural ones, the test has been to determine whether the documents describe coherent ways to fulfil the principles of the Act for all children.

First of all, it was important to examine the *organisational* messages of the documentation. Were they helpful in:

- reinforcing the continuity of planning and reviewing;
- encouraging the preparation of comprehensive and specific plans;
- establishing in participants' minds a clear and appropriate framework of expectations about procedures;
- contributing to a cohesive (though not necessarily unified) system of plans and reviews for all children who might be or were being looked after;
- identifying who may authorise decisions;
- and describing a system for monitoring plans and reviews?

Secondly, it was important to discover whether the documentation helped:

- to ensure the wishes and feelings of children, parents and other significant people were appropriately ascertained and taken into account;
- to encourage multidisciplinary working, especially with health and education.

The second domain therefore covered themes of *partnership* and *co-working*.

A third major domain was the treatment of *substantive* themes in the care of the child:

- family links;
- culture, language, ethnic origin and religion;
- health;
- and education.

Each of the specific topics which we identified in the Guidance and Regulations was translated into a detailed checklist which was used to consider how accurately and comprehensively the items were covered within the documents submitted by each local authority. The complete package of documents submitted – policies, procedures, forms and information – was evaluated in this way.

The five-point evaluation scale was used for each topic. The categories in the scale rose from 'missing', 'limited', 'adequate', 'positive', to 'excellent'. 'Limited' meant that one or more significant aspects of the topic were omitted or poorly explained, while 'adequate' implied that the minimum obligations were observed by, for example, simply quoting Guidance and Regulations. 'Positive' or 'excellent' were reserved for documents that clearly embodied the fundamental thinking behind the formal government directives. The following sections give examples of how the evaluation proceeded and suggest some of the issues which require attention. In order to illustrate the discussion, extracts from the documents are quoted anonymously. We begin therefore with the *organisational* messages.

The evaluation of organisational themes

Continuity of planning and reviewing

The Guidance makes clear that plans and reviews form part of a continuous process in which key decisions are made and re-examined periodically. To fulfil the terms of the Guidance it seemed necessary that the documentation endorse planning for children before they are looked after and recommend that a plan exist at the first statutory review, within four weeks of being looked after. Thereafter, the minimum time intervals stated in the Regulations had to be brought to the attention of staff, emphasising the need for continuous information collection and the possibility of holding a Review at any time the child's welfare demanded it.

See DH, 1991b, Vol.3: RCC 3; Ch.2.9, Ch.8.1, 8.6, 8.12.

The following example shows the procedures we would expect to see.

Planning meetings should be first convened when the need for accommodation of a child is being seriously considered, or, alternatively, when the local authority is first considering an application for a care order.

When a child starts being looked after, a further meeting is convened within five working days to confirm the initial arrangements contained in the care plan.

Attendance at planning meetings is to be kept at an absolute minimum, with the list of prospective participants being discussed with the child beforehand.

The **care plan** is a core document and should be the focus of all planning meetings.

Review meetings scrutinise previous planning and operational work to ensure that the work has been accomplished to the required standards.

Unlike planning meetings, reviews take place at specified intervals (and so on). (emphasis in original)

In this authority the Regulations on reviews were also quoted in full. Though the specific arrangements for planning and for reviewing were somewhat different from each other in this authority, the procedures were faithful to the Regulations and clearly rated as positive in the evaluation.

One central issue to be faced was the organisation of plans and reviews in the first month of being looked after, when there is a need both to confirm a plan and to review it. There appeared to be a difficulty in deciding how far these are separate and distinct tasks, and how far they could be brought together. As one of the respondents commented:

The first review [within one month] creates logistical problems and [Review Chairs] question how much can realistically be reviewed so soon after the plan has been made.

There is a case for further clarification of the relationship between early plans and reviews.

Comprehensive and specific plans

The Regulations governing general Arrangements for Placement and the Review of Children's Cases require that plans deal with a specific range of issues. These can be grouped roughly into five areas: consideration of changes in legal status; contact with the family (including the appointment of an independent visitor); special arrangements and services (including those for special educational needs); health and education; arrangements for aftercare and for placement in a new family. The translation of assessed needs into aims and objectives is dealt with systematically in the Guidance and Regulations governing placement arrangements. As well as the consideration of options for placement, both immediate and long term, a range of other matters for future action have to be specified. These issues to be actioned in the future include: the allocation of responsibility for carrying out plans (not forgetting the role of parents); provision for changing plans; provision for ending plans, with the possibility of the child returning to live with a parent; and contingency plans.

See DH, 1991b, Vol.3: RCC 4(4), Sch.2 and 3; APC 4, Sch.4; Ch.2.20, 2.62.

An authority which displayed a positive approach had produced a checklist for reviewing officers, reproducing verbatim the items in Schedules 2 and 3 of the Regulations; in addition it used the then current LAC Care Plan form.

A clearly explained procedural framework

The organisation and conduct of review meetings has been made subject to detailed regulation and guidance. The coordination of reviews is based on specific obligations and requirements which affect preparations for the meeting, the meeting itself and the outcome. Participants, including children and parents, are to be informed and consulted, using written records and reports. A chair is to be appointed who will bring objectivity and oversight to the review of the case. A list of suitable participants is laid down, including the child and the parents, and various considerations surrounding attendance and the choice of venue must be taken into account so that the attendance and participation of children and parents are facilitated and encouraged as far as possible. The agenda of the review is also governed by the planning requirements, including the discussion of previous decisions and decisions to be taken. A record of the meeting reflecting the child's and parents' views must be made and checked by the chair. Decisions on the plan must result, with a note of those in agreement and those dissenting. At this point the requirements of planning, such as specifying responsibilities and timescales, should be incorporated in a revised statement and the outcome of the meeting notified within 14 days to all participants.

The Guidance simply states that the chair should be a senior person who can bring a degree of 'oversight and objectivity' to the consideration of issues. In some cases, a line manager assumed that role; in others, it was a manager with no line management responsibility. In a few cases dedicated reviewing officers had been appointed. One authority adopting a minimalist position referred simply to a 'senior officer' taking the chair. An evaluation of these variations required further evidence from another survey which is reported in Chapter 7.

See DH, 1991b, Vol.3: RCC 4 and 7, Sch.1; Ch.2.64, Ch.8.11, 8.19, 8.21–23, 8.25.

The responsibilities of social worker, line manager and reviewing officer were carefully delineated in this encouraging example.

> The Social Worker and the Line Manager chairing the Case Planning Meeting should ensure that the plan is written up by completing form XYZ. Ideally the plan should be written up at the time of the meeting using black ink and bold letters.

Responsibility for key decisions about the conduct of the review was clearly laid down.

> Children and parents should always be involved in both reviews and Case Planning Meetings <u>unless to do so would be against the child's interests and well-being</u>. The reasons for not involving parents or children must be recorded on the <u>review of arrangements report</u> and in the <u>case file</u> for the child. This decision is delegated to the <u>Group Leader</u>. (underlining in original)

This arrangement provided for an exceptional situation to be resolved by a senior person, in line with the emphasis of the Guidance and Regulations on consultation. The broader task of oversight and monitoring was assigned to the Reviewing Officer.

> The Reviewing Officer is responsible for ensuring that:
> (a)   A written plan has been drawn up for the child being looked after;
> (b)   Satisfying themselves that the plan does reflect the needs and circumstances of the child;
> (c)   Preparing a written review of the arrangements of the child following the Department procedures set out in [another section of this document].

A cohesive if not necessarily unified system

Looked-after children can fall into several categories sometimes simultaneously. From the perspective of planning and reviews, there are some distinct categories that arise from the existence of parallel procedures (such as child protection conferences), specific arrangements for types of placement (for example, with parents), for particular needs (such as special educational needs and disability) or for particular carers, such as voluntary and private agencies. It seems highly desirable that the procedures for these various categories should fit together so avoiding unnecessary duplication and delay and affording families the best possible access to the planning system.
See DH, 1991b, Vol.3: RCC 1(2), 2.4(5), 11; Ch.8.1–4, 8.7.

This 'excellent' example indicates a specific link between procedures for child protection and for care planning.

> *If child protection issues come to light as a result of an assessment process, Child Protection procedures must be followed and may include the need to convene a Child Protection Case Conference.* Where a [Child Protection]

Conference decides that a package of services is required, the appointed key worker will convene a Planning Meeting under these procedures.

Planning meetings will take priority over all other work except Child Protection Investigations and Conferences and Review Meetings where these were arranged first.

Creating a cohesive system – the problem of short-term placements

The Regulations sought to define non-continuous short-term placements, lasting for up to 90 days in a year, that would be treated as single placements for the purposes of reviewing (*RCC 11*). But local authorities seemed to be unclear about how to count the days of placement so as to meet the standard timetable laid down for reviews.

If only the actual days of a short-term placement were counted then a 90-day placement would initially require only one statutory review in a calendar year, that is, before the twenty-eighth day of placement. The problem is illustrated in this example.

Children whose patterns of placement fall within (the category of short-term placement) should be reviewed **before the 28th day of respite care**. (emphasis in original)

But it then went on to state,

Any **continuing** or subsequent placement packages should be reviewed 28 days after its commencement. (emphasis added)

It is necessary to ask whether this means that the review cycle begins again in the second calendar year of a continuing placement, with another preliminary 28-day review. The Department of Health has more recently attempted to clarify these points by issuing revised regulations, stipulating that the first review takes place within three months of the commencement of placement (Department of Health, 1995b).

There were also difficulties in making families feel comfortable with the new, more formalised procedures, which also meant confronting more squarely the reasons for the authority's involvement and the likely timescale. As recent research has shown, short-term placements have often been designed as services to carers, thus focusing on carers' needs rather than necessarily on children's (Robinson, Minkes and Weston, 1993). That research indicates that there is a long way to go before these placements are brought into a cohesive system of planning and reviews in which proper consultation takes place.

The authorisation of decisions

It would be contrary to the whole intention of the Children Act if appropriate plans and reviews were not to be implemented. Indeed the authority responsible for the child's case is obliged to implement such

decisions. However, first of all, they have to be authorised. But how was this to be done? Would the coordinator of reviews have a clear role in this? How would the chair 'bring oversight' to such issues? Was there a clear system for instigating a further review if circumstances changed?
See DH, 1991b, Vol.3: RCC 4(3), 8; Ch.8.3, 8.6, 8.13.

It became clear from the documents that supervisors and managers were directly involved in the planning and review process. Such arrangements gave an adequate indication that some way of authorising decisions had been established. However, there was evidence of other managerial decision-making forums which appeared equally, if not more, important, adding a new layer of complexity.

For example, an approach that seemed positive gave an account of which individual managers and placement planning groups were responsible for particular types of decision. In one such model the planning and review meetings could only suggest possible resources, the chairs having no executive power (though team leaders were fully involved at this stage). It was for a set of individual managers and three placement planning groups, meeting regularly, to authorise decisions as appropriate. At least one of these groups was also able to send members to attend the review in complex cases. Such a detailed model demonstrates the importance in complex organisations of having an appropriate system for authorising key decisions. It also highlights the tension between a child-centred system for plans and reviews and a professionally managed system of resource allocation.

Monitoring the planning and review system

The Regulations stipulate that monitoring arrangements be established; a specific monitoring officer is also mentioned in the Guidance. In evaluating local procedures, several aspects seemed important – that such monitoring be based on systematic records of meetings and decisions, possibly using computerised methods; the planning and reviewing system was subject to quality assurance procedures and targets; the monitoring system was able to identify training needs; there was evidence of ways of addressing problems in the operation of the system.
See DH, 1991b, Vol.3: RCC 9; Ch.8.26.

The monitoring requirement was met in an 'excellent' manner by one authority that had created a fully-fledged system. Five Review Managers chaired all reviews; they maintained a database for all children looked after within their cluster of Area Teams; a Quality Assurance Section helped to specify the information required; within this section a Child Care Planning Manager coordinated the system of reviews. Performance indicators had been specified so that outcomes of the planning and review system could be monitored (for example, the percentage of reviews carried out within specified timescales); an annual report was presented to the Director. The system therefore linked operational management with the collection of information so that problems could be appropriately resolved. Unfortunately it was not evident how children and parents were to contribute their opinions about their experience of plans and reviews.

In a contrasting example, the only information on monitoring was that a fostering panel monitored placements – a clearly limited approach.

The evaluation results for the organisational messages

So far we have used examples to illustrate our assessment of the documentation in relation to organisational themes. In Figure 2.1, we summarise the pattern of scores for each of the topics discussed so far. The scores relate to 79 of the 80 packages, with the exception of 'comprehensive plans'. This was because one authority sent only a planning form for our attention.)

In summary, a combined quarter of all the local authority scores implied 'limited' or 'no evidence' of a response to the organisational implications of the Guidance and Regulations. Another group comprising 37 per cent of scores indicated an 'adequate' response, while a further 37 per cent displayed responses that seemed 'positive' or 'excellent'.

There were more frequent positive ratings on the first three criteria – Continuity, Comprehensive plans, Clear procedural framework – than on the second three – a Cohesive system, Authorisation of decisions and Monitoring. In addition there are more cases where we find no evidence relating to the second three criteria. Evidence about Comprehensive planning and a Clear procedural framework was more clearly recognised in the documentation than about a Cohesive system, a system for Authorisation of decisions and a Monitoring system. Nor should we overlook the evidence of limitations in responses, especially to issues about procedure, continuity and authorisation of decisions.

The evaluation of partnership and co-working themes

We turn now to the second major group of topics – partnership and co-working – which one would expect to be promoted through local procedures. The Children Act has highlighted as never before the themes of consultation with the child, partnership with parents and multidisciplinary cooperation. We assess the documentation from each of these three perspectives.

Consultation with the child

The Regulations, first of all, seek to ensure that children are informed

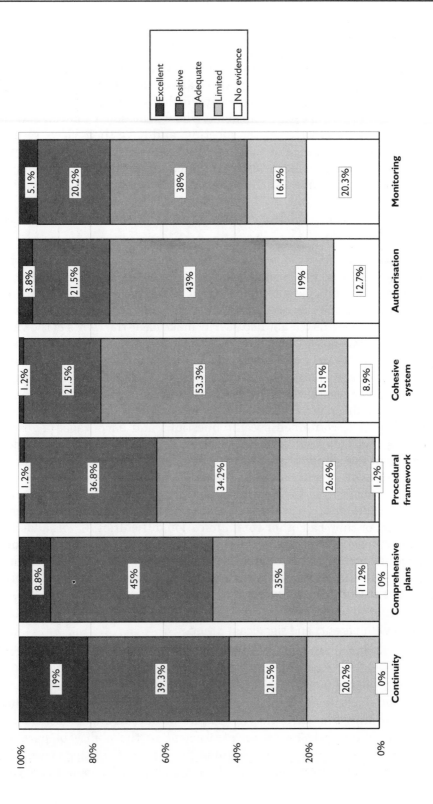

Figure 2.1   Evaluation scores for organisational messages

about their procedural and legal rights under the Act, such as the right to apply for a Section 8 Order, to make representations and to be a party to agreements. There are also in the Guidance specific practice considerations to be noted. Social workers are expected to consult with children not only about their wishes and feelings in general but also about the venue for the meeting and about who will attend. Children may have the help of a supporter at the meeting, and have their views recorded. The right of children, if of sufficient understanding, to refuse medical examination or treatment is also mentioned in the Guidance. Finally, children should be notified of the outcome of the meeting, which should also be explained to them.

See DH, 1991b, Vol.3: APC 3(3)(5); RCC 7, Sch.1; Ch.2.64, Ch.8.11, 8.15–18, 8.20–23, 8.25.

We saw previously how information leaflets for children about plans and reviews were rarely in evidence. The same applied to information for parents. To some extent, consultation forms gave an indication to the child of what the meeting was about and what was expected. However, consultation forms did not necessarily make clear the rights of the various parties. It was important therefore to look at the whole of the documentation in order to see how far the principle of consultation was embodied.

Thus, one authority achieved a positive rating because several features appeared praiseworthy despite the absence of an information leaflet for children. Its consultation form, although designed prior to the Children Act, contained specific questions and encouraged a response rather than demanding one. Moreover, it had adopted inquiry and assessment instruments originated by the Looking After Children project, and these are directly addressed to children's perceptions and views. It was emphasised in procedural guidance that special efforts should be made when children were very young or their first language was not English, or they had other communication difficulties. It was added that support needed to be available for children to cope with difficult issues at meetings and information about complaints should be given. It was not clear, unfortunately, how children's rights in respect of court orders under the Children Act were to be communicated.

Consultation with parents and significant others

The Guidance and Regulations build on the concept of parental responsibility, stressing the various ways in which partnership with parents should be reflected in the planning process. It is expected that, through a process of negotiation, written agreements will be produced, incorporating the parental role in day to day arrangements. A major consideration therefore is an assessment of the ability of parents to adhere to an agreed plan. Reasons for discounting the views of the parents should also be clearly explained, in line with a general obligation to communicate with parents, whatever the circumstances. In cases of disagreement the procedure for representations and complaints is to be made clear to parents. Moreover, there is also an obligation to consult with significant others in the child's life.

See DH, 1991b, Vol.3: APC 3(4)(5), 4(1), Sch.4; RCC 7(1); Ch.2.21, Ch.8.16, 8.25.

To give an example of a positive approach, we can cite a package which dealt with all the points covered by the Regulations. For instance, specific mention was made of the extended family as possible consultants and there was also a definite awareness of the obligations, outlined in the Guidance, to state why the wishes of people consulted had been discounted. The parents' consultation form for this authority also served its purpose satisfactorily. The only possibly doubtful feature of the plan agreement format was an option for parents to sign a statement saying that they had been 'fully consulted' but did not wish to sign the agreement form. Perhaps uncharitably, this sounds like an option it would be impolite to refuse!

On the other hand, a more limited approach was evident in the case of another authority which referred only to the use of written agreements and the representations procedure while saying very little about consultation with significant others. Part of the problem here was the lack of documentation concerning plans, as distinct from reviews.

Multidisciplinary working

Because the development of a child gives rise to a whole range of needs, the Guidance and Regulations has insisted on the application of methods of multidisciplinary working, especially in the formulation of plans. For example, the Guidance points out the advantages of combining assessments under different pieces of legislation, such as the Education Act 1981 (now superseded by the 1993 Education Act). It is also recommended that specific officers in other agencies be contacted so as to facilitate consultation with their colleagues. In the health field, a designated doctor should advise the local authority and carers should have access to advice about the health needs of minority ethnic groups. Procedures for placement necessarily include an assessment of health, prior to placement, if possible, and also require that appropriate notifications be sent to health and educational agencies. The Children Act 1989 also makes provision in Section 27, for cooperation by other agencies in response to reasonable requests for help made by the authority looking after the child and, in Section 28, for consultation about placements with an education component.

See DH, 1991b, Vol.3: APC 5, 7; Ch.2.25–26, 2.52, 2.54, Ch.8.24.

In one authority an extensive list of possible consultants was provided, covering various medical and educational specialists, probation and the police as well as those versed in the needs of children with disabilities or from minority cultures, religions, languages and ethnic groups. Notifications of placement were also necessary. Plans for 'relief' care, as it was called, were also to be shared with the GP and the school. There was a clear acceptance of an obligation to consider arranging specific multidisciplinary assessments, for example, under the Education Act 1981. 'Assessment and Health Managers' were also mentioned as possible chairs for certain planning meetings. For cases where the child was not receiving education the need to consult the Education Department itself was acknowledged. Yet even in this authority it was not very clear whether there was a structure of inter-agency consultation at a senior level. Nor was evident attention paid to Sections 27 and 28 of the Children Act, covering aspects of consultation and implementation. Nonetheless the authority's documentation was given a positive rating.

It appeared that in general the documentation tended to focus on the immediate tasks of the reviewing process rather than on the structure of multidisciplinary cooperation envisaged by the Guidance on planning. The facilitating role of specific officers in other agencies, for example, was not mentioned as frequently as we would have hoped. It was disappointing, for example, when a set of documentation referred only to two points – health assessment prior to placement and the Education Act 1981 – thus receiving a rating as limited.

Figure 2.2 sets out the results of the evaluation for the themes discussed in this section.

The evaluation of substantive themes in the care of the child

We now turn to a group of *substantive themes* in the Guidance and Regulations, which include family links and contact; culture, language, ethnic origin and religion; health; and finally, education.

Family links

The Regulations for planning emphasise the promotion of contact among family members, whether the child is placed in public, private or voluntary provision. Furthermore, there is an important obligation to take account of family contact when making plans, including the duty to give priority to placement with family members or significant others, to placement near the child's home and to the placement of siblings together. The Guidance also highlights the significance of rehabilitation to the family home.

See DH, 1991b, Vol.3: APC 4, 6, Sch.1, 4; Ch.2.12. Children Act 1989, S.23(6)(7).

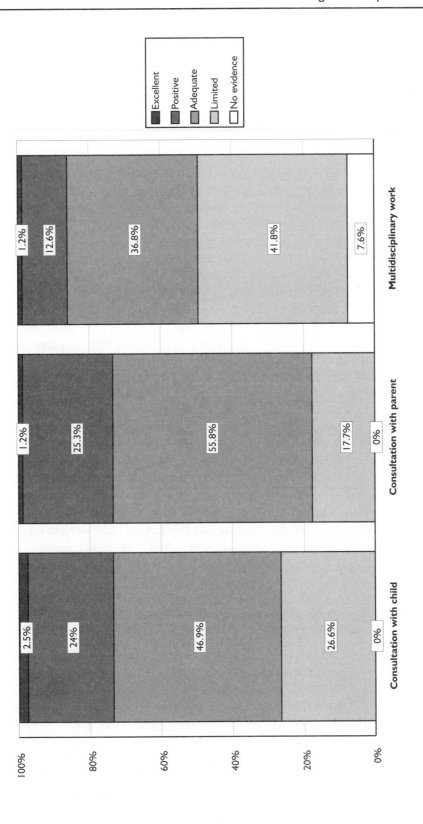

Figure 2.2   Evaluation scores for partnership and co-working

This extract illustrates a positive approach to the issue:

> The Act imposes a duty to *promote contact* between a child who is being looked after (whether in compulsory care or not) and those who are connected with him.

> This would mean facilitating contacts, particularly initial contact following for example removal from home by *paying for transport costs* or accompanying and introducing visitors appropriately. (emphases in original)

Distinctions between arrangements for those in accommodation and those in care were adequately described. Even the possible need to interpret the language of such arrangements was mentioned. Each of the priorities for placement laid down in Section 23 of the Children Act was faithfully followed. Some weaknesses in dealing with these priorities occurred in other sets of documents. An authority with an otherwise sound policy background had omitted these placement priorities, thus receiving a rating as 'limited'.

Culture, language, ethnic origin and religion

A child's culture, language, ethnic origin and religion are accorded significant importance in the Act and are discussed in the Guidance. *See DH, 1991b, Vol.3: Ch.2.40, 2.71. Children Act 1989, S.22(5).*

Language presented some straightforward issues. Examples of positive attention to language needs include the following:

> The District will provide an interpreter, signer or other appropriate assistance so that all significant persons are able to play a full part in the decision making process. Children should under no circumstances be expected to act as interpreters.

A well-organised and positive approach to issues of ethnic origin was shown by a checklist for plans that included the following insertion:

> How these needs are to be met (for a black child this will include
> - developing a sense of black identity
> - developing skills for surviving in the white community
> - developing the cultural and linguistic attributes necessary to function in the black community, when the child ceases to be accommodated
> - developing a positive self image and self esteem).

To some extent, however, the habit of grouping culture, language and ethnic origin together makes it less easy to identify them as separate issues with their own particular implications. They tended to exist in the form of checklist items, perhaps understandably in light of the fact that documentation had rarely been the subject of consultation with representatives of minority ethnic groups.

Health needs

An acceptable approach to health needs had to include the specific matters laid down in the Review regulations, which outline a health agenda for consideration at the review and stipulate the frequency of assessment. In addition some reference to positive health measures (such as self care and sensible health behaviour) and to disability issues seemed desirable. The process of healthy psychological development mentioned in Chapter 9 of Volume 3 of the Guidance was also relevant to the evaluation. Attention to the health needs of minority ethnic groups has been specifically recommended in the Guidance. Protecting young people from injury and infection seemed also a key part of a wide-ranging and positive health care strategy.

See DH, 1991b, Vol.3: RCC 5, Sch.3; RCC 6; Ch.2.26, 2.28, Ch.9.51–53, 9.55. Children Act 1989, Sch.2, Part I, S.6.

An authority was rated as 'positive' where all the matters dealt with in the Regulations had been properly recognised, and in addition, reference had been made to disability, to self care and health education, and to minority group needs. This authority made use of the BAAF Health Passport which provides the basis for a personal health history. In contrast an authority which only dealt with the frequency of health assessment showed a limited approach.

Education

The Regulations make clear a series of practical obligations to be followed during the planning and review of a child's education. In particular, they draw attention to the child's educational development, looking at the child's history and maintaining continuity of education. There is also a focus on needs, especially special educational needs. The Guidance goes on to discuss contact with a child's school, promoting a child's interests and gifts, and ensuring homework is done, as well as thinking about further education and training.

See DH, 1991b, Vol.3: APC 4(1), Sch.3; RCC, Sch.2; Ch.2.35, 2.37, Ch.9.90–91, 9.95.

The achievement of a 'positive' rating regarding education was illustrated by an authority that had a clear view of children's needs and progress, including special educational needs. It distinguished itself by including topics like carers' contacts with school, children's interests and their homework, as well as further education and training. It failed to achieve an 'excellent' rating because it had not made clear how children's educational history and the continuity of their schooling were to be addressed.

The results of the evaluation for family links, health, education, culture and so on

If we bring together the results for the four previous topics, an interesting pattern emerges, as shown in Figure 2.3.

The combined totals show that a quarter of the scores indicated 'limited' or 'no evidence' of responses to the Guidance and Regulations, just over a half appeared to be 'adequate', while 21 per cent were rated 'positive' or 'excellent'. The highest level of scoring was for culture, language, ethnic origin and religion, though none achieved an 'excellent' rating. By contrast, planning for educational needs appeared to be an area of comparative weakness.

Discussion

To summarise then, the evaluation provided evidence about the quality of the documentation and asked how appropriate was the *content*. By this test, it appears that the majority of documents came up to an adequate standard or performed above this level. In these cases, the initial objectives of the regulatory strategy had been fulfilled. But in a significant minority of cases, however, there was little or no evidence that particular messages of the Guidance and Regulations had been absorbed. On a complex subject such as this, some gaps might be expected but it is sobering to consider that, some two years after implementation of the Act, a significant minority of documents were still inadequate. The regulatory strategy is not therefore an instant solution to the problems of practice – simply because the messages are not always effectively communicated to practitioners and those with whom they work. Unless and until all local authorities respond to the urgings of such regulation, there will be some residual doubts about the success of the regulatory strategy in achieving a comprehensive influence and thus helping to structure practice on a national basis. However, there is clear evidence that progress was being achieved in a majority of cases within the timescale of two years. The growing influence of LAC forms since the survey took place is another positive indicator that the Guidance and Regulations are being heeded in more and more authorities. To this extent the regulatory strategy has overcome the first significant hurdle in moving towards the long-term objective of influencing child care practice.

Legislating for good practice?

The very scale and scope of the documentation created by local authorities does raise some fundamental questions about the relationship between statutory requirements, local procedures and ultimately practice in child care. It is to these questions that we now turn.

Firstly, we consider the advantages of a procedural approach and point to some potential disadvantages; then we consider the perspectives of managers on these issues; finally, we suggest how planning and

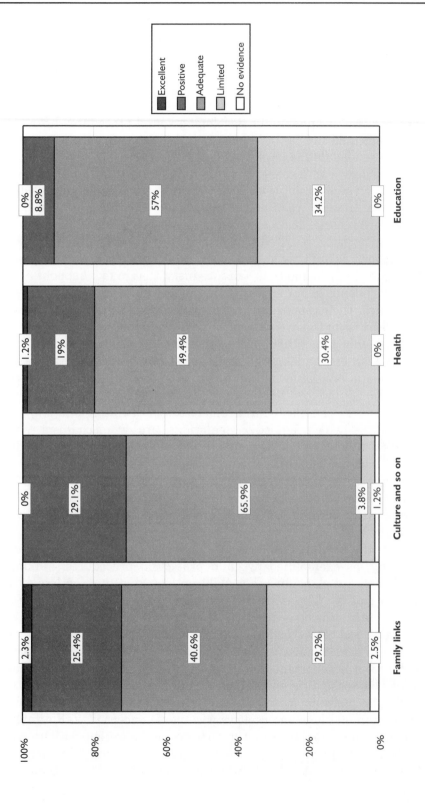

Figure 2.3   Evaluation scores for family links and other substantive themes

review procedures can be implemented in a way that promotes good child care practice.

The benefits of a procedural approach

The positive arguments for developing sound procedures have already been indicated in the first chapter, but it is worth rehearsing them in order to elucidate the implications of the survey.

Procedures can have an important function in *informing users* and working in partnership with them. There is much evidence that children and their families are often unclear about their rights or what they can expect from social services when they are being looked after. However this can only be resolved if procedures are open and shared. For instance, *only* when they know they have a right to receive a written Care Plan can children and their families insist that in fact happens.

The evidence of our survey is that in only a very few authorities were families or their representatives consulted in the drafting of procedures or had access to them; similarly for persons representing minority ethnic groups. Only a handful of authorities had produced any leaflets for children or families explaining the planning and review process. Very little documentation or information was available in forms other than written English.

Procedures can also be a means of *communication with staff*. Those procedures which embody regulations are a mechanism whereby national policies can be mediated to the staff who have responsibility for implementing them. In this way procedures can play an educative role in developing a common understanding of good practice and establishing performance standards. In this regard, the evidence from our survey of the limited distribution of documentation to care staff is a little worrying.

Agreed procedures are also an important component of *inter-agency working*, as exemplified by child protection procedures. Making and implementing plans for other children looked after is no less an inter-agency activity. The evidence from our survey suggests limited engagement with other agencies in the preparation and distribution of planning and review policies and procedures.

So the development and implementation of detailed procedures can serve several important functions. This being so, it is necessary to consider how these different purposes can be met within the design of any particular planning system. It can be argued that, on balance, the documentation on plans and reviews was more concerned with establishing organisational directives and ensuring compliance than with broadening the basis for partnership and co-working. This seems to suggest that there may be unintended drawbacks in operating a planning and review system in too narrow and prescriptive a manner – what might be called an 'administrative model' of planning.

An 'administrative' model

An 'administrative' model of planning is one which *appears* to place greater emphasis on compliance with internal procedures than with meeting the specific needs of the individual young person; where the framing of rules to deal consistently with situations *seems* more important than the exercise of social work skills or professional judgement; where working collaboratively with all those concerned in a child's life *seems* insufficiently valued. Ideally, of course, the procedures should facilitate the use of social work skills to meet the particular needs of each young person. However, in designing and operating systems to deal with the real life complexities of planning for young people looked after it is easy for this balance to slip. For instance an administrative model may be encouraged when organisations or individual workers feel defensive, perhaps because of the nature of past criticism. Or workers may feel that the scope of the procedures and the volume of accompanying paper-work creates an imbalance in their workload.

Our study of planning and review systems points to several such drawbacks that need to be considered if the 'administrative' model is not to detract from soundly based professional decision-making.

- Our survey, supported by field research in local authorities, suggests that the impetus for the development of the new procedures was managerial rather than practitioner-led. We have commented already on the considerable thought and focused attention that went into these and how important this can be in reinforcing messages about why planning procedures are important to the outcomes for young people. When practitioners are not brought into that process from the outset then they are unlikely to have the same feelings of ownership or understanding of the value of the procedures.
- Secondly, the development of procedures by social services has been mainly concerned with organisational matters within its own domain. Indeed, the survey shows that users and other agencies were infrequently involved in the creation and distribution of documentation; there was too little information for people not employed by social services. In this sense it is social services that carry the ownership of the procedures. The 'administrative' model can encourage an inwardness, concentrating upon 'our' procedures rather than promoting sharing and partnership. In such situations, for example, a health or education professional may be simply sent a form to complete, and have very little awareness of its significance or purpose.
- 'Administrative' models like consistency and predictability; they are

not good at dealing with diversity or dynamic situations. The regulations on plans and reviews are intended to apply to all looked after children, from those in long term stable care, to those receiving respite care, to the adolescent whose life is characterised by constant changes. Meeting the diverse needs of all children calls for a system that allows professionals to recognise individual and specific requirements while continuing to fulfil the objectives of the Children Act.

● We have referred to the very important role that procedures play in enabling standards of social work practice to be monitored. However, it is important that the indicators employed are appropriate. For instance, if only procedure-based performance indicators are used these are likely to say more about the system than, say, the quality of the relationship between a social worker and young person. This also carries the danger of appearing to downgrade professional skills.

● 'Administrative' models of planning can give disproportionate time to the processing of knowledge and the management of resources at the expense of working with and caring for children and families: an imbalance in the effort that goes into making decisions compared with putting them into effect.

● Social work practice that appears to be heavily preoccupied with guidance and procedure may inhibit the necessary application of professional judgement based on principle. Such deskilling is not only demoralising to staff, it may also be counter-productive. If social workers are not asked to use their judgement in individual cases, they may come to expect guidance and procedures to make their decisions for them. This could lead to an unwieldy 'procedures culture' in which authoritative guidance is sought for every contingency.

So far, the discussion has been based on the national survey, identifying general problems. But there is another source of evidence about the dilemmas of 'proceduralism' – interviews with seven senior and middle managers in the three authorities taking part in the second, fieldwork stage of the research.

Management perspectives

One of the fundamental questions posed in interviews with managers was about the relationship between regulation, procedure and practice. Did managers regard the Guidance and Regulations as effective? Were they appropriate? What were the implications of the highly structured LAC materials for planning and reviewing? How did the managers see the role of written procedures in controlling, guiding and improving practice?

The impact of regulation

In each local authority, managers perceived a variety of positive changes in planning and reviewing since the Children Act 1989. In Midshire there was a common perception that the Guidance and Regulations had been fairly effective in influencing practice. The introduction of middle managers more specialised in child care was regarded as one factor in this progress. In the Midshire district where the fieldwork took place, the changes had been palpable. Prior to the Act, reviewing had been an administrative routine allocated to Friday mornings, bringing together the Area Director, the Manager and the team leaders. A far more systematic approach, including children and families in the process, was now in operation. However, over-large meetings in sometimes unsuitable settings were a drawback of the new arrangements.

In Northborough, the Guidance and Regulations were depicted positively, as 'a bedrock' on which practice could build. With the support of the Guidance, independent reviewing had become the norm rather than the exception in the borough. In this respect, planning and reviewing was felt to have progressed since the Children Act.

In Westside, perceptions of the impact of regulatory changes seemed to be a function of how actively the managers monitored their cases. One manager was confident that planning took place at an early stage, setting short-term goals, including assessment. It was not simply about the major options for permanency:

> 'You have to have a stab at a plan and look at it again.' (Manager, Westside)

There were other positive changes since the Children Act: the clarity of information provided by the recording system; and greatly increased attendance of young people at meetings.

In Midshire and Westside there was criticism of the content of the Children Act Guidance and Regulations. One manager made a fundamental criticism, believing that the Guidance issued under statutory powers was dangerously misconceived; it extolled minimum standards and good practice without often clarifying which was which. It was argued that this created a 'no-win' situation for social workers. It should have concentrated fully on clarifying the minimum or baseline requirements so that good practice could be described and built up on them.

The criticism of the Guidance as misconceived does raise major questions about the proper scope of procedures. In considering the functions of the review one manager wished to emphasise the different timescales for accomplishing different objectives.

> 'I'd have put in more flexibility; to have reviews as and when appropriate with the family.'

This manager argued that there were different objectives to be attained by reviewing: therapy; involvement; resolving issues that concerned some people and not others: 'They're trying to kill too many birds with one stone.' He contemplated a possible change so that the statutory review would be a 'low key' check on the whole process, dealing with the results of other, different meetings that might happen more frequently.

In effect, such a model seeks to use Guidance to oversee the continuity of practice – somewhat different from the one implied in Midshire. However, both criticisms lead to reflections on the complexity of the work expected to go into one single review and its corresponding meeting. They remind us that the requirements of both the Guidance and Regulations have been understood to culminate in a set-piece review event. The concept of a review process with different components taking place at different times would seem to call for some rewording of the guidance, which frequently refers to the review as a single process though holding more than one meeting is not excluded (Volume 3, Ch. 8.3). Later, in the final chapters of the report, the questions highlighted by such comments will be reconsidered at greater length.

The LAC packages

The interviews with managers presented an opportunity to explore different perceptions of the LAC materials, the use of which was spreading during the fieldwork period (Ward, 1995). While Westside had extensive experience of the pilot materials, Midshire and Northborough had so far only organised some experimentation. However, by the end of 1994, both Midshire and Northborough had chosen to adopt the system.

Westside's experience of the LAC system enabled managers to comment from a more informed perspective. In Westside, the piloting of LAC materials applied to the full set – the Essential Information Record, the Care Plan, the Review form and the Assessment and Action Record. These were fully revised during the fieldwork period. Consultation forms also became available at a midpoint in the fieldwork. Making sure the Assessment and Action Records were completed had proved to be a challenge for managers. Some children refused to do them but they were popular among carers. For social workers the LAC system created a lot of work. However, the social work rationale for paper recording was to ensure that things happened.

> 'A lot of people feel they're overwhelmed by paperwork. Social workers have always felt like that. In my view the record is as important as the review. If it's not written up, the process fails – people don't do things if they're not written up.' (Manager, Westside)

Paperwork was perceived as a part of the chain of implementation – a prerequisite for continuity in the process. There were, however, two problems associated with this more pre-structured recording system.

One problem was that the use of structured records, while covering relevant issues effectively, created some difficulties of interpretation.

For example, what did the spaces left blank mean? Were they irrelevant issues? How could the reader tell? Another perceived consequence of structured recording was to introduce a more clinical and less humane approach than in the past – especially with the LAC Review form.

> 'I lose any sense of the child from the reviews. The old reviews were good on humanity, on dilemmas, but not so good on content. Answers are now more clinical, answered by rote, succinctly. If a child had only copies of (his or her) old reviews, God help them! . . . They are not unit chapters in a life story book.' (Manager, Westside)

On the other hand, the Assessment and Action Records were seen as positive vehicles for stimulating discussion with the child and allowing more space for comment. Further initiatives were necessary if a real dialogue with children was to be conducted: a young people's forum where managers and children could meet; more surveys of young people's opinions; and high quality leaflets written in consultation with young people.

Procedures and professionalism

Managers' perceptions of the LAC materials raised a much broader question – the relationship between good procedural frameworks and good practice. Comments from managers brought out a tension between professionalism and regulation: in essence, good social workers did not need regulation, but poor social workers did.

> 'Written guidelines are essential, but not for a good social worker. It's seeing all the issues are covered – the standard of quality . . .'. (Senior Manager, Northborough)

> 'Most staff would say it's over-regulated. Public opinion tends to think that lack of professionalism means it should be regulated.' (Senior Manager, Midshire)

> '[Written guidelines are] . . . a mixed blessing . . . . [It's a] guarantee of the minimum necessary. The trouble is you have so many that people don't read them and people think their judgement isn't trusted.' (Manager, Westside)

The usefulness of written guidelines lay therefore in addressing inadequacies and lapses of professionalism. Good professional work went beyond the demands of regulation.

> 'I'm not a procedure person – I do believe good quality planning is to do with relationships, using your relationship with the family. Far more important than ensuring all the boxes are ticked.' (Senior Manager, Northborough)

> 'In child protection now we have so many procedures we have to reassert the value of good practice.' (Manager, Westside)

Managers were in general ambivalent about regulation, accepting that it was necessary as a control on poor practice yet wishing to transcend its limitations. Over-prescription could turn into a constraint on good practice and deskill social workers if it merely led to defensive practice – going through procedures in order to avoid possible criticism in future.

> 'There's a tension between offering procedures as tools for good practice (that is, you decide if it's of use) versus people saying "I must do the procedures because a public inquiry will ask me if I have done the procedures and, if not, will blame me."' (Manager, Westside)

In the last analysis professional judgement was the key to the dilemmas of practice.

> 'The issue is how you *judge* what to do when you have pressures.' (emphasis added) (Manager, Westside)

Such views cast doubt on any simplistic notions about the scope and impact of regulation and suggest a significant tension between regulation and professional judgement.

Discussion

When managers were asked about the function of procedures and paper systems, they raised some puzzling problems. There is an obvious dilemma here: are procedures and systems designed primarily to regulate out poor practice or to act as a tool to aid good practice? If the aim is to eliminate poor practice, then procedures have to be detailed and mandatory. If the aim is to aid practice, then it is less clear how detailed, or indeed how mandatory, they need to be.

The concept of procedures as an enabling 'tool' means that attention needs to be focused on the practitioner, not the procedure: tools can be used selectively to address the individual task. The idea of the 'tool' is seen as empowering good professionals to trust their own judgement; but it may present a message to poor professionals that is confusing and inappropriate.

The questions posed by managers go to the heart of the issues about standards which were broached earlier in this book. The point about good standards is that they are not simply meant to be lists of do's and dont's to be followed mechanically in every case. They should be framed so as to be capable of being usefully applied in a variety of circumstances.

So how can planning and review systems documented in our survey be developed to comply not only with the letter, but more importantly with the spirit of the Children Act? To achieve this will require systems that are structured enough to ensure that children's needs are appropriately assessed, care plans made and reviewed, but which have sufficient responsiveness to deal with the diverse and changing circumstances of children being looked after.

Guiding principles of planning and reviewing

Here we suggest a set of criteria for guiding the planning and reviewing process – criteria that help to promote both sound procedures *and* professional judgement, in the best interests of children. So we shall discuss in turn how the following criteria can be applied successfully:

- openness and sharing
- cogency
- integration
- flexibility
- sensitivity
- responsiveness
- continuity

Openness and sharing. The survey suggests that social services have established ownership of their procedures with insufficient means of involving children, parents and other agencies. To open up and share the procedures it is necessary that social services go beyond simply inviting people to meetings and sending out letters. They must consult with participants about their procedures. They must provide information that empowers participants, explaining not only administrative details but more importantly how the views of families and other agencies can influence decision making, taking account of privacy and confidentiality. In this way the communication system will offer participants opportunities for conscious influence and power.

Cogency. The Guidance makes clear that consultation forms part of a process that begins with inquiry and assessment and culminates in decision making. This involves an explicit listing and appraisal of options, before settling on the best available. Rational decision making is not, however, about a simple choice. It has been suggested that a decision does not consist of a single step in a particular direction, but involves a number of lesser steps, each of which needs to be clarified and understood (Lewis, 1994). When a decision has been about any aspect of a plan, it should be possible for all concerned to see how the steps in the reasoning behind that decision fit together logically. A purely administrative or checklist approach cannot provide the necessary cogency.

Integration. To meet all the needs of a child properly it is important that the plan is more than a collection of separate items. It should be integrated so that the participants can identify common themes and work together, so that, for example, work by a social worker with a parent can be reinforced at contact sessions by the foster carer. In cases of disability this requirement is often pressing, where a need arising from a particular disability has consequences not only for children's care but also for their education – for example, the need to learn skills that can be taught at home as well as in school.

Flexibility. Planning and reviewing should be organised flexibly. In some cases, it may be apparent that issues to which the Guidance draws attention are in practice irrelevant – children without disabilities or language needs, for example. In others, there may be agreement that a particular issue has been settled for the foreseeable future. Reviews need therefore to be capable of focusing sharply on current areas for decision making, as well as checking that well-established arrangements are going satisfactorily.

Flexibility also means making a decision about the appropriate balance between 'evidence' gathered prior to meetings, written 'evidence' and that given in person; between topics that need further exploration and those that can be covered by reports.

There is also an argument for going lightly over ground that can be covered effectively elsewhere – perhaps in an educational or health forum. The Guidance makes it clear such forums can be used to advance the planning process in a flexible way. It is important, however, that the basic standards applied in reviews are also adopted in other settings so that flexibility does not lead to a casual disregard of the rights of children and families.

Sensitivity. Reviewing in child care can never be impersonal; necessarily it touches the emotions of all its participants, to a lesser or greater degree. A review will be child-centred to the extent that it succeeds in properly appreciating the sensitivities of the child. Consultation forms are only part of the answer here, and only for a proportion of children. Also needed is direct work with children which calls for definite skills and training. Establishing trust, identifying sensitive issues, establishing common ground – all depend on consistent work which should be taken forward in the preparation and conduct of planning meetings. It would be disastrous if meetings were to be perceived by children or families as ways for authority figures – teachers, social services and others – to 'gang up' on children or family members. Similarly, children's or parents' absence from a meeting should not be looked upon simply as a personal choice, nor as an expression of lack of interest or commitment. It should be regarded as possibly signifying something problematic about the process as it personally affects an individual.

Responsiveness. The planning and review process must be able to deal with new circumstances and fresh demands. This may entail bringing forward the review at the request of a child or family member as the Guidance suggests. It may involve setting a review date to fall in with a particular deadline, such as a court hearing. Or there may be concerns that require prompt action leading to a fundamental review of the plan.

Administrative requirements may, on the other hand, deter professionals from arranging reviews if over-methodical arrangements are necessary each time. It is important that planning and reviewing are part of the natural process of work, rather than a periodic event. Planning for children also should take into account an accumulation of new facts that signal the possibility of reassessing part or all of the plan.

Continuity. If the process for making decisions is too separated from that of reviewing, the planning system is likely to suffer from discontinuity, disjunction and repetition – which will leave children and their families at best confused, at worst marginalised. Similarly, if the administrative systems for arranging reviews are not sufficiently flexible, then either decisions will be made in other venues or review meetings will be faced with confirming de facto changes to care plans. The rapidly changing circumstances of adolescents demand this responsiveness, just as much as the developmental progress of infants. The survey findings show that some local authorities have not fully come to terms with this need for continuity.

The layout of the Regulations has not been altogether helpful, dividing placement, planning and reviewing into separate regulations. However the Guidance makes clear that reviews are designed to monitor and amend the care plan as necessary. They are an opportunity to stand back and appraise the progress of the plan. Furthermore, any planning meeting should meet the standard set by reviews:

> *Any* meeting which is convened for the purpose of considering the child's case in connection with *any* aspect of the review of that case falls within the scope of these Regulations. (Department of Health, 1991b, p.80) (emphases added)

Only considerations of complaints or line management meetings are exempted from this provision. The materials prepared by the Looking After Children project have tried to reinforce the message that only a review can change the care plan.

Another enormous dilemma which local authorities have struggled to resolve is the relationship between responsibility for making plans for individual children and that of allocating the resources to fulfil those plans. Here again the survey findings demonstrate the power of panels and other bodies to decide on resource distribution. All this must be made clear to families, as far as possible; without this participation there is a danger that the planning process will be seen as purely an occasion for making lists of good intentions.

These then are some of the criteria that can be used to combat the influence of administrative complexity or inflexibility and to focus attention on the practical needs and circumstances of individual cases. The remainder of the study is devoted to exploring practice in planning and reviewing, thus evaluating the success of the regulatory strategy. In this investigation, the issues covered by the documentation survey are examined in relation to individual cases. The criteria described here will help to orient the investigation by reminding us of the importance of making systems work for individual children, rather than the other way round.

Key findings

- A national survey of documentation about plans and reviews drew responses from 80 authorities in England and Wales.
- When 42 policy and 72 procedure documents were examined, it was found that health and education authorities and other local authority departments had been consulted about them in less than a third of cases. Consultations with child or parent advocacy groups or with representatives of minority ethnic groups took place in less than one tenth of cases.
- Though three quarters of authorities gave copies of procedures to social workers, they were reported to have received copies of policies in just less than two thirds of cases; care staff received such documents in no more than half the cases.
- No more than two fifths of health and education authorities received copies of such documents, while very few representatives of minority ethnic groups were given them. A similar pattern was found when the distribution of forms and of information about plans and reviews was investigated.
- Significant information about parents' rights to be consulted was identified in no more than 14 cases, while similar information in respect of children was found in only ten. In no more than six cases were any documents reported to be available in minority or special languages.
- When the documentation as a whole was evaluated it was found that in about seven out of ten cases the minimum requirements of the Guidance and Regulations had been incorporated.
- Interviews with senior managers in three authorities where the subsequent fieldwork study took place suggested that positive changes in planning and reviewing had occurred since the Children Act 1989. But there were still issues to be resolved about the balance to be struck between supporting sound professional judgements and putting effective procedures into place.

3.   From procedure to practice

Introduction

This chapter explores the implications of selecting the three sample authorities for a study of practice in planning and reviewing. The locations of the fieldwork were intended to reflect a range of social and geographical characteristics across the country as a whole. Areas representing the countryside, the inner cities and the capital were therefore chosen, so as to maximise the relevance of the study. A more detailed area profile is contained in the full report of the project (Sinclair and Grimshaw, 1996).

The chapter goes on to look at the organisation of services for children and, in particular,the local frameworks for the organisation of planning and reviewing. Finally, the chapter examines the methodology and samples of children that featured in the field research.

The research context: fieldwork areas

The first of the three areas selected for the research was a large Midlands County, 'Midshire', within which a rural district was chosen for study. 'Rural Midshire', as it will be termed in this research, was a large district with a major town and many villages dotted across its agricultural landscape.

The second fieldwork area was located in a northern industrial city, 'Northborough'. The research focus lay on inner city areas in Northborough. Two social services area offices were selected, which are here termed Northborough A and B. The great majority of the study cases in the city came from Northborough A. A significant part of that area attracted national attention before and during the research as an area of high deprivation and social malaise. However, Northborough A also extended to a less deprived sector of the city and local data suggested that its pattern of deprivation was similar to the city as a whole. Northborough B was situated on the opposite side of the inner city zone to Northborough A.

The third area was a small inner London borough, 'Westside', all of which could be covered by the research. One of the features which made this borough of special interest was its decision to pilot the Looking After Children Project materials. The area sample therefore consisted of Rural Midshire, mainly inner Northborough and Westside.

Population

The most glaring difference among the areas was in the distribution of population. There were marked contrasts in population density between county and urban areas, ranging from 160 people per square kilometre in Rural Midshire to 12,467 per square kilometre in Westside.

In size, the total child population in the main sample areas was fairly similar, at between 21 and 23 thousand. The exception, Northborough B, had a child population less than half that of Northborough A, but it contributed only a small number of cases to the sample. The similarity in population size belies, as we shall see, their different organisational settings. Table 3.1 shows the child population according to ethnic origin, spotlighting differences in the proportion of black and ethnic minorities.

Table 3.1   Child population aged 0–15 years, by ethnic origin and area, 1991 (percentages)

	England and Wales	Midshire		Northborough			Westside
		All	Rural	All	A	B	
White	90.4	93.1	98.7	89.6	70.2	82.5	75.1
Black	2.6	2.5	0.4	2.4	8.4	1.9	10.8
Asian	5.1	2.9	0.3	5.9	15.9	13.1	3.4
Other	1.9	1.5	0.5	2.2	5.4	2.6	10.7
Total	100	100	100	100	100	100	100

Social and economic conditions

There is good evidence to suggest that the number of children being looked after is linked to social indicators of poverty and deprivation (Bebbington and Miles, 1989). Given the significant geographical differences among the fieldwork areas, were there any relevant differences in social and economic conditions that would help explain the composition of the research samples?

Superficially, the facts of industrial change have been most observable in the North and Midlands. Both Midshire and Northborough were included in European regional initiatives, begun in 1989, 'to promote the conversion of areas affected by industrial decline.' During the 1980s, London and the South East, with their expanding service sector, were regarded as an economic success story. In the early 1990s, however, the position deteriorated with unemployment in the South East rising more rapidly than the national average (Mohan, 1995).

The economy of Rural Midshire itself appeared to be doing better than Midshire as a whole, though there were local problems. A local authority study using 1991 census data showed that 30 per cent of Midshire's population lived in areas of social need compared with 16 per cent in Rural Midshire. Out of the eight county districts, Rural Midshire was, by this standard, the fifth most deprived. Similarly, in July 1995, Rural Midshire ranked fifth out of the eight districts in its rate of unemployment. However, there were pockets of high unemployment, especially in some former mining areas: 6 of the 31 wards in the district had rates above the county average.

A comparison of the urban areas – Northborough and Westside – showed their similarities. These common features are emphasised by a recent analysis of socio-demographic change using data for 1989–90 (Boddy and others, 1995). In fact, Westside and Northborough were found to belong to a cluster of 11 districts (out of 57 inner-city authorities) with similar demographic, social and economic characteristics. The two areas were also found to belong to a grouping of 19 districts with similar patterns of deprivation and poverty. In particular, these areas had intermediate scores for welfare dependency and homelessness but scored poorly on two indicators of child welfare – low birth weight and infant mortality.

The organisation of services for children and families

The structure of services was influenced by the geography of the local authorities and by the degree of their commitment to specialisation.

Midshire was divided into nine districts, each with one or more specialist children's services manager who was responsible for the work of several teams. There was a county management team which produced policy and procedures and monitored information.

Northborough was organised into three main divisions containing 18 areas, the boundaries of which had recently been redrawn. There was a central management team but the manager for each area had a wide responsibility.

In Westside there were only three areas, each with a manager who formed part of the management group headed by a principal officer for children and families. The local managers had become purchasers of the services provided by the fostering and residential sections.

There were significant differences in the organisation of work to meet the needs of children and families. In some respects Midshire had the most specialised organisational structure: most child care work was divided between teams responsible for assessment, children in need and long-term child care. The long-term teams, which held most 'looked

after' cases, contained social workers as well as specialist support workers for children. Some adoption cases were held by the fostering and
adoption team and some 'looked after' cases were held by the youth justice team.

In Westside there were specialist children and families teams composed of case-holding social workers, with a broad remit for child care.
As in Midshire they were supported by specialist teams.

The least specialised structure was found in Northborough where
generic teams remained the norm. A youth court specialist for one area,
for example, was assigned to a local generic team. This had implications
for the scope of supervision: Northborough team leaders oversaw the
work of mental health and social welfare officers as well as social
workers responsible for children. Child care was therefore only one of
the team leaders' responsibilities. Offices were shared with home care
workers who were formally allocated to the area teams but had a
specialist manager of their own.

Given their specialist team structures, it is interesting that neither
Midshire nor Westside had introduced a system of 'independent' review
chairs; only Northborough had gone down that road. Northborough
opted for reviewing by peers from neighbouring areas, rather than by a
specialist reviewing officer. It seemed that in Northborough there was
more emphasis on mingling patterns of work at a local level while in the
other authorities the main focus was on managing work on a discrete
basis.

The local procedural frameworks and the operational context for planning and reviewing

Next, we consider the extent to which the procedural frameworks in the
fieldwork authorities met the criteria set by national Guidance and
Regulations – a significant methodological step prior to the evaluation
of practice. Broadly speaking the frameworks met the prescribed
standards. However some problems and issues about organising and
monitoring reviews were noted.

The frameworks of documentation

The evaluation scores for each of the fieldwork authorities indicated
that on the *organisational* criteria their arrangements were adequate or
above this minimum standard. Midshire's procedures showed only one
area of difficulty, which concerned the authorisation of decisions. In
order to control the large number of S.20 accommodation cases, District
Child Care Panels had been established. They were composed of senior
fieldwork and resource managers and chaired by the Service Manager
responsible for children's services.

After an initial planning meeting between the family and child care professionals, a formal panel meeting would be held to which the family were invited. The Panel would then decide whether the plan should be authorised. It seems doubtful whether this procedure meets the requirement in the Guidance for meetings to be organised in ways that are 'user friendly'. According to a subsequent departmental research report, the sheer size of the Panel's membership was acknowledged by social workers to be 'intimidating' for families. Accordingly, the question of family attendance at the Panels was reconsidered at a policy level during the fieldwork. Apart from this function, the Panels had other important tasks, in monitoring child care careers and the effectiveness of statutory reviews.

The evaluation exercise also considered the extent to which the documentation encouraged *partnership* with children and parents, and *multidisciplinary working*. None of the authorities, unfortunately, had produced information leaflets for children and families specifically about plans and reviews. But, in other respects, most of the documentation was again adequate or better. Westside clearly addressed the issues of children's participation at a level above the minimum standard. However, on this topic there were small but significant gaps in the documentation of the other authorities. For instance, in Northborough, it was not clear that young people could expect to have support at the meeting or be consulted about the venue.

On a few points, Midshire's documentation on reviews presented a somewhat imprecise picture. For instance, information about complaints and representation procedures was not specifically signalled as an issue for the review process. Neither was it clear how young people were to be consulted about the venue of meetings. Attendance at meetings could be substantial: apart from the chair and the social worker it was possible for up to three 'essential attenders' from social services to be identified, including supervisors and the fostering officer. Nonetheless, there were other valid and significant messages about children's participation in the documentation of both Northborough and Midshire.

There were no problems in other areas of partnership and co-working. In each authority's documents, the value of partnership with parents was adequately embodied. In relation to multidisciplinary working, Westside's arrangements rated as adequate, Midshire's as positive and Northborough's as excellent.

Similarly, on a number of *substantive* child care topics – promoting family contact, addressing aspects of ethnicity, education and health – the evaluation indicated that the authorities' arrangements were adequate or better. For these substantive topics, Northborough's ratings were consistently positive.

The results of the evaluation imply that the authorities had established a sound basis for the practice of planning and reviewing, with clear expectations that practitioners should be able to understand. However, it was essential to ask managers more about the way in which the procedural framework was operationalised.

The operational context for reviewing

Working in an organisation is a more complex business than a study of its procedural frameworks would suggest. Interviews with a total of seven senior and middle managers in the three authorities made it plain that the *operational* context for reviewing was different in important ways from the *procedural* framework: not all the things outlined on paper were present in reality.

Midshire

The county of Midshire consisted of nine extensive districts, of which Rural Midshire was only one. A major issue particular to this local authority was how to address the difficult challenge of coordinating such a far-flung organisation.

Local managers were seen as responsible for the coordination of reviews. In Rural Midshire an administrative system provided a print out about the due reviews, which was meant to alert social workers and team leaders. The list also went to the local manager. The team leaders who line-managed the social workers would chair the reviews. This system meant that some line managers – those in the long-term teams – were much more heavily committed to reviewing tasks than their colleagues, causing a particular burden.

The districts' practices were not monitored centrally. 'It's not something we've actively monitored, whether (the districts) follow the format' (Senior manager, Midshire). Monitoring at the centre consisted largely of examining broad outcomes for particular categories of case, for example Section 20 admissions. Policy makers were mainly concerned with obtaining a strategic overview, occasionally backed up by detailed in-house research in the localities. Quite reasonably it was pointed out that the size of the county precluded blanket surveillance of every case. Sampling procedures would be necessary in order to focus on trends and patterns. But there was no target or performance indicator for the implementation of child care decisions – 'no scientific assessment of the gap between need and provision'.

Monitoring, therefore, in practice was local. It was intended to be carried out by the District Child Care Panels overseen by District Managers. Local monitoring was perceived by a manager at the centre to be inadequate, leading to drift in the implementation of decisions.

'One of our biggest issues is lack of involvement by District Managers in individual cases – the need to have quality control sampling of what is going on . . . District Managers need to be in helicopters (so to speak) . . . and swooping down [to check out practice].' (Senior manager, Midshire)

The Rural Midshire manager confirmed that quality assurance was not carried out and saw it as a significant problem which needed to be remedied.

The local manager made a check simply on whether reviews were done. It was the responsibility of the team leaders to see that decisions were implemented. The local manager became aware of implementation though chairing certain meetings – case conferences and fostering panels – and through payments – S.24 allocations, for example. In practice, the local District Child Care Panel did not carry out a monitoring function of the kind that the local manager would have liked.

Northborough

By comparison with Midshire, Northborough was, of course, smaller in area. But its number of children looked after was not dissimilar. Northborough's policy initiatives on planning and reviewing stemmed from a children's operations group chaired by an assistant director. It was the only authority in the fieldwork sample to commit itself to a form of 'independent' reviewing in which a senior person other than the line manager takes the chair.

The first review was normally chaired by the team leader with line management responsibility. Subsequent reviews were chaired by a team leader without such responsibility. Team leaders from the same office were allocated groups of social workers for whom they became 'independent reviewing officers'. This system seems to be one of the most simple variants of 'independent reviewing'; other authorities have appointed specialist independent reviewing officers with a larger caseload. These issues are explored more fully in Chapter 7.

The arrangements for chairing in Northborough had clearly led to intensive thinking about the concepts of 'plan' and 'review'. There seemed to be agreement that planning was itself a process separate from reviewing.

'[We are] trying to reinforce independent reviewing – not planning. Planning is for the first line manager and the social worker.' (Senior manager, Northborough)

'People are more clear [since the Children Act 1989] about the reviewing function as opposed to planning . . . . I see them as rather different. The manager of the case, the social worker, child and so on make the plan. The reviewing officer is reviewing it . . .' (Local manager, Northborough)

The rationale given for independent reviewing was to increase the objectivity of reviewing the process.

'it was collusive to have a line manager [doing reviews]. It's hard to be objective.' (Senior manager, Northborough)

Yet it is difficult to see how the intentions of the Guidance can be fulfilled unless the planning process is linked to the review in a purposeful way. In this respect some problems were reported.

Organising reviews in Northborough was neither simple nor straightforward. The system was described as depending heavily on social workers' initiatives. A print out about reviews due was supposed to be given to the social worker. However, there were administrative problems affecting computer output and the local manager admitted that there was 'always slippage'. This deficiency was acknowledged to be a citywide problem. Staff shortages were another drain on the system's efficiency. Despite their systems for parcelling out reviews among team leaders, these areas of Northborough appeared to be struggling to perform reviews.

Once the review was completed, what happened that might reinforce the continuity of the process? In Northborough, reviews were ratified by the local manager. One of the reasons given for this procedure was to reconcile any differences between the views of the line manager and the reviewing officer. The local manager also assumed a responsibility for checking on gaps in the implementation of plans but this was an indirect responsibility, with a generous timescale attached.

'Eighteen months down the track, I'd feel I had some responsibility [for non-implementation of a plan].'

But a responsibility for ratification was not combined with a role in monitoring and quality assurance. Indeed it was confirmed that the authority did not have a monitoring system.

'I don't think there is one. Information isn't collated . . . we've not been asked to do it departmentally.'

Though there were managers of greater seniority who were supposed to look at area performance, there was no systematic information base for this task. The senior managers could only look at reports on resource use, or scrutinise individual cases referred to them, such as requests for placements outside the authority. The absence of monitoring was confirmed by an internal report written in 1992 which recommended a programme for regularly surveying and monitoring reviews. In practice, by the end of the fieldwork period, there was no evidence of such a programme.

Westside

Westside was by far the most geographically compact authority of the three involved in the fieldwork and looked after less than a fifth of the number of children who were the responsibility of the other authorities. Here local managers were influential figures.

In Westside, team leaders normally chaired the reviews of social workers in their own team, as the procedures suggested, though one manager pointed out that by agreement a child protection specialist in his area chaired some reviews.

In Westside, computerisation was used as a tool much more evidently than in the other two authorities. There was a detailed individual computer record for each child, showing all previous and forthcoming conferences and reviews, together with basic details about the individual's care episodes. Using the record, the team review clerk was able to flag upcoming reviews, the dates of which had been agreed at the previous review. The system was felt to be working well. As a quality control, one manager also read each review record.

> 'I look for gaps, questions not answered, lack of explanation and I ask questions.' (Manager, Westside)

Monitoring in this detail was not carried out in each Westside area. It seemed to be an easier task in areas where the local manager had an office at the same site as the teams, compared with areas where the teams were dispersed.

Methodology and fieldwork samples

Introduction

This section outlines the research methodology and profiles the samples drawn from the fieldwork areas.

The field research was designed to include a number of related components. The primary task was to identify a target sample of 60 cases in each fieldwork area, generating a total of 180 cases. Data about planning and reviewing were collected from the social work files on these children.

For 45 cases within the target sample, review meetings were to be observed. From these cases, a further small sample was to be selected so that interviews with all those attending the meeting would be undertaken. These objectives were achieved.

Focus group meetings for young people were also planned to take place in each local authority area. In practice, only one authority was able to help arrange a session, and a voluntary group made it possible for one further focus group to be organised.

A survey of the social workers responsible for the cases in the main sample was successfully conducted.

Finally, the implications of the research results were discussed at three regional workshops for local authority representatives.

As we shall see, there are children in the main sample who were born not just in different counties or boroughs but in different continents. Despite this, there are also many things, like schooling or being in foster care, which the children share. Profiling the sample makes us aware of that mixture of features and warns us against any tendency to stereotype them.

Methodology

Selection of the main sample cases. A sample was drawn by means of systematic sampling, which involves selecting a target number of cases from a list at proportionate intervals (Hoinville and others, 1977, p.61). However, the available listings were not always comprehensive, so efforts had to be made to seek out cases that might have been overlooked (Sinclair and Grimshaw, 1996).

Table 3.2 shows the number of teams contributing cases to the samples in each area. The Westside sample was the most extensive, spread over the caseloads of 13 teams, compared with almost half that number of teams in the other two areas.

Table 3.2   Teams contributing cases to the samples

Midshire (N=6)	Northborough (N=7)	Westside (N=13)
Rural Midshire	*District A*	Local area (11)
Long term (2)	Local area (4)	Homelessness (1)
Adoption and Fostering (1)	*District B*	Hospital (1)
Juvenile Justice (1)	Local area (2)	
Rural Neighbourhood (1)	Community Learning Disabilities (1)	
Community Mental Handicap (1)		

From each authority's set of teams, 60 cases were selected. Information about a total of 180 cases was therefore collected from the available records. Not unexpectedly, some information was found to be missing from particular files. One or two files were transferred beyond reach of the study before the data collection was complete. Very occasionally, reports of meetings that had been observed by the researcher proved to be unobtainable. Despite such individual difficulties, a body of data was collected which substantially fulfilled the original aims.

Observations of meetings. In addition to case records, it was felt that review meetings had a major significance for the practice of planning and reviewing. Forty-two meetings involving 48 cases within the main fieldwork sample were therefore observed, after access had been negotiated. Only four children or parents actually refused when approached by a social worker or team leader. In all, access was gained to 42, out of a possible total of 57 meetings. Chapters 5 and 6 provide more details about the meetings sample.

Case study interviews. Case studies were undertaken in order to find out more about the qualitative experience of planning and reviewing and to compare the viewpoints of children, parents and professionals. Case studies were performed on a small sample of cases after the meeting had been observed.

In carrying out the case studies, it was a priority to interview children and parents attending the reviews. An interview was sought, firstly, with the young person attending the review and then with the other people present. If it was not possible to interview the parents who attended, further cases were chosen and as many attenders as possible were interviewed. Interviews with all attenders eventually took place in 12 out of the 15 cases where interviews were begun. The breakdown of case study interviews is shown in Table 3.3.

Table 3.3   Interviews with review meeting attenders

Family group	Young people	12
	Parents	6
	Other relatives and friends	3
Primary care	Carers	14
	Social workers	12
Secondary care	Chairs	12
	Fostering officers	2
	Residential managers	2
Other disciplines	Teachers	2
	Health professionals	1
	Total	66

Focus groups with young people. The individual interview method is not always successful in encouraging people to articulate general viewpoints. Focus group forums were therefore organised in order to encourage young people to express their general attitudes towards reviews. This strategy of group interviewing was an adaptation of the focus group session developed mainly for adults. In a relaxed and comfortable environment, a group of six to eight people is brought together for a guided discussion, subject to ethical guidelines agreed beforehand (Krueger, 1994). The comments made during the two focus group sessions appear at several points within the chapters which follow.

Survey of social workers. In order to add a practice perspective to the research, a postal survey of social workers responsible for the sample cases was undertaken. The questionnaire explored their experiences and opinions, using a mixture of attitude scales and open ended questions.

Out of 82 social workers contacted, 49 responses were obtained. The main reasons given for non-response were that social workers were on leave or had changed their employment. Data from the survey have been included at various appropriate points in the following chapters.

A broader policy perspective on the general findings of the research was later obtained by organising three regional workshops with a wide group of local authority representatives.

The main fieldwork sample

Using the case file records, data was collected about the characteristics and background of the children, whether they were on the child protection register, their legal status and reasons for being looked after, their current home circumstances, their placement, their education, and the periods of time that they had been looked after by the local authority. This section gives a selective profile of the children who form the main sample for the study as a whole.

As previously indicated, the process of sampling was rather different in each local authority. Where relevant, therefore, the characteristics and background of the children in the sample were compared with data about the population of looked after children in the local areas included in the study. However, because the sample was selected over time rather than on a particular day, there are likely to be some differences between the composition of the sample and the 'snapshot' data collected by the local authorities. Selecting cases over time is a more thorough procedure because a greater number of cases is potentially available.

The first two sections of this profile outline major personal characteristics of children in the main sample: gender, age, ethnicity, language and religious affiliation.

Gender and age

The gender distribution of the sample (52 per cent males; 48 per cent females) was within the usual expectations (Rowe, Hundleby and Garnett, 1989).

Figure 3.1 shows that their age distribution was relatively normal: a fifth were less than five years old; a quarter were aged from five to nine years; over a third were from 10 to 15 years old; and just over a fifth were at least 16 years old. There were significant differences among the local authority samples (chi-square p<.01).

In Midshire, the proportion of children under five years old was significantly lower than in the other samples. In Northborough, the proportion of very young children in the sample was significantly higher than elsewhere. The Northborough sample also contained the highest proportion of children aged from five to nine years, while having a low proportion of young people aged 16 years and over. As we shall shortly see, the age of the Northborough sample was linked to other characteristics that defined them as vulnerable. The Westside sample presented a different pattern: it had the lowest proportion of five- to nine-year-olds; a majority of its sample were at least ten years old.

The proportions of young people aged 16 and over were somewhat lower in the samples than in the official figures for the sample areas and this discrepancy was most marked for the Northborough figures. The sampling procedure was, of course, quite different from a 'snapshot' on a particular day which may understate the throughput of younger children and exaggerate the representation of adolescents (Rowe, Hundleby and Garnett, 1989).

Ethnicity, language and religion

Almost two thirds of the sample were white. The black and minority ethnic groups represented most frequently were: Africans (mostly from Ethiopia or Eritrea) (14 per cent); those of mixed white/other parentage (10 per cent); and African-Caribbeans (5 per cent). There were only two children from the Indian subcontinent (1 per cent). Nearly a fifth of the children's first languages were other than English, and the most frequent of these were African. Figure 3.2 summarises the distribution of ethnic categories and shows large differences among the three local samples ($p < .01$).

As expected, Rural Midshire's sample had a very low proportion of children from black and minority ethnic groups. In Northborough, it was sometimes difficult to establish the child's ethnic identity but, on the information available, Northborough seems to form an intermediate case, while in Westside the majority of children were identified as from black or minority ethnic groups. The largest minority ethnic group – Africans – were represented only in Westside. The distribution in Westside was therefore heavily influenced, as we shall see further, by the arrival of unaccompanied refugees from Africa (Sinclair, Garnett and Berridge, 1995). In general, the differences are very striking and emphasise the variation of social work tasks in these metropolitan, urban and rural areas.

In nearly four out of ten cases, no information about the child's religious affiliation (or lack of it) was found. Of those cases where information was recorded, 70 per cent of the children were described as Christians. The Muslim religion and other faiths accounted for slightly

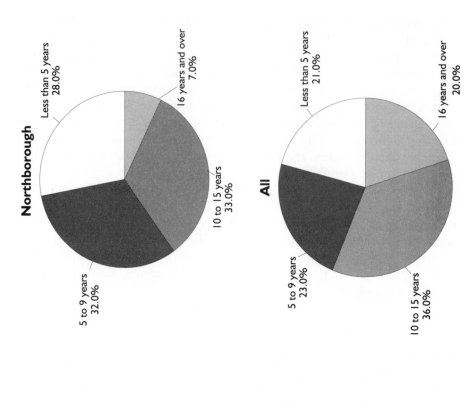

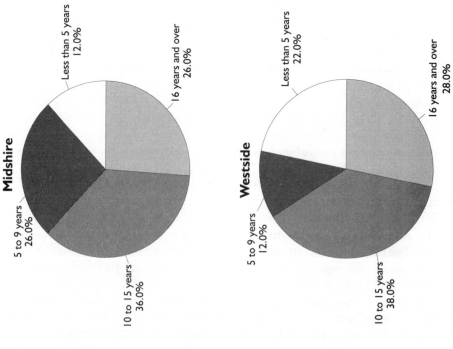

Figure 3.1   Age group, by local authority sample

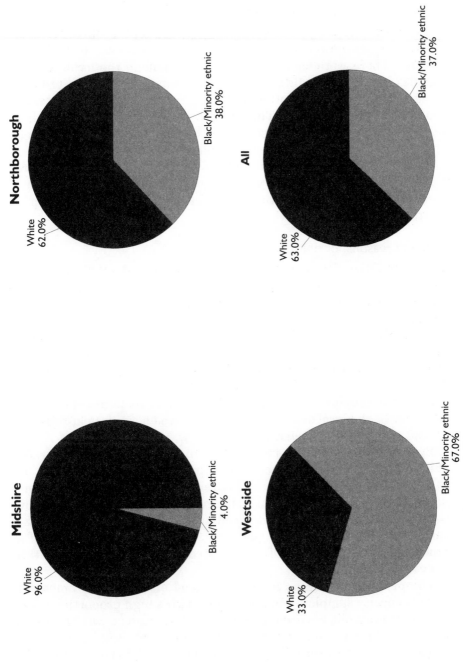

Figure 3.2   Ethnic categories, by local authority sample

less than 10 per cent of cases. A fifth were recorded as having no religious affiliation.

Placement on the Child Protection Register

A quarter of the sample were currently placed on the Child Protection Register. Registration was significantly associated with the child's age (p<.01). There were significant differences among the local authority samples (p<.01). Two fifths of the cases in Northborough were registered, compared with about one fifth of Westside cases, and less than a sixth of those in Midshire. This pattern is broadly consistent with the normal local practices of registration. The high proportion of registered children in Northborough seemed again to be linked to their ages: for example, 14 of the 16 children under five years of age were registered. Young children who were looked after were therefore generally considered to be vulnerable and this was a particular focus of work in the Northborough cases.

Legal status and reasons for being looked after

In all, two fifths of the cases were accommodated under S.20 and the rest were in care. Most of the latter group had been the subject of full Care Orders. There was a significant difference among the local authority samples which is demonstrated in Figure 3.3.

The lowest proportion of children accommodated under S.20 was in Northborough. This proportion was very similar to the last 'snapshot' figures for each Northborough sample area (Districts A and B) and for Northborough as a whole. The intermediate case was Midshire, while the highest proportion was found in Westside. In terms of children's legal status, the local authority samples showed a similar pattern to the official area figures (Sinclair and Grimshaw, 1996).

By far the most common reason for being looked after was the risk to children from abuse or neglect, accounting for 45 per cent of cases. The other significant reasons were: children being refugees (12 per cent); parental ill-health (10 per cent); children being at risk from their own behaviour (9 per cent); parents needing relief because of the stress of caring for a disabled child (6 per cent); and parents needing relief for other reasons (4 per cent). Offence-related reasons applied to only three per cent of the children.

The pattern of reasons for being looked after differed among the local authority samples. With Northborough's high proportion of care orders, it was not surprising that abuse or neglect was the reason given in 70 per cent of its cases, compared with much lower proportions in Westside (36 per cent) and Midshire (26 per cent). The low figure for Midshire seems related to the fact that some of its records were unclear about the reason for being looked after: only

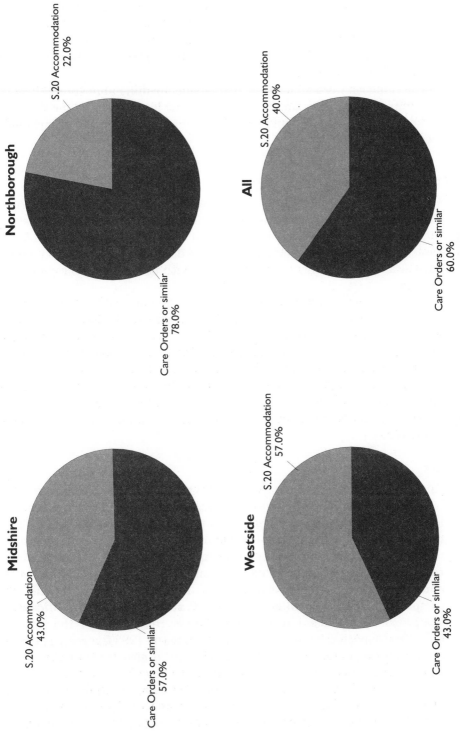

Figure 3.3   Whether in S.20 accommodation or in care, by local authority sample

about three quarters of the Midshire case records clearly contained this information. However, there were indications that, in Midshire, the parents' own difficulties, such as health problems, were more frequently cited as reasons for being looked after, though the numbers in these categories were small.

The refugees were all located in Westside, forming almost one third of its sample. This proportion is in line with the local statistics for children looked after. Their age profile was older than in other cases: nearly half were at least 16 years old.

Current home circumstances

Where possible, information was collected about each child's current 'home base', in other words, a household where a parent figure was living. Some kind of home base was in fact identified in nine out of ten cases. For refugees, in particular, it was difficult to identify any home base at all because they had lost contact with parents in their countries of origin.

In all, the most common home base consisted of a mother living alone (two fifths of cases). The proportion of home bases with a lone father was less than a twentieth. In only a sixth of cases was a household containing both natural parents of the child identified as the home base. A new partnership formed the home base in only an eighth of cases.

This pattern of data indicates that, though many children had a home base, this was unlikely to be in a two-parent household or in a new relationship which one of the parents had formed (Bullock, Little and Millham, 1993).

Placement

In all, a sixth of the sample lived with their parents or in other settings within the community. Almost six tenths of children were placed in foster care while only an eighth were placed in residential homes. The remaining tenth were in semi-independent placements or other settings.

The Midshire sample contained the highest proportion of children currently living with their parents or in community settings (29 per cent), and a tiny proportion – just one child – in a residential placement. By comparison with the available 'snapshot' statistics for Rural Midshire, the proportion of foster placements (50 per cent) is lower than would have been expected (66 per cent, according to the 1993 figures). The very low proportion of residential cases (2 per cent) is also less than the 'snapshot' figure (9 per cent); in this instance, we have been advised that the high 'snapshot' figure is unrealistic, and may be attributable to court remands. The Midshire sample therefore seems to reflect the more fluid aspects of child care placement, as children moved between substitute care placements and settings in the home and community.

The Northborough sample had the highest proportion of children in residential placements (22 per cent). This proportion was consistent with the local 'snapshot' figure (17 per cent).

The Westside sample had the highest proportion in foster care (67 per cent) and the lowest proportion living with their parents or in the community (7 per cent). Its proportions of cases in fostering and residential placements (67 and 15 per cent, respectively) were close to the most recent (1994) 'snapshot' figures for the borough (63 and 19 per cent, respectively).

Education and employment

Just over two thirds of 3- and 4-year-olds were in educational placements. Three quarters of 5- to 10-year-olds were in mainstream schools but a fifth were in special education. There was a similar pattern for 11- to 15-year-olds, but the proportion in other provision, outside the school system, increased from just 2 per cent to 10 per cent of cases. Two thirds of those over 16 years of age had an educational placement. There were no significant differences among the local authority samples in these patterns.

Placement for special educational needs had been arranged for a very high proportion of the sample. Indeed, a quarter of the sample had, at some stage, either received a statement of special educational needs or had been referred for one. These findings confirm the prevalence of special educational needs among children looked after, which has been suggested by recent research (Ofsted/SSI, 1995).

With so many young people in education, data about employment related to only a small part of the sample. Of ten young people over school leaving age and not in any form of education, five were unemployed, one was in part time employment, three were undergoing Employment Training and the remaining young person was doing voluntary work. If these small-scale findings illustrate anything, it is that young people who have finished their education occupy a weak position in the current marketplace (Sinclair, Garnett and Berridge, 1995).

Continuity and discontinuity in being looked after

Over seven out of ten children had experienced one single continuous episode of being looked after. There were significant differences between children who had been looked after continuously and those who had not.

As expected, continuity was more frequent among children in care than among those accommodated under S.20. It was most frequent among those who had been looked after for more than a year and among those whose current plans did not involve a return to the birth family.

Over eight out of ten children looked after because of abuse or neglect had experienced a single continuous episode, as had all the refugees.

There were also significant differences among the local authority samples in this experience of continuity (p<.01). The Midshire sample had the lowest proportion of children looked after continuously (57 per cent) compared with higher proportions in Northborough (75 per cent) and Westside (83 per cent).

The data indicate that repeated episodes had been experienced by a minority of children who were most likely to be currently accommodated under S.20. By contrast the majority had experienced only one continuous episode up to the point when our main sample review occurred. Discontinuity was more frequent in the Midshire sample, whose current placements, as we have seen, were also more likely to be in the home or the community.

Total length of time looked after

Data were collected about the total period over which a child had been looked after. For those who had experienced more than one episode, all the recorded episodes of being looked after were added together.

The largest group of children – two fifths – had been looked after for less than one year; the proportion of the sample looked after for one to two years was only a sixth, with similarly low proportions for subsequent yearly intervals. The maximum period during which a child had been looked after was over 16 years.

There was a clear difference between cases accommodated under S.20 and those in care (p<.01). Children in care were more likely to have been looked after for longer than a year. Indeed, nine out of ten children looked after for more than four years were in care (Rowe, Hundleby and Garnett, 1989).

When the local authority samples were compared, it emerged that the Midshire cases tended to have been looked after for a longer period of time, as shown in Figure 3.4.

The case study sample

Case studies were selected so that some of the major characteristics of 'looked after' cases would be included, as well as cases from each of the local authority areas. As explained earlier, the target was to conduct 12 complete case studies. After some difficulties, this target was achieved. Before reaching it, three further studies were started but, for various reasons, could not be finished in every respect. The 15 children consisted of nine boys and six girls.

Because a priority for the research was to interview the child, the great majority of the case studies (12 out of 15) concerned young people who were at least 12 years old. Most were white and belonged to the

Figure 3.4   Time looked after, by local authority sample

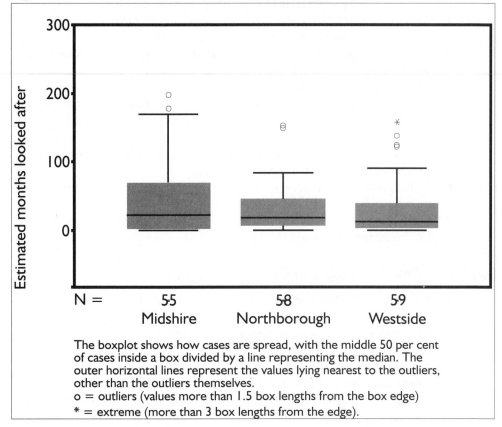

The boxplot shows how cases are spread, with the middle 50 per cent of cases inside a box divided by a line representing the median. The outer horizontal lines represent the values lying nearest to the outliers, other than the outliers themselves.
o = outliers (values more than 1.5 box lengths from the box edge)
* = extreme (more than 3 box lengths from the edge).

Christian faith: three of the 15 were from black and minority ethnic groups (two African and one Pakistani) and just one was brought up in the Muslim faith. The first languages of two children were other than English. One of the children used a special language in order to communicate, while no less than five were placed in special education of some kind. Most had been looked after for over a year and a majority had received full care orders; the risk of abuse or neglect was the most common reason for being looked after.

Each local authority sample contributed to the case studies (five from Midshire; four from Northborough; and six from Westside). As intended, this small subsample of case studies covered a range of different child characteristics and situations, but was mainly focused on those at least 12 years old.

Key findings

- A comparison of the three fieldwork locations – Rural Midshire, mainly inner Northborough, and Westside – showed similarities in the social characteristics of the two urban areas.

- The most specialised structure of social work services was found in Midshire and the least specialised in Northborough.
- The three authorities had established procedural frameworks that adequately fulfilled the regulatory requirements.
- In Midshire and Westside, reviews were chaired by the team manager who supervised the social worker responsible for the case; in Northborough, chairing was usually performed independently, by neighbouring team managers who shared out the cases amongst themselves. In Northborough, there was a clear belief that planning was a separate activity from reviewing.
- The monitoring of reviews was variable and tended to concentrate on whether or not reviews were being done.
- Only in Westside were the pilot versions of the *Looking After Children* materials widely used.

Summary of methodology and fieldwork samples

- A total of 180 cases, drawn equally from the three fieldwork areas, was selected for study. These formed the main fieldwork sample and were drawn from the caseloads of 26 teams.
- Forty-two review meetings involving 48 children within the main sample were observed.
- Case study interviews were conducted with all the meeting attenders in 12 such cases. In a further three cases, some interviews were carried out. Focus group interviews took place with young people in one of the local authorities and in a voluntary organisation not involved in the fieldwork.
- A total of 49 social workers responsible for cases in the main sample responded to a questionnaire survey.
- Three regional workshops were held in order to discuss the implications of the findings as a whole.

The main fieldwork sample

- Table 3.4 summarises the principal features of the sample according to their distribution in the local authority samples.
- Two thirds of three- to four-year-olds and the same proportion of those aged at least 16 years were in educational placements. Almost a fifth of 5- to 15-year-olds were currently in special educational placements, while a quarter of the whole sample had, at some stage, either received a statement of special educational needs, or had been referred for one.
- Children in care and those looked after for more than a year were more likely to have been looked after in one single continuous

episode than those accommodated under S.20 or looked after for less than a year.

Case study sample

- Fifteen cases from the main sample were selected for special attention. Twelve out of the 15 children were at least 12 years old, while three were from black and minority ethnic groups.
- A majority had received full care orders and the most common reason for being looked after was the risk to a child of abuse or neglect. Most had been looked after for more than a year.

Table 3.4   Summary of the main cases, by local authority sample

Midshire	Northborough	Westside	All
A clear majority over ten years old	A clear majority under ten years old	A clear majority over ten years old	A small majority over ten years old
Less than a tenth from black and minority ethnic groups	Over a third from black and minority ethnic groups	Two thirds from black and minority ethnic groups	Almost four out of ten from black and minority ethnic groups
Less than a sixth placed on CPR	Four out of ten placed on CPR	A fifth placed on CPR	A quarter placed on CPR
A majority in care	A majority in care	A majority accommodated under S.20	A majority in care
One quarter looked after because of abuse/neglect	Seven out of ten looked after because of abuse/neglect	One third looked after because of abuse/neglect	Over four out of ten looked after because of abuse/neglect
No refugees	No refugees	Almost one third refugees	One eighth refugees
Half in foster care	Almost six out of ten in foster care	Two thirds in foster care	Almost six out of ten in foster care
Almost six out of ten looked after in one continuous episode	Three quarters looked after in one continuous episode	Eight out of ten looked after in one continuous episode	Seven out of ten looked after in one continuous episode
Mean estimated months looked after = 46	Mean estimated months looked after = 31	Mean estimated months looked after = 26	Mean estimated months looked after = 34

4. Inquiry, consultation and assessment

Introduction

This chapter examines the preparation which should occur prior to a review meeting. What kinds of information are available to decision makers? And how adequate are they? The Guidance distinguishes four typical stages in the planning process: inquiry, consultation, assessment and decision making (Volume 3, Ch. 2.43). This chapter therefore deals with the three stages before decision making. It was not possible to study these stages at the time they occurred. However, information from the case files, interviews and the social workers' survey will be used to build up a picture of how the different stages combined in practice.

A major purpose of this study was to investigate how far the prescriptions of the Guidance and Regulations on planning and reviewing have exerted an influence on practice in three distinctive local authority settings. In order to identify such influence, a set of evaluative criteria were created, closely following the framework laid down by official directives. Ratings were made of the evidence of inquiry and consultation in the case files, using a five-point scale in the following ascending order: 'missing', 'limited', 'adequate', 'positive' and 'excellent'. The use of evaluation ratings for assessment deserves further explanation. No particular format for general assessment, such as the LAC system, is specified by the Guidance. The broad contents of assessment are described by the Guidance in general terms that resemble the specifi- cations for the plan (Volume 3, Ch. 2.54–58 and 2.62). In order therefore to focus the evaluation and avoid unnecessary duplication, it was decided that the general plan (rather than the general assessment) should be evaluated. A report of this evaluation is a task for a later chapter. However, because health and education assessments are relat- ively specific and represent the work of separate agencies, ratings of these particular assessments were made. The range of other assessments, including Assessment and Action Records, is also quanti- fied and discussed.

The findings were then analysed in order to discover whether they were associated with any particular features of the cases in the main sample. Thus, the analysis drew on information about the children's gender, age, ethnic group, legal status, placement and the period that they had been looked after. Information from interviews and the survey is used to put these findings in a broader context. The conclusion examines the implications of the findings, especially in considering how far specified procedures and paperwork have become part and parcel of practice.

Sample

The major sources of data in this chapter were the records associated with a single review within a case file. In principle a review was to be selected for full study and evaluation from each file in the main target sample of 180 cases but owing to the unavailability of records or the failure to hold a review, this was sometimes possible only on a partial basis. Table 4.1 shows how the target sample of major reviews was reduced by such factors to a core of 165 cases (N indicates numbers, not percentages). The review sample was affected to a greater degree in Northborough and Midshire than in Westside.

Table 4.1   Core review sample, by local authority

	Midshire	Northborough	Westside	All
	N	N	N	N
Target sample	60	60	60	180
Review document unavailable	4	6	0	10
No core review	2	2	1	5
Core review sample	54	52	59	165

Because some of the detailed information within such files was also unavailable, a number of the tables in this chapter present even lower totals. However, in other cases, the totals are somewhat higher because assessment information (such as evidence of inquiry) was available even though the final review report was not. In order to arrive at as fair a view of the evidence as possible, the individual totals have not therefore been uniformly standardised.

Inquiry

The case file records pertaining to the selected review were scanned for evidence of inquiry. The main purpose was to identify factual information that had a bearing on the current handling of the case. Was there, for example, an up-to-date note of the addresses of parents and other significant people? Was there a social history or a summary of key features, such as the LAC Basic Facts Sheet (used only in Westside)? The next example shows a case where the information-finding was rated as 'positive'.

> *Case 63*. Following difficulties associated with his mother's mental health, a boy was placed on the child protection register and made subject to an interim care order shortly after his birth. As part of a systematic assessment of the father's parenting potential, enquiries were made to the Home Office and International Social Services about his background.

On the other hand, the following cases illustrate the kind of information rated as 'limited':

> *Case 9*. An 11-year-old white boy, the subject of a care order, was in a stable foster care placement. Though the addresses of some family members had been systematically recorded on the file, there was no clear evidence of the addresses of his GP or school.

> *Case 20*. A nine-year-old girl of unrecorded ethnic origin was receiving respite care. There was no factual information about the progress of the placement arrangements during the period of more than a year since they had started.

> *Case 144*. The siblings of a 15-year-old refugee from Eritrea were apparently living in the UK but their addresses had not been ascertained. The young person's immigration details were recorded on the files as missing and her Basic Facts Sheet had not been updated.

Table 4.2 compares the results in each local authority sample. Evidence of inquiry was found in over eight out of ten cases; the range was from 74 per cent of cases (Midshire) to 92 per cent (Westside).

Table 4.2 Evidence of inquiry, by local authority sample

	Midshire		Northborough		Westside		All	
	N	%	N	%	N	%	N	%
Evidence of inquiry								
	40	74	42	79	55	92	137	82
Total	54	100	53	100	60	100	167	100

The clarity and comprehensiveness of the information contained in the case file was then evaluated on the five-point scale, using the categories 'missing', 'limited', 'adequate', 'positive' and 'excellent'. Figure 4.1 compares the evaluation scores for the different local authority samples. The results for the whole sample indicate that over half the cases of inquiry were given an 'adequate' rating. But when the local ratings are compared there appear to be some differences.

The Midshire sample had the highest proportion of 'adequate' scores but the lowest proportion of 'positive' or 'excellent' scores; the Northborough sample results were more diverse, having the highest

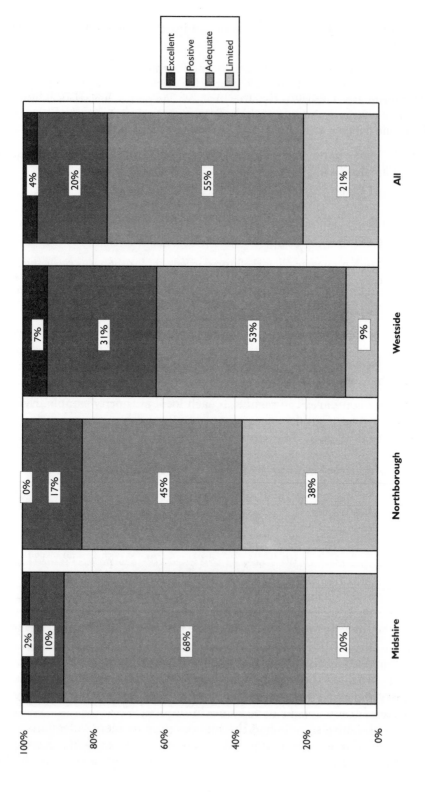

Figure 4.1   Comprehensive and clearly presented facts, by local authority sample

proportion of 'limited' scores but a higher proportion of 'positive' or 'excellent' ratings than Midshire. Westside's performance seemed to be superior: nearly all of its scores were distributed in the middle and upper ranges. In Westside, the Basic Facts Sheet, predecessor of the Essential Information Record, was in common use throughout the research period. No similar document was used in the other areas. A form designed to collate basic information seemed to make some difference to the presentation of facts in case files, suggesting that the LAC approach has been effective.

Consultation

Consultation with children

The Guidance makes clear that consultation should take place with children, subject to their understanding. This means obtaining their wishes and feelings (Volume 3, Ch. 2.46–47). It was often difficult to determine from the records whether their views had been ascertained before the review meeting. However, consultation with children which had occurred at some stage in the process was evident in the records of over two thirds of the sample. Table 4.3 shows how the frequency of consultation was associated with the child's age.

Table 4.3 Consultation with children, by age group

	Years of age									
	Under 5		5 to 10		11 to 15		16 and over		All	
	N	%	N	%	N	%	N	%	N	%
Consultation with child	3	9	23	56	46	88	32	91	104	65
Total	32	100	41	100	52	100	35	100	160	100

Young people over 11 years of age were very frequently consulted but the rate of consultation for five- to 10-year-olds fell to almost a half and then dropped to a tenth, for those under five. The data on children aged five to 10 years shows a particularly interesting pattern, in that just over half the age group were consulted. To see whether age differences within this group helped to explain the frequency of consultation, a further analysis was undertaken, which confirmed this hypothesis.

Table 4.4 shows that, unlike those aged five to seven years, a majority of the subgroup aged from eight to 10 years were consulted. This older category clearly accounted for most of those consulted at primary school age. Since children's understanding of a review may have been associated in professionals' minds with their education, did their educational placements affect whether or not they were consulted? An investigation into a possible relationship between the type of schooling and the frequency of consultation revealed no association between these variables for children of primary school age; a child in special education seemed no more or less likely to have been consulted than a child in a mainstream school. Age appeared therefore to be a more significant variable than schooling. If professionals did link schooling with a child's degree of understanding, there was no sign that any such assumption was a significant influence on the frequency of consultation. The child developmental issues surrounding consultation with five- to seven-year-olds are delicate but there is clear scope for talking with them about significant topics, for example, the people who are important in their lives (Wassell and Wilson, 1992).

Table 4.4   Consultation with children of primary school age

	Years of age					
	5 to 7		8 to 10		All	
	N	%	N	%	N	%
Consultation with child	10	38	13	87	23	56
Total	26	100	15	100	41	100

There was no evidence that features of the case such as gender, ethnic group, or placement were connected with the frequency of consultation with children. No significant difference was found among the local authority samples.

Consultation with mothers

The records of reviews were studied in order to find any evidence of parental consultation, though it was not always possible to establish whether this had occurred prior to a meeting. In looking at this evidence, the rate of consultation with mothers was examined separately. This measure excludes 19 cases (such as unaccompanied refugees in Westside) in which consultation seemed to be impossible. Taking this into account, Table 4.5 shows that two thirds of mothers were consulted, but this varied with the child's age group.

There was some evidence of a difference in the rate of consultation with mothers of children in different age groups (chi-square p<.05). The rate of consultation for children under ten years of age was over seven out of ten, but from the age of 16 years this slipped just below half the relevant cases. There was no significant difference linked to the children's gender or ethnicity. The rate of consultation with mothers was not significantly different among the local authority samples.

Table 4.5 Evidence of consultation with mother, by age group

	Years of age									
	Less than 5		5 to 10		11 to 15		16 and over		All	
	N	%	N	%	N	%	N	%	N	%
Mother consulted	25	78	29	74	21	54	11	48	86	65
Valid cases	32	100	39	100	39	100	23	100	133	100

Not surprisingly, there was a very high rate of consultation with mothers (94 per cent) when the child was living with a parent. Mothers of children accommodated under S.20 were significantly more likely to be consulted than those with children in care (p<.01). But there was no significant statistical difference between the rate of consultation with mothers of children in foster care, compared with mothers of children in residential placements. Consultation was more frequent at important transitional stages in a child's career within the system. For example, when children were on the child protection register, mothers were significantly more likely to be consulted (four fifths of cases) (p<.05). The rates for those on different kinds of care order show the pattern of consultation at different stages. Table 4.6 compares these rates with the rate for all legal statuses combined.

Table 4.6 Evidence of consultation with mother – care orders

	Interim Care Order		Care Order		Deemed Care Order		All legal statuses	
	N	%	N	%	N	%	N	%
Consultation with mothers	17	74	16	48	11	39	84	64
Valid cases	23	100	33	100	28	100	131	100

The table shows a decline from a higher than average rate during interim care orders to a lower than average rate thereafter. By comparison the rate for S.20 accommodation cases (not short term) was 84 per cent – well above the rate for the whole sample; a lower rate would have been found if the unaccompanied refugees accommodated under S.20 had been included. The rate of consultation with mothers peaked in the first year of the child being looked after.

Consultation with fathers

Both sexes are acknowledged to have a positive role in parenting children (Fox, 1988; Parkinson, 1992). Unfortunately, the involvement of fathers in services for children has been problematic in the past (Hamill, 1996). Not surprisingly, there were more cases where information about consultation with fathers was missing (18 per cent compared with 15 per cent for mothers). As before, there were 24 cases (largely unaccompanied refugees in Westside) in which consultation seemed to be impossible. These factors reduced the sample size considerably. Table 4.7 shows how in little more than a quarter of cases were fathers consulted, but the distribution was similar to the consultations with mothers.

Table 4.7   Evidence of consultation with father, by age group

	Years of age									
	Less than 5		5 to 10		11 to 15		16 and over		All	
	N	%	N	%	N	%	N	%	N	%
Father consulted	11	38	13	36	10	28	1	5	35	29
Valid cases	29	100	36	100	36	100	21	100	122	100

The table reveals that the rate of consultation for fathers decreased significantly for children in older age groups (chi-square $p<.05$). There were no differences linked to the children's gender but, even after the refugees had been removed from the analysis, fathers of white children were consulted significantly more often than fathers of children from other ethnic groups ($p<.05$).

Just as for mothers, there were no significant differences among the area samples in the rate of consultation with fathers. Nor was there any significant evidence of statistical associations between the consultation rates for children placed in foster or residential care. In cases where the two natural parents lived together, the majority of fathers were consulted. But unlike the rate for mothers, the rate for children accommodated under S.20 was similar to the rate for children in care. A higher rate was found for fathers with children on the child protection register ($p<.05$). Table 4.8 also shows a decline in consultation for those on care orders, similar to that observed for mothers.

Unlike the evidence for mothers, the rate for cases with full care orders was slightly above the rate for the whole sample. Another difference was that the rate for cases under S.20 accommodation (not short term) was only 21 per cent and thus fell below the rate for the whole sample even after cases such as the refugees had been excluded. No significant statistical relationship was found between the rate of consultation with fathers and the period that the child had been looked after or with the implementation of a recent contact plan.

Table 4.8   Evidence of consultation with fathers – care orders

	Interim Care Order		Care Order		Deemed Care Order		All legal statuses	
	N	%	N	%	N	%	N	%
Consultation with fathers	9	43	11	34	4	17	34	28
Valid cases	21	100	32	100	24	100	120	100

The age of the child therefore seemed to be the most straightforward feature connected with the rate of consultation with fathers. In addition, fathers were consulted more frequently at transitional points, when the child was placed on the child protection register or during an interim care order. Accommodation under S.20 was not linked to a higher rate of consultation – a clear contrast to the evidence for mothers.

Consultation with other significant people

In about a fifth of the main sample, there was evidence of consultation with another significant person; in nearly one out of ten cases, one other significant person was consulted. There was no evidence of a statistical association between such consultation and a number of other variables: whether or not a child was in accommodation; the length of time a child had been looked after; or the child's broad ethnic category. The rates were fairly similar in the three area samples.

Table 4.9   Consultation with other significant people, by local authority

Consulted	Midshire		Northborough		Westside		All	
	N	%	N	%	N	%	N	%
Other significant person (1)	13	24	11	21	10	17	34	21
Other significant person (2)	7	13	5	10	2	3	14	8
Total	54	100	52	100	59	100	165	100

Consultation and language needs

The Guidance advises that attention be paid to fulfilling language needs (Volume 3, Ch. 2.57). Yet in only two cases was there concrete evidence of consultation with the child formulated in a language other than English (such as a translated document on the file). In six cases, however, there was evidence that an interpreter had figured at some stage in the consultation with children. This compares with a total of 27 children whose first language was recorded as being not English. Similarly, in only one case was there concrete evidence of a consultation with an adult formulated in a language other than English, but in 12 cases interpreters were involved in consultation with parents and in four with other significant people. One of the five children with special language needs was consulted using a special language.

Social workers were asked in the survey to indicate how easy it was to obtain help in fulfilling particular language needs. Their responses are detailed in Tables 4.10 and 4.11.

Table 4.10   Ease in obtaining interpreters in languages other than English (Social work survey)

Language	Very difficult N	%	Fairly difficult N	%	Neither N	%	Fairly easy N	%	Very easy N	%	No experience N	%
Bengali	1	2	7	16	3	7	5	11	3	7	25	57
Urdu	1	2	7	16	3	7	5	11	2	4	26	59
Hindi	1	2	6	14	3	7	5	11	1	2	28	64
Gujarati	1	2	7	16	3	7	4	9	1	2	28	64
Punjabi	2	4	5	11	4	9	5	11	1	2	27	61
Chinese	2	5	2	5	4	10	2	5	2	5	30	71
Arabic	3	7	0	0	3	7	5	12	9	21	23	54
Cantonese	3	7	0	0	3	7	1	2	2	5	32	78
Vietnamese	3	7	2	5	3	7	2	5	1	2	31	74
Turkish	3	7	1	2	3	7	2	5	2	5	30	73
Welsh	3	7	2	5	3	7	0	0	1	2	33	79
Other	1	3	0	0	3	8	6	17	7	19	19	53

It is not easy to draw definite conclusions from such a table because most social workers had no experience of obtaining interpreting services in languages other than English. However, rather more of them had experience of arranging interpreters for languages associated with the Indian subcontinent than for languages associated with South Asia and elsewhere. The former languages were also those for which difficulties were reported more frequently. On the other hand, reports of difficulty were typically balanced against favourable reports.

Table 4.11 Ease in obtaining interpreters in special languages (Social work survey)

	Very difficult		Fairly difficult		Neither		Fairly easy		Very easy		No experience	
	N	%	N	%	N	%	N	%	N	%	N	%
Makaton	2	4	4	9	1	2	5	11	1	2	32	71
Bliss	3	7	3	7	2	4	1	2	2	4	33	75
Sign	1	2	4	9	2	4	4	9	2	4	32	71
Braille	1	2	3	7	3	7	1	2	2	5	33	77

The level of inexperience in obtaining interpreters for special language needs was similar to the level for languages other than English. Those few social workers with relevant experience held mixed views about the ease with which interpreting help could be accessed.

Evaluating the consultations

The Guidance lays stress on the importance of recording consultations (Volume 3, Ch. 2.53). Two complementary ratings were made of the consultations recorded in the case files: the first rated the extent to which the consultation record reflected people's independent voices, using their own words; the second evaluated the comprehensiveness of the consultation in terms of the topics laid down by the Guidance. The first criterion was meant to give some indication of the validity of the consultation, while the second measured how far it fitted the specified purpose.

The following case illustrates a comprehensive consultation which clearly gave an independent voice to the child, parent and family members.

> *Case 78*. This child was a nine-year-old girl of mixed African-Caribbean and white parentage. Her views were recorded on a consultation form, describing her placement as 'awful' and giving comments on contact with her family, her education and her hobbies.
>
> Her mother presented her views on a consultation form, referring to her daughter's placement, health, education and the contact arrangements. Comments were made about child protection issues. She complained about the lack of reports on the case.
>
> An older female relative and her partner used a consultation form to express views about the young person's placement and education.

In contrast, it was sometimes impossible to determine what the person consulted had actually said or written and so, by this criterion, the consultation was rated as 'limited'.

Case 168. A 16-year-old young man was attributed with personal views about his placement at a residential school but it was not possible to identify clearly how these had been obtained and whether they had been recorded in his own words.

Figure 4.2 shows the distribution of ratings on the first criterion – giving an independent voice – for each local authority area.

Though some of the frequencies in Figure 4.2 are too small to make statistical inference possible, there appear to be differences among the ratings in the local authority samples. Northborough's evaluation results seem to be the most encouraging – certainly compared with Midshire's, where nine out of ten ratings were 'limited'. The scores for Westside correspond to the distribution for the whole sample, making it an intermediate case.

In seeking an explanation for these differences, it is worthwhile looking at the use of consultation forms for parents and children. In Northborough two-sided forms devised by the local authority were in routine use, while in Midshire nothing similar was observed. The history of consultation forms in Westside was more complex but will help to bring out an important point about the availability of forms.

Before Westside agreed to the piloting of the *Looking After Children* materials, it had developed its own consultation forms. When the LAC materials were first brought into use, this led to the abandonment of the old consultation forms. Social workers for a time were using Assessment and Action Records without any consultation forms. The pilot Record was focussed on fact finding and assessment. Specific consultation forms were then introduced as part of the *Looking After Children* materials at a midpoint during the research.

It is unfortunate that the piloting of the materials was handled in such a way as to reduce the clarity of the consultation process. This seems partly attributable to the evolving nature of the LAC project. The Record had started out simply as an assessment instrument. Only later did the project develop a full range of documents designed to fit into the planning and reviewing cycle. But the difficulties also bring out an important point about the relationship between practice and recording. Consultation was recorded to a higher standard if social workers had the appropriate forms. Comparisons of the evaluation results in Midshire and Northborough tend to support this claim. By issuing appropriate forms to social workers, local authorities made it possible for people consulted to present their views in their own words. These findings bear out a longstanding conclusion of research that consultation forms have a useful role, especially for children (Stein and Ellis, 1983b; Cadman, 1988). More recent advice on good practice has made the same point (Wassell and Wilson, 1992).

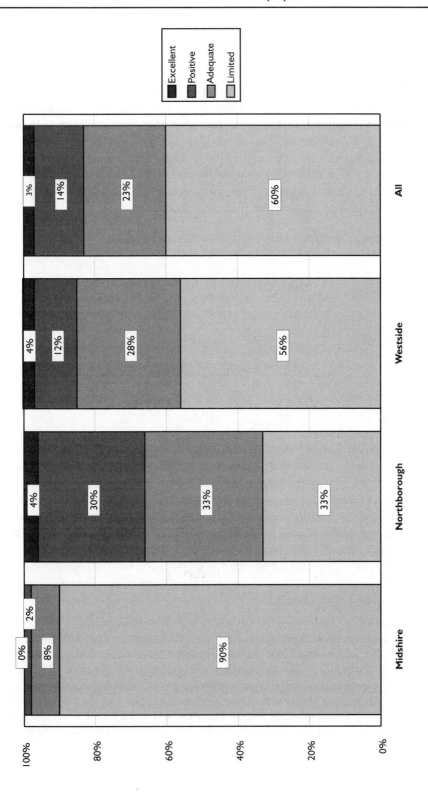

Figure 4.2   Evidence of independent voice, by local authority sample

There was no statistical evidence to show that the evaluation results were linked to the period of years that the child had been looked after or the type of placement. The distribution according to ethnic category is shown in Table 4.12 and indicates that black and minority ethnic groups were better served. The percentages in the table are therefore proportions of the column totals. An explanation for this finding lies in the distribution of ethnic categories among the local authority samples: the Midshire sample had virtually no children from black and minority ethnic groups and also the greatest proportion of 'limited' ratings. When the legal status of the child was brought into the analysis, this failed to shed additional light on the distribution of scores.

Table 4.12   Broad ethnic category, by evidence of independent voice

	Limited		Adequate		Positive		Excellent		All	
Ethnic category	N	%	N	%	N	%	N	%	N	%
White	59	72	14	47	13	65	0	0	86	63
Other ethnic groups	23	28	16	53	7	35	4	100	50	37
Total	82	100	30	100	20	100	4	100	136	100

In sum, the analysis indicates that the explanation for the distribution of these ratings lies with the availability of consultation forms, rather than with features of the cases.

The second rating of the consultation was designed to assess how comprehensively the recorded responses addressed issues referred to by the Guidance and Regulations (Volume 3, Ch. 8.20). A checklist was used to record the topics of consultation: legal status; contact with the family; placement; education; physical health; psychological health and well-being; behaviour; culture; language; ethnic origin and religion; disability; aftercare; and placement in a new family. There was space to record other issues. As before, the ratings were made on a five-point scale. The following example shows a consultation rated as 'positive', given the circumstances of the case.

> *Case 64*. A seven-month-old white boy had been made subject to an emergency protection order and was currently looked after under an interim care order. The review occurred at a time when a parenting assessment in a residential setting had gone through a period of crisis.
>
> The consultation produced evidence of wishes and feelings expressed by the two parents and a maternal grandparent. Even the child's feelings had been noted. The topics of family contact and the placement were dealt with by the consultation, as well as the mother's views on the child's health.

As children grow up, the range of significant topics of consultation is likely to become more extensive. The next example illustrates a case where the scope of consultation was limited.

> *Case 114.* A 12-year-old white boy was subject to a care order and living in a residential home. His independent visitor was due to be replaced. Three years ago he had been given a statement of special educational needs focussing on his learning and behavioural difficulties. Currently, no social worker was allocated to his case. Consequently, no social work report was available.
>
> The only evidence of his wishes and feelings in the review records concerned family contact and the placement; no reference to his education was made.

A similar limitation in the scope of consultation was apparent in a rather different case.

> *Case 154.* A 17-year-old young man had come to this country six weeks previously as an unaccompanied refugee from Eritrea. A specialist worker from the fostering section was involved in the case.
>
> The young man's views on the placement were recorded but the only other opinions noted were about financial matters and learning to cook.

As Figure 4.3 shows, about half the consultations were rated as 'limited', while a little less than a third were rated as 'positive' or 'excellent'. In the light of the previous findings about the consultation rating for evidence of an independent voice, the distribution of ratings for the local authority samples was examined.

The results again indicate that the performance of the Northborough sample was the most successful, though the differences were not shown to be statistically significant. The legal status of children did not seem to be linked with this rating (just as it was not associated with the first consultation rating). Nor was there any statistical evidence that the distribution of ratings was associated with the child's gender, ethnic category, the placement type, or the period of time during which a child had been looked after.

The results of the second rating of consultation suggest similar conclusions to the results of the first; consultation forms made a difference to the authenticity of the consultations and seemed to facilitate a comprehensive response.

The range of assessments

As the introduction to the chapter explained, a primary objective of the study was to look at the range of assessments. For this purpose, an assessment was defined as a preliminary consideration of evidence, and assessments were divided into routine and distinctive forms. No particular practical format for routine assessment is identified in the Guidance. Routine assessments for reviews have been conducted in

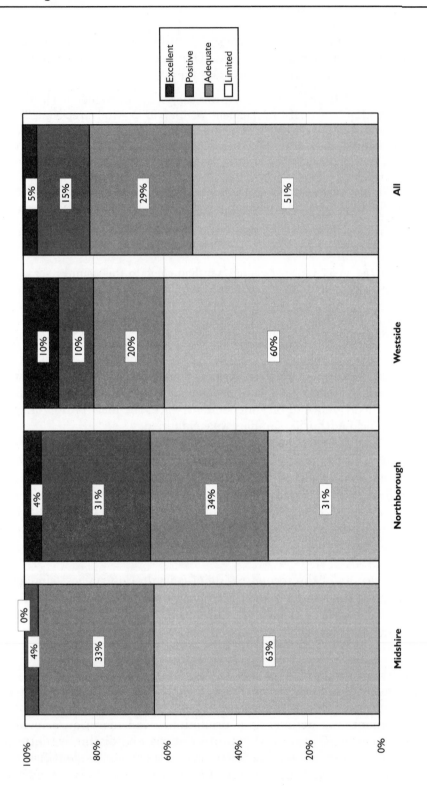

Figure 4.3 Evidence of comprehensive consultation, by local authority sample

formats selected by local authorities, most of which have devised their own paperwork, including forms for health and educational assessment. A small number of authorities, such as Westside, had chosen a distinctive written framework – the LAC Assessment and Action Record (Sinclair and Grimshaw, 1995). But this was completed annually and therefore not repeated for every review.

In examining distinctive assessments, it was possible to consider two aspects – the structure of the recorded assessment and its purpose. A structured approach usually takes the form of specific checklists or schedules. Educational and psychological tests are examples of this approach (Levy and Goldstein, 1984). In social work the LAC Assessment and Action Record and Orange Book assessments (DHSS/WO, 1988) are similar. Other distinctive assessments are produced for specific purposes by particular professionals – psychologists and psychiatrists – and by independent assessment agencies (such as the NSPCC). These are not necessarily structured but they remain distinctive because they do not form part of a routine assessment for a review. Instead, they contribute to other kinds of decision making, such as the determination of special educational needs (SEN) or care proceedings. The data on the various assessments contained in Table 4.13 indicates how frequently they were considered in 166 cases where such information was available. In some, more than one kind of distinctive assessment was conducted.

Table 4.13 Distinctive assessments, by local authority sample

	Midshire		Northborough		Westside		All	
	N	%	N	%	N	%	N	%
Assessment and Action Record	0	0	0	0	22	38	22	13
Parenting or Orange Book	2	4	6	11	1	2	9	5
Psychological	2	4	3	5	2	4	7	4
Independent	0	0	2	4	0	0	2	1
SEN advice	0	0	2	4	0	0	2	1
Any distinctive	4	8	10	18	26	46	40	24
All cases	53	100	56	100	57	100	166	100

In general, only a quarter of the cases were the subject of any distinctive assessment. The Assessment and Action Record was by far the most frequent distinctive form of assessment relevant to the sample of reviews. As previously stated, Assessment and Action Records were being completed annually in Westside. In the Westside sample there were many cases for which there was no relevant Record because, for example, it had not been completed before the review in question. There was also an absence of similar kinds of structured assessment, such as published tests or the materials appended to the *Patterns and Outcomes* study (Department of Health, 1991a). Assessments of parenting were the next most frequent type, followed by psychological or psychiatric reports. Specific assessments by other agencies were much less frequent. Distinctive assessment activity took place most often in Westside but included more types of assessment in Northborough. Cross-sectional sampling of reviews therefore showed that distinctive assessments were relatively infrequent and highlighted how the Assessment and Action Record marked a break from existing assessment practice. In the great majority of cases, assessments followed a routine pattern and were normally recorded on forms designed by the local authority.

This pattern of assessment seemed questionable in cases where children experienced significant transitions yet did not receive a distinctive assessment: there was evidence of a formal parenting assessment in less than a quarter of those cases where the child was on the child protection register and had been looked after for up to a year; only one child in this category was given a psychological or psychiatric assessment. The evidence in general raises issues about when certain kinds of assessments are best performed so that children obtain the benefits of objective and expert appraisals at appropriate stages.

Educational assessment

The Guidance and Regulations demand that an educational assessment covering specific issues should take place for each review (Volume 3, Ch. 2.35, 2.37; RCC, Sch. 2). The assessments considered ranged in style and format, from detailed reports to 'broad-brush' expressions of opinion. The definition of assessment used in the study is therefore wide and inclusive. Data was collected from all available case records about such assessments which were finally rated on the five-point scale.

In nearly six out of ten cases in the main sample, there was evidence of an educational assessment. The rates for children of compulsory school age were over two thirds, while for other groups, the rates declined below half of the relevant cases (see Table 4.14).

A more detailed analysis was possible by examining the children's educational placements (see Table 4.15) The totals in this table are somewhat different from those in Table 4.14 because of missing values.

Table 4.14   Educational assessment, by age group (N=178)

	Less than 5		5 to 10		11 to 15		16 and over		All	
	N	%	N	%	N	%	N	%	N	%
Educational assessment	15	41	36	78	40	68	14	39	105	59
Total	37	100	46	100	59	100	36	100	178	100

Table 4.15   Educational assessment, by educational placement (N=162)

	Educational Assessment		Total	
	N	%	N	%
Mainstream	61	76	80	100
Special Education				
Day	18	86	21	100
Residential	4	100	4	100
Other pre-16	12	86	14	100
Post-16	3	30	10	100
None	7	21	33	100
All	105	65	162	100

The highest rates of assessment were for pupils under 16 in placements outside mainstream schools – a difference of ten per cent compared with mainstream schools. Only three of the ten young people in post-16 education received an assessment. Those without educational placements form a mixed group but all six of the children excluded from school or not attending for other reasons were given assessments.

There was no apparent link between assessment and the type of placement: the proportions of those in residential and foster placements who had educational assessments were very similar – about two thirds. There were no differences among the local authority samples.

Table 4.16 provides information about who was responsible for the assessment in cases where this could be identified. Two thirds of the assessments were produced by schools while most of the rest were produced by specialists (such as educational psychologists). There were no obvious differences among the local authority samples.

There was hardly any evidence that reports were being coordinated through a link person in education: in only five cases spread across the area samples was there any such person. The Guidance suggests that officers in other agencies should be identified in order to consult with their colleagues (Volume 3, Ch. 2.52). There was barely any evidence that such an arrangement was being applied to reviews.

Table 4.16   Educational assessor, by local authority

	Midshire		Northborough		Westside		All	
	N	%	N	%	N	%	N	%
School	17	65	24	73	23	62	64	66
Specialist	6	23	6	18	4	11	16	17
School and other	2	8	0	0	3	8	5	5
Other including social worker	1	3	3	9	7	19	11	11
Total	26	100	33	100	37	100	96	100

Evaluating the educational assessment

The contents of the educational assessments are prescribed by the Guidance and Regulations (Volume 3, Ch. 2.35, 2.37; RCC, Sch. 2). These topics were formed into a checklist to be used in evaluating the assessments. In some cases, however, assessment documents were not placed on files. Where a relevant set of documents could be scrutinised, an evaluation was possible, using the five-point scale. Sometimes, only opinions were reported and, for the purposes of the research, these were regarded as 'assessments' and evaluated accordingly.

The example below illustrates an assessment rated as positive.

> *Case 166*. A report was prepared on the education of a 15-year-old boy in a residential special school. It contained subject reports linked to the National Curriculum. The pupil's progress and examination prospects were discussed. There was an account of his special educational needs and his behaviour; his interests and gifts were described.

The following examples show a variety of circumstances in which the educational assessment was considered 'limited', ranging from a child with special educational needs to an unaccompanied refugee requiring help with English.

> *Case 8*. A five-year-old pupil at a day school for children with learning difficulties was receiving respite care in a foster home. Apart from a nurse's comment that he was 'progressing well' in school, there was no educational assessment informing the review process.

> *Case 79*. A 12-year-old pupil in a secondary school was described by her headteacher as making 'average' progress. Her positive as well as negative

behaviour was mentioned, including the fact that she had run away from school on two occasions.

Case 179. A 17-year-old refugee attending a college was felt to need extra English tuition but no assessment report had been filed. The eventual decision was to discuss the issue at the next review.

In each case, it was a lack of systematic information that made it more difficult to share knowledge and to promote the child's education positively. This meant that opportunities to produce more integrated and effective plans were missed.

Figure 4.4 shows the results of the evaluations; no significant differences can be seen among the evaluations in these age groups. Two fifths of assessments were rated as 'limited', about a third as 'adequate' and only about a quarter as 'positive' or 'excellent'. There was no evidence that the ratings were associated with the gender or ethnic category of the children, or with the local authority concerned. Nor was there any evidence of a link with the placement type or the length of time that the child had been looked after.

Health assessment

The Guidance and Regulations lay down the frequency and content of health assessments for all children being looked after (Volume 3: RCC 5, Sch. 3; RCC 6; Ch. 2.26, 2.28, Ch. 9.51–3, 9.55). First of all, the rate of assessment of children in the sample was examined and analysed in relation to gender. In practice, an assessment may vary from a full physical examination to simply a discussion (Gardner, 1987b). Building on the Guidance, the introduction of the LAC system also highlights the possible contributions of nurses and non-medical staff in promoting health. Hence a broad definition of assessment was used in the research, including, where relevant, contributions from nurses and other staff.

A health assessment was identified for three quarters of the children. There was a significant difference in the gender distribution (see Table 4.17): more males than females were assessed (chi-square $p < .05$).

Table 4.17   Health assessment, by gender

	Male		Female		All	
	N	%	N	%	N	%
Health assessment	70	82	55	69	125	76
Base total	85	100	80	100	165	100

Health assessment decreased as the age of the children increased (chi-square $p < .01$) (see Table 4.18) but for young women the issue was more complex. The gender difference was most obvious for young women

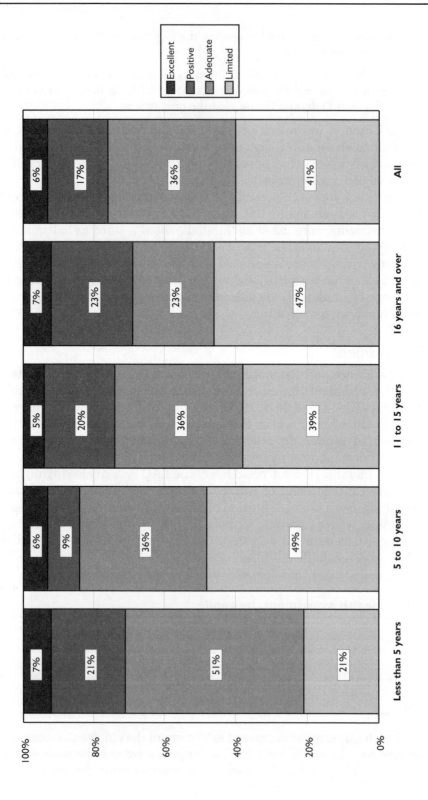

Figure 4.4 Adequacy of educational assessment, by age group (N=99)

from 11 to 15 years old. They accounted for less than one third of the 11- to 15-year-olds assessed. After the age of 16, this gender distribution became even.

Table 4.18   Health assessment, by age group

| | Years of age | | | | | | | | | |
| | Less than 5 | | 5 to 10 | | 11 to 15 | | 16 and over | | All | |
	N	%	N	%	N	%	N	%	N	%
Health assessment	30	91	39	89	40	71	17	52	126	76
Base total	33	100	44	100	56	100	33	100	166	100

Ethnicity was unconnected with the rate of assessment. There was no link between placement type and health assessment, but there were significant differences among the local authority samples (chi-square $p<.05$). Westside's rate of assessment was significantly higher than the rates in the other area samples.

Table 4.19   Health assessment, by local authority

| | Midshire | | Northborough | | Westside | | All | |
	N	%	N	%	N	%	N	%
Health assessment	35	64	41	77	50	86	126	76
Base total	55	100	53	100	58	100	166	100

Responsibilities for health assessment

The Guidance suggests that a doctor be designated to advise the local authority in reviewing health arrangements (Volume 3, Ch. 2.25). There was evidence of a medical link person in 55 cases in the whole sample but a significant difference among the local authority samples was identified: Westside (30 cases); Midshire (17 cases); and Northborough (8 cases). In Westside, an individual community consultant paediatrician performed this linking role as well as undertaking a substantial number of assessments. The compactness of the Westside area may have been a factor here but, if it was an important one, it is hard to see why in a large area like Rural Midshire this rate was higher than in Northborough.

Where possible, the role of the professional making the assessment was identified and the results are categorised in Table 4.20. It was sometimes difficult to identify the role of the doctor making an assessment; this accounts for the 'unspecified doctor' category in the table. While about half the sample were found to have been assessed by a consultant, this was true of more than two thirds in Northborough, compared with only a quarter of the Midshire cases. The pattern of data suggests that it may be more difficult for consultants to carry out assessments in rural areas, so that the link person role in such areas is crucial, rather than merely desirable.

Table 4.20   Health assessor, by local authority (N=115)

	Midshire		Northborough		Westside		All	
	N	%	N	%	N	%	N	%
Consultant	8	24	24	68	25	53	57	50
GP	15	44	3	8	4	8	22	19
Unspecified doctor	7	20	6	17	15	3	27	23
Nurse	3	9	0	0	1	2	4	3
Other	1	3	2	6	2	4	5	4
Total	34	100	35	100	47	100	115	100

Health needs of minority ethnic groups

The Guidance refers to the importance of considering the specific health needs of minority ethnic groups (Volume 3, Ch. 2.26). Evidence of this consideration was identified in 11 out of 44 cases where it was considered relevant. Some differences were found between the two local authority samples which contained the vast majority of children from minority ethnic groups: five out of the ten Northborough cases had specific consideration given to health needs connected with ethnicity, compared with only six of the 34 Westside cases. However, there was some indication that the findings were linked to the children's age group: eight of the 11 cases given specific consideration were children under 11 years of age.

Assessments of disability

Issues of disability are meant to be taken into account in planning. Yet there was little evidence that significant assessments were brought into the review process. It was expected that an assessment would deal with a range of needs – financial, domestic, personal and social – as well as functional issues, like communication or mobility. The following example was rated as 'adequate' in these terms.

Case 174. An 11-month-old white girl with signs of cerebral palsy was being looked after under an interim care order.

The assessment conducted by a medical consultant and a physiotherapist focussed in detail on her medical needs and her physical functioning.

In other cases, the available information was thin and was rated as 'limited'.

Case 37. A seven-year-old white girl with Down's syndrome was receiving respite care. Yet the only information that might be considered as an assessment was a reference to the family's need for 'relief'.

Table 4.21 sets out the distribution of ratings. Part of the reason for the low frequency of disability assessment may be that it is conducted in specialist agencies according to different timescales and procedures and this knowledge does not necessarily contribute to the review. If this is the case, the integrated process of planning referred to by the Guidance seems to be some distance from reality.

Table 4.21   Evaluation of disability assessments, by local authority

	Midshire	Northborough	Westside	All
	N	N	N	N
Limited	2	1	0	3
Adequate	6	1	2	9
Not assessed	6	4	0	10
Total	14	6	2	22

Timing of health assessments

The Guidance requires that (if practicable) a health assessment should take place immediately prior to placement unless one has already taken place within three months of the placement date (Volume 3, Ch. 2.27). In many cases, placements were longstanding and so this requirement was widely inapplicable. Table 4.22 shows that prior assessment was achieved in just over a third of relevant cases, with wide differences among the local authority samples.

The Regulations stipulate that children should be assessed within certain intervals according to their ages (RCC 6). The data in Table 4.23 indicate that three quarters of the assessments were made within the intervals specified by the Regulations. No differences were found among the local authority samples.

Another requirement of the Regulations is that assessments should refer to a child's health history, in order to ensure continuity of care (RCC, Sch. 3). The records were therefore scanned for references to children's health a year before the review. Table 4.24 presents data for children at least one year old.

Table 4.22   Prior health assessment, by local authority

	Midshire		Northborough		Westside		All	
	N	%	N	%	N	%	N	%
Prior assessment	2	10	17	55	12	35	31	36
Relevant cases	20	100	31	100	34	100	85	100

Table 4.23   Timely health assessment, by local authority

	Midshire		Northborough		Westside		All	
	N	%	N	%	N	%	N	%
Timely assessment	26	74	31	76	36	72	93	74
Health assessments	35	100	41	100	50	100	126	100

Table 4.24   Health history, by local authority

	Midshire		Northborough		Westside		All	
	N	%	N	%	N	%	N	%
Health history	15	44	10	28	21	47	46	40
Health assessments	34	100	36	100	45	100	115	100

Only two fifths of such assessments contained a reference to a child's health history a year previously. The rate in Northborough was much lower than in the other authorities. One partial explanation for this difference seems to be that health reports in Northborough were often investigations of alleged incidents of abuse, rather than routine health assessments. However, looking across the areas, the absence of reference to health histories in so many assessments is a significant general finding.

Evaluating health assessment

Using the Guidance and Regulations as a benchmark, the content of each health assessment was finally rated on the evaluation scale. The following case illustrates an assessment rated as positive, though its approach to minority ethnic needs was unclear.

Case 132. A consultant paediatrician assessed a 12-year-old boy of mixed African-Caribbean and Mauritian background. The report referred to the young person's past immunisations and general health history. A check on the boy's vision was made and an audiological test was recommended.

Other specific health difficulties were noted, such as asthma, migraine, and an allergy to shellfish. Health behaviours such as smoking and drinking were also given attention.

The young person was described as 'a thin, well dressed Asian boy' and also as a 'thin Indian boy'. There was no other reference to his ethnicity in the health assessment.

A 'limited' approach was exemplified by a case where only specific problems had been the subject of assessment.

> *Case 75.* A 13-year-old white boy had been treated for epilepsy and allergic rhinitis by a senior clinical medical officer. There was no report of normal checks on aspects of development and function, such as hearing or dental fitness.

There were clear limitations in cases where the only available record had been compiled by a professional without medical training.

> *Case 173.* A social worker had tried to complete a Basic Facts Sheet on a case involving a young woman aged 16: there was an unresolved query about her immunisation record. Her mother also claimed that she was not using the inhaler prescribed for her asthma.

Figure 4.5 shows a breakdown of the results in each local authority sample.

Comparing the four scale points, there were differences among the local authority samples which just failed to reach statistical significance: in Westside, over half the assessments were rated as 'positive' or 'excellent', compared with the general rate of only two fifths. A difference according to gender was identified but this also did not reach statistical significance. There were no significant differences in the ratings according to the children's age group, ethnic category, placement, legal status, or the period of years that they had been looked after.

A final hypothesis was to consider the role and status of the professional responsible for the assessment. The difficulties in identifying which type of doctor had carried out the assessment meant that it was impossible to compare the ratings thoroughly on this basis. A number of assessments were also absent from the files. However, of 52 assessments for which consultants were found to have been responsible, three fifths were rated as 'positive' or 'excellent' and only one fifth were rated as 'limited'. By contrast, all of eight assessments conducted by nurses or other professionals were considered to be 'limited'. Such findings indicate that medical practitioners have a key role to play in ensuring that the standards required of health assessments are fulfilled, whether or not other professionals are involved.

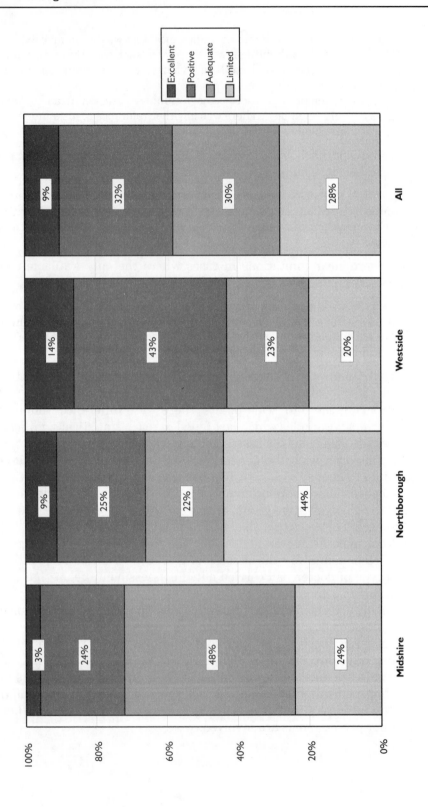

Figure 4.5   Ratings of health assessment, by local authority sample

The perspectives of young people and their parents

Twelve young people were interviewed after their review meetings and asked what had happened beforehand. Only three could remember receiving any information about the review and this had been either a letter or a consultation form, rather than a leaflet. One of these was looked after by a voluntary agency which provided him with a consultation form that it had developed independently. Half the young people had been given some explanation about the meeting.

Almost all said they had been consulted about their wishes and feelings by a professional, whether by a residential carer or a social worker. Some found the process straightforward.

> 'We had to fill in forms. I was fine where I am. There was nothing else I wanted. It was easy.'

Others, such as a young person with learning difficulties, appreciated help with the consultation form.

> 'I asked [my key worker] to write it for me. [She] and I talked. [She] wrote it down. It was easy for me to talk but hard to write.'

Presenting young people with a consultation form did not on its own help them to decide what to say. On a sensitive personal matter, a consultation form created not only an opportunity to express views but also a dilemma about exactly what to say.

> 'I filled it out. I sent it back to my social worker. I had to ponder a few things. I put things [in] about my relationship with my Mum. I didn't want to say in front of everyone else that my Mum is out of her head. That was difficult.'

Young people were also interviewed in the focus groups; they gave similar answers about the consultation process.

> 'When I was living in a children's home . . . my key worker used to help me.'

However, some prepared on their own for the meeting.

> 'I usually have to get my reports out from school.'

> 'I just jotted down some notes. That was basically it.'

> 'If I've got questions, I write them down.'

Filling in a consultation form might be preferable to the ordeal of talking at a meeting. As one young person in a focus group put it:

> 'I just write it and give it to her. I ain't gonna say nothing. I just sit down there [at the meeting].'

Focus group participants seemed almost to equate Assessment and Action Records with homework assignments that had little relevance for young people's futures.

Young person (1): 'We had a review last time. They had a book actually about the things we do . . . before . . . to fill in that asked about 100 questions. You just write them down one after another and it just gets filed away.'

Young person (2): 'You get bored, just see the first question and tick "Yes" [throughout the form]. Just to get to the next page.'

Young person (3): 'They didn't, like, phone me up once I'd done it.'

Focus group participants were also asked about any information which they might have received. One who lived outside the fieldwork areas had been given some information about reviews by the local authority looking after her. But these young people normally did not know what would happen at the review.

Group One

Young person (1): 'I've only just started asking "What's the agenda?". I never really knew what they're talking about until I got in there.'

Young person (2): 'I don't know what they're going to talk about until we actually get there and they start reeling off this stuff.'

Young person (1): 'I asked my social worker "What's on the agenda?" and she timidly said "Help!". I am thinking "Well, it took her a long time to say it."'

Young person (3): 'I mean, information is power.'

Group Two

Interviewer: 'How easy is it to think of what to say?'

Young person (1): 'It's not easy.'

Young person (2): 'Apart from that, I think they should send you a review beforehand so that you can think about [it]. They come into the review and just come straight out with all these questions.'

It was possible to interview just seven parents after the review meetings had taken place. All of these had been sent letters about the review and one received a form to fill in, but none mentioned being given a leaflet. Four of these parents said they had been consulted before the review. Of the remainder, one said she had been consulted in the past but not on this occasion, another said the consultation had not been clear and the third believed that consultation was irrelevant because he had no parental rights.

Two points emerge from this interview evidence. Young people and their parents clearly stated that they had been consulted. But they had not received information which might have enabled them to play a full part in the review. These two points should be borne in mind for future reference when considering the evidence about meetings in the next two chapters.

The perspectives of social workers

As the link with young people and their parents, the social worker responsible for a case plays a fundamental part in the preparation for decision making at a review. Through the survey, evidence was collected about the way in which they approached this task and about their priorities. They estimated the minimum number of hours which they devoted to preparing for different reviews: the mean estimate was six hours. They also estimated the maximum number of hours: the mean was over ten hours. These estimates may represent extreme and exceptional cases. Table 4.25 shows their estimate of the most frequent number of hours spent on this task.

Table 4.25 Most frequent number of hours spent preparing for a review (social workers' estimate)

Hours	% response
Up to 1	9
2–3	34
4–5	38
6–9	17
10–15	2

These figures shed some light on the work performed before a review. They suggest that, on the whole, the time put in by social workers ranged from a minimum of about half a day up to a maximum of about a day and a half. A typical review fell in the lower part of the range; indeed, 81 per cent of respondents indicated that most frequently they spent five hours or less on a review. While almost one in ten social workers typically devoted one hour or less to a review, nearly seven out of ten spent two to five hours, whilst a fifth spent from six to 15 hours on the task.

Some evidence was also collected about social workers' priorities in spending that limited amount of time. Asked to comment on preparations for a review, social workers responding to the survey mentioned a number of aspects such as ensuring involvement, organising administrative tasks, and good time management, but few mentioned work with families. Those who did were keen to see it as part of ongoing work, rather than as a special task. As Table 4.26 shows, their views indicate that reviews usually did not involve new assessments of children.

Social workers were confident that in the great majority of cases the children were well known to them prior to a review. High proportions of children were considered to be well known to social workers within either one or four months of becoming looked after. Hence nearly half the respondents often had a good knowledge by the end of the first review. It follows that initial reviews are not seen as 'paper exercises' or 'holding operations' while knowledge about the child is accumulated. The confidence of social workers in claiming good knowledge of children at these early reviews suggests that the timescales for initial reviews represent a widely acceptable schedule for assessments leading to substantive decisions about a child's future. It seems that most social workers went into review meetings with a body of knowledge about children which they regarded as reasonably satisfactory. Most reviews did not involve new assessment work and some assessment was presumably undertaken before children became looked after.

Table 4.26   Social workers' attitudes to assessment at reviews

	Very rarely true	Rarely true	Sometimes true	Often true	Very often true
	%	%	%	%	%
Children well known prior to review	0	4	12	33	50
Good knowledge after one month of being looked after	4	19	28	30	19
Good knowledge after four months of being looked after	2	2	30	32	34

The perspectives of social workers suggest that the limited time specifically allocated to reviews was devoted to a variety of tasks which did not usually involve a new assessment of the child.

Interpreting the findings

In this section a number of points emerge which require further discussion. There was evidence that forms and information made a difference to the reviewing process. For example, the Basic Facts Sheet and the consultation forms used by local authorities had an impact on the quality of recorded information. In addition, though young people and their parents said they were consulted, they did not receive written information about the reviews. Without this, it is doubtful whether they can become full participants in the review – a point discussed at more length in the next two chapters.

For the majority of reviews, assessments were routine rather than distinctive. The reasons for this began to emerge: social workers typically thought that they had a good knowledge of children; limited social work time was devoted to reviewing. Distinctive assessments from non-social work professionals were not frequently linked to reviews. Completing LAC materials on a regular basis therefore marks a clear break with existing assessment practice.

It has been recently argued that assessment takes a helical form in which current assessments build on previous knowledge (Sinclair, Garnett and Berridge, 1995). Hence assessments did not start from scratch each time there was a review. Important assessments may, for example, take place before the young person is looked after. A cross-sectional sample of reviews will not therefore necessarily identify a high proportion of distinctive assessments because these are not likely to be repeated at set intervals in the same way that reviews are. However, even for children having been recently found at risk of significant harm, a distinctive assessment was not commonplace. The data from the current study tend to confirm that distinctive assessments have been infrequently conducted for reviews.

There were some variations in the rate of educational assessment. Educational assessments were most frequent for young people under 16 years in special education and other educational arrangements, compared with a lower rate for those in mainstream education. These differences tend to suggest that reports appeared more frequently from educational sectors with higher ratios of staff to pupils. These differences in the rates of assessment highlight the absence of educational coordinators. A lack of structures for practical coordination is reflected in other authorities, according to a recent inspection.

> Liaison between the SSD, social workers and teachers was too patchy and often ad hoc. (Ofsted/SSI, 1995 p.36)

There were significant variations too in the rate of health assessment, which was lower for females and for the older age groups. The lower rate of assessment for adolescents echoes recent findings (Sinclair, Garnett and Berridge, 1995). More specifically, the findings reveal a particular problem – the low rate of assessment for adolescent young women. Further data on this issue will be discussed in Chapter 9. The results raise questions about whether this group was being helped to gain access to appropriate assessment and health services. Evidence of negative attitudes to 'medicals' among young women was found by research conducted before the Children Act, suggesting a regrettable lack of progress in recognising their needs (Gardner, 1987a).

Health assessment, like educational assessment, was influenced by organisational and procedural factors. Authorities differed in their use of designated medical experts to coordinate reviews but they were more evident than in education. There were some small indications that the role and status of the professional responsible for the health assessment influenced the quality of the outcome. In general, the content of health assessments met the requirements of the Guidance and Regulations more often than did the content of educational assessments. One possible explanation is that better lines of communication were established between health and social services.

A final general observation is worth making at this stage. In many instances, there was limited evidence that features of the case such as placement type were associated with features of the preparation for decision making. In this respect, at least, the traditional distinctions between residential and other cases seemed not to have any influence (Sinclair, 1984; Gardner, 1985). Legal status seemed a more significant factor in relation to parents than to children. Several aspects of the preparation were found to be connected with the gender, age and development of the child. There was therefore relatively more scope for changes in child care practice than if many different case features had been found to have been influential. Much depended on the general organisation of practice rather than on the idiosyncrasies of case status, a point neatly illustrated by the use of consultation forms.

Key findings

- Evidence of inquiry was found in over eight out of ten cases. A fifth of the cases of inquiry were rated as 'limited', while a quarter were rated as 'positive' or 'excellent'.
- Two thirds of children were consulted before the review. Young people over 11 years of age were very frequently consulted but the rate of consultation for five- to 10-year-olds fell to almost half and then dropped to a tenth for those under five years of age.
- In two thirds of cases mothers were consulted but this rate dropped to a half for young people over the age of ten years. In about a quarter of cases fathers were consulted, the rate decreasing similarly for children in older age groups.
- In about a fifth of cases there was evidence of consultation with another significant person; in almost a tenth of cases one other significant person was consulted.
- There was evidence that an interpreter had figured in some stage of the consultation with six children, and in 12 cases of consultation with parents. One of the five children with special language needs was consulted using a special language. A minority of social workers had experience of using interpreters; they held mixed views about the ease with which such help could be obtained.
- Sixty per cent of the consultations recorded people's own words to a 'limited' extent. Half of the consultations gave less than adequate responses to the full range of topics specified in the Guidance. There was evidence that consultation forms made a difference to the quality of recorded consultation.

- Only a quarter of the cases were subject to any distinctive assessment, whether in a structured form (like the LAC materials) or produced for specific purposes (such as special educational needs advice). The Assessment and Action Record was by far the most frequent structured format for assessment.
- Over two thirds of children of compulsory school age received an educational assessment. Three quarters of children in mainstream schooling received assessments, while nearly all children in special education received them. But those young people in further education received assessments in less than a third of cases.
- Two thirds of assessments were found to have been performed by schools; less than a fifth were performed by specialists such as educational psychologists.
- There was barely any evidence that educational assessments were being coordinated by appropriate professionals working in education.
- Two fifths of educational assessments were rated as 'limited' in terms of the expectations set by the Guidance, while about a quarter were rated as 'positive' or 'excellent'.
- Three quarters of the young people received health assessments; significantly more males than females were assessed. Health assessment decreased significantly as children's ages increased. A category with a particularly low rate of assessment consisted of girls aged from 11 to 15 years.
- There were significant differences among the local authority samples in the rate of health assessment and in the system of responsibility for it.
- One quarter of the children from minority ethnic groups had attention paid to their specific health needs.
- Few significant assessments of disability were associated with reviews.
- About three quarters of the health assessments were made within the intervals set by the Regulations.
- An assessment of health was made prior to placement in just over a third of cases.
- Two fifths of assessments contained a reference to a child's health a year previously.
- Just over a quarter of health assessments were rated as 'limited', compared with two fifths that were rated as 'positive' or 'excellent'.
- Young people who were interviewed said that they had been consulted about their wishes and feelings. However, a number said they had not been given information about the review and about what would be discussed. Similar comments were made by parents.

- The great majority of social workers responsible for the cases indicated that they typically spent five hours or less on preparations for a review. Most felt that they had a good knowledge of most children prior to reviews, even the initial ones.

5. The organisation of the review meeting

Introduction

The previous chapter looked at evidence about the stages of inquiry, consultation and assessment, prior to decision making. This chapter takes the study forward to the point where, in principle, decision making occurs. In particular it examines the practice of holding a meeting as part of the review. Typically, a single meeting took place though the Guidance, as we shall shortly discuss, does not rule out multiple meetings. Using the data from the main sample of up to 180 cases, the first section describes the venues of meetings and the identities of those who chaired them. The next section analyses the attendance of children, parents and professionals at meetings, and considers some of the factors behind the attendance of professionals.

In the light of this information, a description is given of the way the meetings were run and how this influenced the discussion and decision making that took place. This data is drawn from a subsample of 42 meetings observed by the researcher.

Data from the survey of social workers responsible for the main sample cases is used to show how practitioners interpreted the review process. In the next chapter, evidence about the degree of participation by children and parents will be discussed.

Meetings and reviews

The Guidance and Regulations make clear that a review should be a consideration of the plan for the child (Volume 3, Ch. 8.4). A meeting is a means to this end. The Guidance and Regulations state that several meetings can form parts of the same review (RCC 4(4), Sch. 1; Volume 3, Ch. 8.3). The recommendations about attendance, the venue and so on suggest that the same requirements apply for any meeting that forms part of a series of connected meetings together forming one review. Having said so much about how a meeting should be conducted, it is difficult to conclude that the Guidance envisages a review combining meetings of different *kinds*. Therefore a series of meetings would be necessary exceptionally, when, for example, the business could not be concluded on one occasion. The language of the Guidance, moreover, implies that normally a single meeting will take place (Volume 3, Ch. 8.21). Moreover, the fieldwork data indicate strongly that the Guidance has been read to mean that a single meeting takes place for each review. Decision making was therefore concentrated at the meeting.

The subsample of meetings observed

A subsample of 42 meetings, concerning 48 children, was observed. Family members attending the meeting were informed about the research beforehand and observations took place with their consent.

The cases were drawn evenly from each authority: 15 each from Midshire and Northborough and 18 from Westside. The distribution of these children's ages and ethnic origins is set out in Tables 5.1 and 5.2.

Table 5.1   Children in review meetings subsample, by age group (N=48)

Years of age	N	%
Less than 5	10	21
5–10	12	25
11–16	14	29
17–18	12	25
Total	48	100

Table 5.2   Children in review meetings subsample, by ethnic origin (N=48)

Ethnic origin	N	%
White	35	73
African	5	10
African-Caribbean	3	6
Asian	2	4
African/White	1	2
Unrecorded	2	4
Total	48	100

Slightly more than two thirds of the children were in care; the rest were accommodated under S.20 (two in short-term respite care placements). Thirty per cent were on the Child Protection Register at the time of the review. Over three quarters were placed in foster homes; the subsample thus under-represents children in residential and other placements. This profile of the subsample helps to prepare the way for an analysis of how meetings were organised, beginning with the choice of venue.

Venue of meetings

The venue for a meeting needs to be carefully chosen especially as a major aim is to make children and parents feel comfortable. The Guidance specifically suggests that the venue for the meeting should be a matter for consultation with the child. Before the Children Act 1989 the administrative structure of social services departments influenced the arrangements for meetings and many took place in offices (Sinclair, 1984). How much had changed since the Guidance and Regulations came into force?

It is not possible to draw conclusions about the venue of the meetings from the main sample because review forms did not systematically record this information. This is also true of the LAC Review form in its pilot and revised versions. However, it was possible to analyse the venues for the meetings observed during the research.

Table 5.3   Venue of observed meetings (N=48)

	N	%
Foster home	23	48
Team office	13	27
Residential home	6	12
Secure unit	1	2
School	2	4
Clinic	1	2
Supported living unit	1	2
Independent living	1	2
Total	48	100

The great majority of the observed review meetings were held at the placement, indicating that the office-based meetings of the past have been superseded to a significant extent. The data on foster placements shows that 69 per cent of these were reviewed at the placement; for the rest, office venues were chosen (with two exceptions – a clinic and a school). However, it is not possible to draw definitive conclusions because of the nature of the subsample, particularly about reviews in residential facilities.

Office-based meetings were more frequent in one authority, Northborough, where independent reviewing officers usually took the chair. It was not wholly clear why this should have been so, since the distance of placements was similar in the other urban authority, West-side. In Midshire, travelling to and from the placement was a time constraint upon staff yet office meetings were untypical. In a rural area, as the local manager explained, it was more difficult to find a neutral venue within a reasonable distance of the placement. While local schools offered possibilities, the practical and financial arrangements for using them as venues were felt to be an obstacle, even if they were acceptable to children, which might not be the case.

Some of the practical advantages and disadvantages of particular venues became evident. For instance, reviews in foster care homes were often affected by an embarrassing lack of comfortable seats. Three piece suites could not accommodate more than five attenders. Given a core attendance of four (one young person, one carer, the social worker, and the chair) it was easy to predict when some improvisation would be needed. However, this did not always appear to go smoothly; the researcher's presence merely compounded a problem which was often inherent. The hospitable attitudes of the foster family meant that 'guests' usually got the best available seats; one foster carer stoically sat on the carpet throughout.

Another problem arose when young children had to be minded during the meeting – clearly a distraction for the foster carer. After such a meeting with a lively six-year-old and a toddler, the chair described the event as 'chaotic'. Even older children had to be considered: one review of a new adoption placement was attended by all the young people in the adopters' family. Afterwards, the chair expressed some disquiet about the presence of siblings at the meeting.

> 'I was a bit put off by the presence of the [other] two sisters. I felt a bit un-easy . . . . She should have space on her own.'

It appeared that this issue had not been clarified prior to the review meeting. In general, if specific arrangements had not been made about who from the family would be present, there was a possibility of both confusion and a breach of confidentiality.

Other homes had similar drawbacks. A review took place in a young person's flat which had seating for only one visitor. By comparison, schools and residential centres were better designed for holding meetings. They sometimes had meeting rooms available; otherwise, reviews were carried out in vacated offices. However, this apparent convenience should not be over-rated: from a child's point of view, both residential homes and schools are likely to carry very personal and particular connotations, which it is necessary to take into account before any meeting is arranged (Fletcher, 1993).

Departmental office venues varied in their degree of formality and comfort. One review took place in the social work team office with chairs formed into an impromptu circle. On the other hand, formal conference rooms were frequently used: these tended to be large and impersonal, with office chairs set around a wide table. Some, however, took place in designated family meeting rooms containing comfortable chairs and toys to amuse young children.

The chairs of meetings and social workers clearly had a variety of options in choosing a meeting venue and the practical arrangements for each occasion demanded individual consideration and foresight.

Though the Guidance suggests that the children should be consulted about the meeting venue, this was just as likely to happen as not being consulted, according to the children's interviews. There was also evidence that their preferences were not given priority. Social workers were asked in the survey questionnaire how often it was true that 'wherever possible, children's preferences about the venue of a review are given priority'. Only 16 per cent thought that it was 'often true'; 27 per cent that it was 'sometimes true'; and 57 per cent thought this was 'rarely true'.

None of the meetings took place in the parental home. This meant that support for parents' attendance was a significant issue. There was variation in the support required and the support offered. Placements remote from the family home obviously tended to call for support. A parent interviewed complained of always having to take time off work and travel by bus to a neighbouring town in order to attend the review at a residential placement. Even meetings nearby could give rise to needs. A parent who came from an Asian background was particularly grateful for the social workers' escort to the meeting because she feared a random street attack. Parents with cars were at an advantage but this was not always checked out. A father said he did not know if the social worker was aware that he had a car.

Chairs of meetings

Records about the main sample provided information about the identity of chairs and their relationship to the case. The percentages in Table 5.4 relate to the total number of cases for which information was available.

Table 5.4   The identity of review meeting chairs (main sample)

		N	%
Status	Team leader	163	98
Relation to case holder	Line manager	121	74
Whether the chair was the nominated person	As nominated	156	98

The data from the main sample show that the chairs were virtually always people 'senior' in status to the social worker (Volume 3, Ch. 8.13). Senior departmental managers chaired only one per cent of meetings. The relation of chairs to the case holder conformed to the system in each local authority; even in Northborough, line managers chaired initial reviews. If not in the chair, the line manager never attended. The actual chairs were the persons with nominated responsibility; the substitution of a chair was virtually unknown. The local system of chairing was therefore taken seriously in practice.

Social workers' views about who should chair a meeting

Social workers were asked in the survey to describe their preferences about the appointment of chairs and the presence of line managers at reviews. There were mixed views about line managers as chairs: 36 per cent both for and against; with 26 per cent undecided. But 73 per cent were in favour of line managers being present.

There was some support for independent chairing: 51 per cent in favour compared with 20 per cent against. In some authorities, specialised officers are appointed, one of whose main tasks is to chair reviews. Social workers were not quite as convinced that a specialised officer should be chair: 36 per cent were in favour; 37 per cent undecided; and 24 per cent against.

Attendance

Before considering the data on attendance we need to look at the minimum requirements compatible with the Guidance. It recommends that the core group of attenders should include the carer, the social worker, the parents and the child, where appropriate (Volume 3, Ch. 8.23). The line manager should also attend. Midshire and Westside dealt with the last point by making line managers into chairs; in contrast, after the first review, Northborough's line managers did not attend their social workers' reviews. The systems in the local authorities therefore had different responses to the requirement about line managers' attendance.

The size of the meetings in the main sample is shown in the first bar chart (Figure 5.1). The attendance figures, including the chair, range from a minimum of two to a maximum of thirteen. The most frequent total was five – a number close to the core attendance identified by the Guidance. However a substantial number of meetings rose above this level and the mean attendance was 6.2. These figures show little difference from the attendances at comparable types of review before the Children Act 1989: for residential reviews see Sinclair, 1984 and for reviews in Scotland see Cadman, 1988 and Kendrick and Mapstone, 1991.

The next bar chart (Figure 5.2) concentrates on meetings in the main sample attended by young people. Here the distribution of attendance is

Figure 5.1 Attendance at meetings, all cases (N=168)

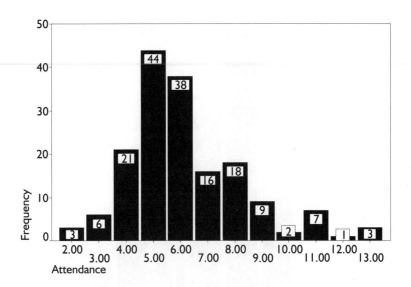

very similar. A significant proportion of children were therefore attending meetings with five to 12 other people present. The next task of analysis is therefore to compare data about the core group mentioned above with data about other professionals and those from different agencies, such as health and education. According to the Guidance the attendance of these more peripheral figures has to be justified. This is important if large meetings that overwhelm young people are to be avoided (Fletcher, 1993). Data on such individuals therefore deserves closer scrutiny.

Table 5.5 shows attendance frequencies for four main groups – family members, those primarily responsible for the child's care, those with a secondary responsibility, and other agency representatives. As well as showing the proportion of relevant cases attended, the table puts these proportions in rank order. The chairs have been excluded from this table.

The first category consists mainly of family members: the children attended in just over half the cases, mothers in four ninths and fathers in a fifth of cases. 'Other significant people' included siblings and other relatives, who attended in almost a quarter of cases. People who were not family members but offered support were very few.

The second category of attenders to be considered is those primarily responsible for the child's care. Table 5.5 shows that social workers, foster carers and residential carers almost always attended reviews. The

Figure 5.2   Attendance at meetings, child present (N=92)

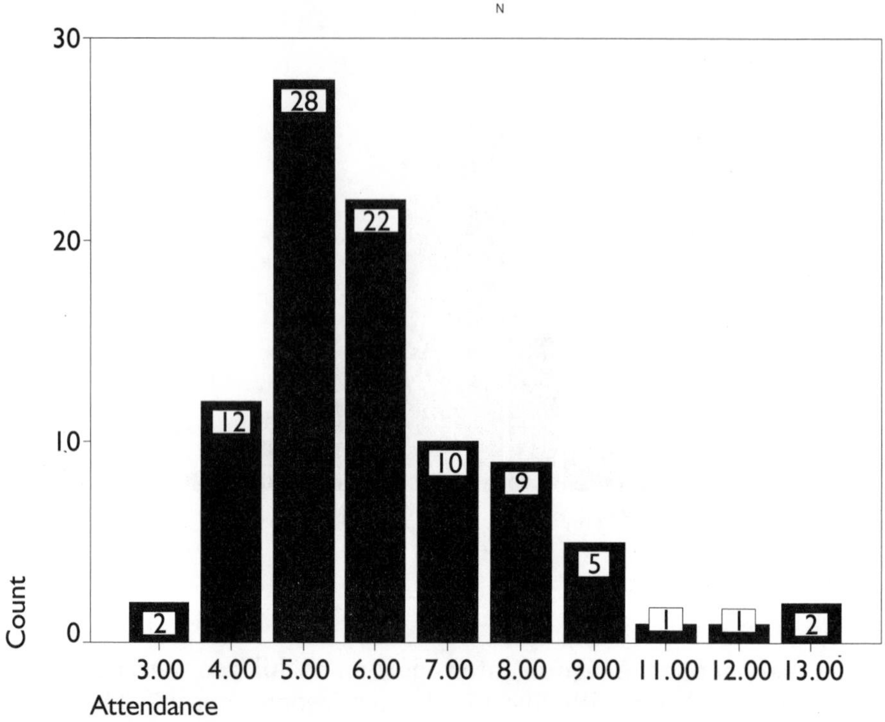

high involvement of foster carers contrasts significantly with the situation prior to the Children Act 1989 (Vernon and Fruin, 1986).

The third general category of attenders consists of social care professionals (other than the social worker for the child) who played a variety of roles: Guardians ad litem who represented the child; fostering and adoption officers; residential managers; other senior officers; other workers providing services. (As previously explained, line managers did not appear in this category either because they held the chair or because it was common practice for them not to attend.) In the table, this general category was divided into two, in order to differentiate social services department employees from the rest. These miscellaneous departmental workers attended over half the meetings – more frequently than the parents, or any other professional group (apart from the social workers responsible for children). The other professionals, such as Guardians or workers in independent settings, attended in a fifth of cases.

A fourth general category includes professionals from other disciplines: education (26 per cent), followed by health (14 per cent), and, lastly by other organisations, such as the police (10 per cent).

Table 5.5 Attenders at review meetings (main sample)

	N	%	Rank
Family group			
Child	92	55	5
Mother	63	44	6
Father	29	21	9=
Independent visitor	2	1	13
Other significant people	38	23	8
Primary care			
Social worker	153	94	1=
Foster carer(s)	114	94	1=
Residential carer	27	93	3
Secondary care			
Other SSD	93	56	4
Other social work	35	21	9=
Multi-agency			
Education representatives	42	26	7
Health representatives	23	14	11
Others	17	10	12
All valid cases	168	100	–

Note: the percentages in this table relate to the proportion of relevant cases for which information was available

The information discussed so far concerns the representation of individuals and groups at meetings; one way to judge whether their attendance was necessary was to look at the numbers of attenders from the same grouping. This is summarised in Table 5.6 which again refers to the main sample. These figures relate to the proportions of meetings at which there was single or multiple representation. Thus, in 59 per cent of cases, there was just one foster carer and, in 34 per cent of cases, more than one foster carer present at the meeting. Some foster carers had their own respite carers who also attended. In 36 per cent of cases, there was one person and, in 19 per cent, more than one person from the 'other social services department' category. If the intention is to produce child- and parent-friendly meetings, it is not easy to justify multiple representation from the same category. Hard questions must be asked about the number of social services department professionals in attendance.

Table 5.6   Size of representation by category of attender (percentages)

	1 person	2–3 persons	4 and over
Foster carers	50	31	2
Other significant people	10	11	1
Other SSD	36	18	1
Other social workers	18	2	1
Health representatives	11	1	1
Education representatives	21	5	0
Others	8	1	0

By examining the attitudes of social workers to attenders it was hoped that the pattern of attendance could be better understood. The survey asked social workers to rate the priority of various attenders on a scale from zero to ten. The results are compared in Table 5.7 with the actual pattern of attendances. The first column gives the actual rank order of attendance and the second shows the mean priority scores for these individuals and groups. An asterisk in the second column indicates a match between the actual attendance and the priority rating given by social workers.

In order to clarify the analysis, the line managers are discounted from these conclusions since they attended mainly as chairs. Leaving them aside, the results for ten of the ratings exercise correspond to the actual rank order. There are three clear exceptions: children, parents and the area manager. Area managers in fact attended few reviews, so the ratings are still consistent with the findings on actual attendance. For children and parents, it is perhaps understandable if fewer attend than social workers would ideally like. For example, children may be too young to understand the review, or parents may be living far away.

Nonetheless, the ten matched priority ratings for other individuals are interesting when compared with the actuality. Social services professionals (such as residential managers and fostering officers) achieved higher ratings and attended more often than other groups, including other significant people. Education representatives were rated more highly and attended more often than other significant people and health representatives. The relatively low ranking of friends and supporters is striking, especially in the light of the Guidance's endorsement of their role. These priority ratings by social workers seem to reflect the working practice of reviewing and suggest that social workers exercised significant influence over the invitations that were made.

Table 5.7 Comparison of actual attendance and social workers' priorities

	Rank order of attendance	Priority rating (0–10)
		*Marks correspondences with rank order of actual attendance
1=	Foster carer	9.7*
3	Residential carer	9.7*
4	Other SSD	8.3 – residential manager* 8.2 – line manager 7.1 – fostering officer* 2.7 – area manager
5	Child	9.1
6	Mother	9.6
7	Education representatives	7.0*
8	Other significant people	6.7 child's supporter* 5.5 parent's supporter* 5.2 other relative*
9=	Other social workers	(not included)
9=	Father	9.5
11	Health representatives	6.4 health visitor* 4.6 doctor*
12	Others	(not included)
13	Independent visitor	(not included)

Beyond this, was there evidence of background factors influencing the distribution of attendance? Educational representatives attended about a quarter of children's cases: of these, significantly less than half (40 per cent) had a statement of special educational needs or had been referred for assessment. Health representatives attended in fewer cases (14 per cent): of these, just over a third (35 per cent) had a statement or had been referred for assessment; only a quarter (26 per cent) had some form of disability.

The multidisciplinary network of child protection also seemed to have some influence: 55 per cent of health attendances were for children on the child protection register, compared with 38 per cent of education attendances.

A more significant background feature for health attenders appeared to be the child's age: 78 per cent of the meetings they attended concerned a child under 11 years old. Education attendances were related to a broader age span: 38 per cent of their attendances concerned a child aged from 5 to 10 years compared with 43 per cent for 11- to 15-year-olds.

The attendances of professionals from health and education were thus only partly distributed according to indicators of need, such as special educational needs, disability, or child protection issues.

In the complex world of individual care planning described by the Guidance and Regulations, there is a great deal of work to be done in bringing together the joint views of all concerned with the child's welfare. Currently a single meeting is used to bring all the significant people together. The next chapter shows how some young people felt intimidated by large groups and particularly by the questions of those professionals who to them were strangers. It does seem that the attendance of all concerned at a single meeting presents difficulties. The Guidance does not, however, suggest that the review consists of one single meeting; more are possible. This is a key issue for further discussion and reflection. In the sections which follow, the data from observations supplemented by other findings will be used to present a picture of how the meetings were managed. The main focus is on detailed description in order to achieve a better understanding of the typical processes at work. The examples are meant to illuminate aspects of those processes, thus emphasising the qualitative dimension of the research (Bryman, 1988).

Running the meeting

Preliminaries to the meeting proper, such as personal introductions, were generally informal and completed quickly. Chairs tended to begin by briefly outlining what they saw as the tasks of the review. There was no discussion of procedural formalities, such as the standing of the chair and the rights and obligations of attenders. In general, it would have been impossible for an uninformed visitor to tell that the meeting was governed by statutory Guidance and Regulations.

When asked afterwards about their preparations for the review, chairs spoke about the limited amount of time they could give. Case conferences and child protection meetings were regarded as more important than reviews. Before the review took place, chairs concentrated on the substantive issues that they would need to know about. In some cases, therefore, the agenda was not set out; nor were copies of an agenda often available. Similar weaknesses in fixing the agenda were observed before the Children Act (Gardner, 1985).

Documents were treated as a basis for verbal reports, rather than as independent evidence which needed careful scrutiny from all concerned. Sometimes it was difficult to see any documents at all, apart from the chair's notes. There was also little attention to who had read which reports. Any reports or agendas that had been circulated beforehand were not treated as significant tools.

Copies of reports were also rarely available. Some independent agencies caring for young people produced copies of their reports to be read at the meeting but even this was not always true. The usual approach was for attenders to speak to reports which they kept in their hands. In some cases, chairs read out the contents of the reports produced by people who were not attending. Documentary evidence was not, on the whole, a key focus of the meetings.

Minutes were normally taken by chairs as they went along. Specialist minute-takers did not attend, unless, as in some cases, the child care review was combined with a child protection review. Some chairs actually filled in the review form as they went along. One spoke of how this interfered with his chairing responsibilities.

> Chair, Northborough: 'The review form tends to disrupt the consultation and discussion – all the tick boxes.'

However, going through the current LAC form and recording the meeting simultaneously was regarded as extremely difficult. The practice of recording 'as you go' may help to explain why review records were often very concise and kept well within the boundaries of official review forms. Few chairs added appendices to review records, filling out the detailed content of discussions and decisions.

> Chair, Northborough: 'You have to be very concise. It might be disadvantageous for the record, for people who want to look at the reasons for previous decisions. It would be scantily available.'

The method of recording therefore had dubious implications for anyone trying to determine how cogent the decisions were – a significant issue for any system of monitoring (Volume 3, Ch. 8.21).

In formulating their agendas, chairs briefly consulted with participants. Some were more methodical about firming up the agenda and clearly invited participation, as the following example illustrates.

> *Meeting 146.*
> Chair: 'I've been through the review form and drawn up the agenda. There are items from [the young person] and [the foster carer]. It would be helpful to talk about the agenda. OK?'

> Parent: 'Yes.'

> The chair then listed an agenda with 11 items. The social worker confirmed that the parent had seen the consultation form but preferred not to complete it. The chair helpfully encouraged the parent to contribute at any stage.

> Chair: 'Just stop me and we'll add [something].'

The fostering officer mentioned a letter he had received from the young person that day but the young person declined the offer to talk about the letter at the current meeting. This agenda discussion lasted for about seven minutes.

Monitoring the implementation of previous decisions

The Guidance declares that the agenda should 'include consideration of progress in implementing the plan . . .' (Volume 3, Ch. 8.3). In practice, the decisions of the previous review were often dealt with cursorily or not at all. While chairs agreed during research interviews that this kind of monitoring was a review function, it was not given central importance; nor did social workers greatly value the monitoring function, according to the survey. Such monitoring as did take place was mainly factual, rather than exploratory or investigative.

> *Meeting 155.* Four minutes were spent discussing outcomes of the last review decisions. The doctor and the child had changed their minds about the medical decision. The college placement had been successful. There were still problems with transport for the disabled young person. Family contact was taking place in line with the plan.
>
> These topics were later discussed separately as current issues within the main agenda.

There seemed to be a wish to concentrate on the current situation and to move forward, rather than to find out why particular plans had turned out as they had. Hence there was little opportunity to reflect on the past or to record obstacles for future reference. In the following example, confusions about responsibilities for the previous plan were exposed, yet what had been learnt was not brought out into the open.

> *Meeting 151.*
> Chair: 'What about the vaccination?'
>
> Social worker: 'I don't liaise with the GP. I believed the school nurse would deal with vaccination.'
>
> Teacher: 'The nurse is not able to do it.'
>
> Adoption worker: 'The foster carer [who was absent from the meeting] dealt with it.'
>
> Chair: 'So [the social worker] will follow that up.'

The distinction between factual and evaluative monitoring was made by Sinclair (1984). In the present study too, the form and purpose of monitoring remained unclear – an important issue which affects both the assessment and the planning processes. More than that, it prevents any routine recording of information that could assist the better management of child care cases as a whole.

The substantive agenda

The Guidance and Regulation set out a minimum list of issues for consideration at each review (Volume 3, Ch. 8.20; RCC 5, Sch. 2). The list seems designed to cover the major decisions that are relevant to children looked after. Yet its wide scope raises a problem, in that it takes little account of the progression of plans. Its list of issues could be taken to imply that at each review similar options remain open. Yet the evidence of this study is that care planning implies a career path for children that markedly narrows down those options. In practice, this meant that the substantive agendas did not follow the detailed minimum checklist in any rigid sense – for example, in considering whether children should return to their parents or existing family members.

If children were accommodated under S.20 (other than short-term placement), the possibility of a return to their family setting was, in principle, significant; but, in practice, it was a relatively rare objective (less than a fifth of those cases in the main sample). An example of the discussions at meetings reveals how such options were sidelined.

> *Meeting 32*. The chair tried to encourage a young person in supported lodgings to keep in contact with his mother. The young person who was impatient to leave the meeting said he would see her that night. A discussion about transport followed. There was no consideration of rehabilitation or a long-term plan.

When a review took place on a case due for care proceedings, there was typically little evidence of substantive discussion about the issues that would be decided in court. It seemed, for example, that there would be little or no possibility of halting the proceedings in the light of the review's findings.

> *Meeting 105*.
> The child was already accommodated. The plan was for care proceedings to take place shortly. One of the parents was present at the meeting. During a seven minute verbal report, the social worker stated the date of the hearing and said that a care order was expected. She concluded:
>
> Social worker: 'We shall have rights to ensure [the child] is properly looked after.'
>
> The chair then moved the discussion on. He later summed up the review recommendations, the first of which was as follows.
>
> Chair: 'A care order to establish his status as a looked after child, to protect his future.'

For those children in care the evidence from the main sample showed that rehabilitation with family members was again an infrequent objective – only a fifth of cases. Not airing that option at the meeting meant that in practice it was shelved.

Meeting 160. The general plan was for the long-term placement of a child in care at a residential special school, with a supplementary residential placement for the holidays. In a meeting lasting over 90 minutes there was no discussion of legal issues or the possibility of rehabilitation.

Again, when a placement had lasted for a number of years, reunification was typically regarded as a remote possibility and barely discussed, if at all.

Meeting 153. The plan was for the young person to stay in the foster placement on a long-term basis. This was stated at the outset. The young person agreed to talk about contact with his parents but there was no discussion of reunification. Fifteen minutes before the end, the long-term plan was raised as an issue; the young person and the foster carer signified their agreement.

Finding a new family was equally a minority objective (14 per cent of main sample cases). When a plan for adoption had been decided, the emphasis was on implementation and only a fundamental setback such as the failure of an adoption placement would prompt a major reconsideration.

Meeting 151. The general plan was for adoption. A final court date had been fixed, so when the chair introduced the agenda item about the child's future, the plan was simply restated. The guardian and the adoption worker had a five minute discussion with the foster carer about their future roles. These points were noted by the chair at the end of the meeting.

Evidence about the perspectives of social workers showed that they held a mixture of opinions about the impact of reviews as factors for change. About half the social workers in the survey were positive about the review's function in helping to create plans for effective rehabilitation (53 per cent positive; 11 per cent negative). But their views were divided about the impact of reviews in preventing delay in making permanent placements (30 per cent positive; 30 per cent negative) and most (63 per cent) were unsure if reviews helped to prevent the accommodated child going into care.

The evidence of the discussions showed that, while new information might help to sensitise decision makers to planning issues, review meetings were not occasions for fundamental rethinking. The reasons had partly to do with the progression of care plans; going down a certain road made it difficult to retrace those steps and opened other doors. Social workers' views reflected this problem: while half were positive about reviews as a means of promoting rehabilitation, there was much less faith in reviews as a means of preventing entry to care. In other words, it was possible to move back along the path, but there was a smoother route onto the next stage. In practice the minimum checklist contained in the Guidance was drawn upon selectively as children's situations developed.

The substantive agenda was therefore focused on those issues within the Guidance and Regulations that were of more immediate concern – placement, contact, health and education. These were the staple constituents of the agenda. Disability, special needs and aspects of ethnicity were sometimes integrated into discussion of the standard topics or sometimes subdivided into topics of their own, such as transport for a disabled child. As expected, aftercare was a major topic at reviews for older children.

Discussion of specific issues

The limited amount of time given to preliminaries and document reading meant that a great deal of meeting time was devoted to reporting and discussion. Chairs took responsibility for starting each topic, inviting a key person to give a verbal report. Discussion tended to open up quickly, putting an onus on the chair to hold the meeting together. Social workers responding to the survey frequently valued chairs who kept to the agenda while listening to everyone's viewpoint and allocating time for this. The importance of listening was clearly expressed by this chair's description of her objectives.

> Chair, Northborough: 'To listen to everybody. To consider any written reports. Look at the issues raised and the plan.'

If a plan was missing or unclear, discussion was intended to help deliver it. Asked to describe a review's objectives, another chair emphasised the centrality of defining a plan which had continuing significance.

> Chair, Northborough: 'A **clear** plan, because I will review it again. It's a **benchmark** for further reviews.' (emphasis in original)

At an initial review there was an urgent emphasis on planning, as this list of objectives, recalled after the meeting, suggests.

> Chair, Westside: 'To look at the issues on the review form, settle the agenda, make plans for the placement for [the young person] and look at her future placement, whether at home or in other accommodation. Then the medical and school. . .'

But in reviews where the plan had been already formulated, there was a more cautious approach. As outlined in the previous section, the scope of discussion was defined primarily by the current care plan.

Legal issues

The discussion of alternative legal options further illustrates the way in which the current plan exercised an influence. Though the Regulations insist that reviews inform young people about their legal rights, such as the right to seek the revocation of a care order, this was a serious issue at few reviews. Even in a case where information was provided, it was not followed up in the review.

Meeting 166.
The question of revoking the care order came up in a preliminary conversation before the review meeting started.

Young person: 'Can I have my care order revoked?'

Chair: 'Yes.'

Young person: 'I want my care order because it affects my benefits.'

Chair: 'No, it won't.'

Unfortunately, the implications were passed over, as others gathered for the meeting. Several minutes later, the chair went on to introduce the review proper mentioning that, 'you'll be **looked after** till you are 18.' (emphasis added) This formulation avoided the question of whether the young person should be in care or accommodated under S.20. The young person's legal status was never mentioned again.

Here is another example where the same issue was somewhat glossed over.

Meeting 50.
Chair: 'I think we should continue the care order and give you more support.'

Key worker: 'Do you want continuing support?'

Young person: 'Yes.'

The legal issue in this case was therefore closely linked to 'continuing support'; alternative legal arrangements were not considered. Nor was it emphasised that the young person had formal rights in the matter. An application for a residence order was also rarely discussed, one reason being the chair's assessment of its appropriateness, as in the following example.

Chair: 'The residence order wasn't brought up at the meeting. I feel now he wouldn't benefit from a residence order. He'd lose out on aftercare provision. It affects permanency.'

Pragmatic considerations came into play, rather an automatic reference to an inflexible agenda.

Contact

Contact was a regular agenda item. Social workers referred in their reports to the quality and frequency of planned contact and this gave rise to discussion with family members who were present. If parents were having problems or wanted more contact, these issues were addressed.

Meetings 109–110. The mother of a child in a foster placement complained that contact had not been satisfactory because she had not been given a proper address to attend and therefore limited contact had taken place only at a nursery. The chair suggested that individual arrangements be made, commenting to the mother: 'We didn't know why you didn't turn up.'

There was a change in the way contact was approached as young people grew older, with more emphasis on their power to choose.

Meeting 38.
The young person was offered a choice about contact arrangements with her parents.

Young person: 'I want to leave it [as it is].'

Chair: 'We can make an agreement or leave it with you.'

Young person: 'Yeah.'

After chairing a similar discussion, a chair commented on the difficulty of raising a delicate issue like contact in a long-term foster placement. The foster carer's presence had an impact on the discussion.

Chair, Westside: 'It's difficult for [the young person] to talk about his parents **in front of the foster carer**.' (emphasis added)

For some young people, however, there were fundamental reasons why contact was barely on the agenda. Obstacles to family contact were vividly outlined by a young refugee as follows:

Meeting 179.
Young person: 'I know of no relatives other than my father. He was a single child. My mum had another husband previously. One third of the population [in my country] have this problem. It'd be a miracle [if relatives were found]. The new government doesn't want to show the bad. [My father] was arrested by the new government.'

The decision was to try tracing the young person's father through an international agency. For young people such as this, it is unfortunate that so few independent visitors were available to attend reviews. Their absence reflected a systematic problem. One chair began a discussion of independent visitors with a candid admission that there were none in the local authority area!

Placement

The placement was a central focus of discussions, and the very frequent attendance of carers meant that a firsthand perspective was routinely available. Some carers were eager to present as positive and supportive to young people, intervening to clarify matters or add examples of positive achievement and behaviour. They prompted young people to fish out examples of art work or school awards which received the approval of other participants. This attitude was further expressed when carers offered support to young people before the meeting.

Residential carer: 'I said, "Would you like me to say things? Can you do it on your own?"'

Where poor behaviour by a young person had occurred, it was sometimes difficult for carers to avoid a complaining tone when referring to incidents.

Meeting 166.
There was a general discussion of the young person's past behaviour difficulties which, after a stay in a psychiatric unit and a new school placement, had partly improved. The discussion continued:

Residential carer: 'His behaviour was disruptive **on a recent weekend away**.' (emphasis added)

Young person: '[Another carer] was picking on me.'

The young person then explained how an incident had been misunderstood by staff. The young person's discomforted response emphasises the problem of discussing incidents of behaviour at reviews without adding to the stress on young people. This is a point picked up in the next chapter.

Some residential workers gave frank comments about young people's hygiene.

Meeting 74.
Residential carer: 'She's not organised around the house. Personal hygiene is an uphill battle.'

In response, the young person expressed a preference for using a shower tap; the senior residential worker replied that a plumber was due to visit to install the shower.

It is not surprising then if some young people feel thrust under a glaring spotlight at reviews.

Talking constructively with young people about aspects of their behaviour is an extremely challenging task, one which is magnified by the dynamics of a meeting. Carers need support if they are to make their anxieties clear without adversely affecting the situation. There is a good deal of knowledge about effective approaches to behaviour issues which could be usefully incorporated into the shaping of discussions at reviews (Cooper, Smith and Upton, 1994).

In order to make appropriate contributions, carers also needed some background knowledge about the review procedure, as this comment after a meeting suggests.

> Foster carer: 'I'm not sure what is supposed to come up, like education and health . . . there wasn't the link with the school. I feel I'm out on a limb. I'd like to know more about him . . . . We're ordinary foster carers.'

This foster carer's lack of procedural knowledge was one obstacle to raising a key topic – how to understand a child's special needs.

The presence of residential managers and fostering officers at reviews testified to the importance given to maintaining placements.

> *Meeting 134.* The fostering officer pointed to a need for the foster carers to take a break. The foster carer added that last year's break had not been expensive and the chair agreed that 'the powers-that-be' should be approached.

It became clear that the major function of these additional professionals was to support the placement and to see that any burdens were minimised. Hence planning was framed in ways that took account of the 'provider' section of the department. This is not a theme touched on by the Guidance and Regulations which do not envisage the attendance of 'providers' in this sense. Yet it was a significant component of review meetings.

Ethnicity

While the organisation of discussion suggested a cautious approach to the child's legal status and a watchful eye over placement, there were other specific issues, such as ethnicity, that demanded highly sensitive and informed contributions from chairs. All the review chairs for the subsample were white. This meant that they had to call on a particular competence and knowledge in order to overcome any barriers to understanding the needs of children from black and minority ethnic groups.

Solving problems required both tact and persistence in the face of practical barriers and participants' doubts.

> *Meeting 160.*
> Discussions took place about a child's dual placement in a residential school and in an independent residential home run by people who shared the child's Muslim religion.

> The chair's contributions were, first of all, to find out whether staff in the residential home were still committed to maintaining the placement and, secondly, to follow up suggestions made by the staff about maintaining the child's religious observance while at residential school. But the school representative was doubtful about practical issues.

> School representative: 'Nobody on the staff [at the residential school] has that faith. [We'd need] someone to take him to the mosque.'

> Staff at the residential home could assist but there were transport problems. The chair appealed for a joint plan to be made. Afterwards she admitted frustrations about the outcome.

This example was about maintaining a minority cultural identity. Rather different issues of personal identity were discussed at reviews for those children of mixed ethnic origins who were being moved towards adoption.

Meeting 151.
The chair raised the question of how the child saw himself.

Foster carer: 'He still feels he's black . . . he has black origins. It's like a white person can be part of the culture.'

Chair: 'He has black origins. It'll be a continuing issue. People don't treat him as black.'

Guardian ad litem: 'It's ongoing. [There's] a long way to go.'

Chair: 'He needs to feel he can be loved by [a] black [family].'

The discussion here provided a means of sharing perspectives and signifying mutual support for the tasks ahead.

These cases suggest how chairs sought to engage in positive discussion. In order to have a constructive effect it was clear that chairs had to be sensitive and knowledgeable about the issues as they affected individual children. It was not sufficient simply to preside over the contributions of others.

Health

There was very little evidence of medical reports or documents being considered or discussed. Confidentiality was perhaps a constraint on sharing documents but there was no unwillingness to discuss medical matters or to look at possible action. Chairs normally asked about the young person's state of health and confirmed whether or not routine medical checks had taken place.

The age and development of the children and young people were significant in influencing the intensity of medical surveillance. Young children were a particular focus of attention – a point already evident from the data about the attendance of health professionals at meetings.

Meeting 88. The health visitor asked for a three year medical check. This was agreed in addition to paediatric supervision.

For older adolescents, medical arrangements were seen as an area for informed choice and the routine medical was less of a focus.

Meeting 169. Though the previous review had planned for a medical examination, the young person said that it had not happened. The foster carer explained that he did not want one but he did get check-ups from his doctor.

The chair then asked about the arrangement, discussed at the previous review, for the young person to have a particular operation. The young person confirmed that this had happened. Asked if he was worried about doctors, he replied, 'No!' with a smile. 'No one will force you to have a medical', added the chair.

Education

Education issues were routinely given attention; chairs tried to confirm the general progress of the child within the curriculum and explored needs for support. Interests and career choices also came into the discussion. Behaviour was a significant topic which chairs tried to approach sensitively.

> *Meeting 21.*
>
> The chair introduced the topic of education cautiously, aware of behaviour problems at the young person's special school. No one from the school was at the meeting.
>
> Chair: 'I don't like to raise this. You didn't get on with the headteacher in the past. Support is needed.'
>
> Social worker: 'It's about growing up, getting on with people you don't like.'
>
> Foster carer: 'He's had a brilliant week. It's a teenage problem. They're all the same.'
>
> Meanwhile, the young person listened to these sympathetic remarks. The chair then asked him about his examination entries and about a national award scheme. The social worker enquired about his reading. He had little to say and the foster carer intervened to list the magazines that he read. The chair advised him to 'stick with school' and asked about further education. The foster carer agreed to deal with his transfer to technical college. An education grant was going to be sought.

This example illustrates the point that, while the decisions implied action by the attenders, the actual coordination of education and social services around a joint plan was not a major issue. The separation of services was sustained by the fact that education reports were not systematically scrutinised at meetings. The occasions when service coordination was discussed were to do with particular problems such as formal statementing, meeting the needs of a disabled child, or the exclusion of a young person. Even then, there was no evidence of attempts to break procedural logjams through S.27 of the Children Act.

Aftercare

As the young people grew older, their futures were influenced by the stability of their current placement, particularly in foster care. Some long-term placements were planned to continue beyond the age of 18 because of the close relationships that had developed.

Meeting 171. Asked by the chair if she felt part of the family, the young person said that she was soon to become a godmother to the foster carer's daughter.

But there were practical issues to be faced and the meetings presented an opportunity for advice to be given to the foster carer and young person about the financial implications of leaving care. Yet the transition was not easy for foster carers, marking an end to a certain level of social services support.

Meeting 169.
The chair talked about the formal ending of the foster care arrangement. The carer said she felt under an obligation to offer a home.

Foster carer: 'They cut it off at 18 . . . . But that's the rule. Till he's got his own place I feel I'm responsible.'

The relationship of young people with social services changed as they grew up and this was reflected in a partnership approach. Housing decisions, for example, were framed in the context of supporting young people's participation and choice.

Meeting 169.
Young person: 'I'll check the semi-independent flat. I can look.'

Chair: 'Look at two [of them], then decide.'

Young person: 'There's one lady [from the support team] who can take me.'

Sometimes it was clear that young people moving on to independent living situations faced a new set of problems. For one young person, independent living had proved to be a struggle against malicious complaints and unsympathetic housing management.

Meeting 73.
Young person: 'I get dirty looks from people round here. It's envy from older people. They think I'm a drug addict or prostitute.'

The decision was to continue social work support in order to ameliorate the situation.

The evidence of the discussions reinforced the cogency of the Guidance in suggesting that reviews be used to build partnership with young people in order to continue giving support, whatever the nature of their living circumstances at 18.

Decision making

The Guidance identifies decision making as a crucial stage of the planning and review process. The evidence of this study indicated that decisions crystallised at a review meeting. As the meeting proceeded through a topic in the substantive agenda, there was usually a key point at which the chair appeared to assess the situation and to draw a conclusion. It was marked by a brief announcement of a decision, before moving on to the next topic. This skill of summing up the situation at a review was valued by social workers responding to the survey. Chairs clearly saw themselves as responsible for drawing these conclusions and there was no formal reference to other participants. The skill that social workers valued seemed to lie in acknowledging the discussion and at the same time looking for ways of keeping the general care plan on track. Where there was no firm care plan, 'assessment' became the chosen option.

The wording of decisions commonly drew on unspecific formulas (Sinclair, 1984). These had the effect of responding to issues while being open to closer definition in the future. In the following example, a dialogue between social worker and chair shows the purpose served by the word 'explore'.

Meeting 113.
In the absence of parents, only the social worker and chair took part in the review. After some discussion, the chair quickly noted the decisions, talking as she wrote them down.

Chair: 'Assessment and work on appropriate supervision of the child – ongoing.'

Social worker: 'Rehabilitation?'

Chair: 'I'll add that on. "Rehabilitation to be explored once alternative accommodation is secured." "Explored". It's got to be better than the other [accommodation]. It was so cluttered!'

The wording of the plan drew on tried and tested formulas which left room for further definition in practice. The use of such terms meant that the exact scope of the decisions was left undefined.

Meeting 134.
Chair: 'We'll investigate the possibility of additional funding for [educational] help. We'll put pressure on [the local education authority].'

Fostering Officer: '[What about] the complaints procedure?'

Chair: (To the social worker) 'Check it out. [There's a] need to put things in writing.'

Here the decisions were mainly preparatory – 'checking out', 'investigating' – or metaphorical – 'putting pressure on' people – rather than a programme or list of actions. Exactly what was to be done was not specified because how to achieve the goal was sometimes unclear.

Some decisions meant engaging with procedures that the chair could influence but not necessarily control.

Meeting 177.
Chair: 'We **could** find a place [for the child's personal property] in the council [offices]. We'll **have to flag that up**.' (emphases added)

'Flagging that up' was a jargon phrase referring to the seemingly obscure agendas and timescales involved in procedures. Similarly, if the plan was not progressing, the term 'chasing up' was employed.

Meeting 115.
Chair: 'We'll chase up the freeing application.'

Another option was to decide to have a further meeting to discuss some aspect of the plan. This informal signalling of decisions meant that there was rarely any time for spelling out the reasons for decisions. It was assumed that they were evident from the previous discussion.

In announcing decisions quickly, there was a tendency for chairs to say that 'we' would carry them out, as the examples show. Responsibilities were assigned informally and there was no emphasis on obtaining binding commitments there and then, though some staff would volunteer to carry out tasks.

The detailed formulation of decisions into an operational plan or programme was evidently not a major function of review meetings, though some meticulous chairs listed all the decisions at the end. Social workers did not expect chairs to focus on detail. In the social workers' survey, the allocation of tasks to be performed within timescales was barely mentioned as a quality of a good chair. Yet allocation of tasks is a responsibility of chairs (Volume 3, Ch. 8.21). It was unclear how significant non-attenders were to be formally engaged and, where appropriate, committed to the revised plan.

The timescale for action was influenced by the review cycle set by the Regulations (RCC 3). But those intervals in the Regulations were understood to be normal rather than time limits. The influence of such administrative timescales echoes findings from the period before the Children Act 1989 (Vernon and Fruin, 1986). Review dates were fixed three or six months ahead, depending on whether this was a first or later review. Indeed there were examples of review decisions being influenced by these assumptions about the next review date.

Meeting 85.
The plan was for rehabilitation of the child to the mother but the timescale had not been decided.

Chair: '[Revoking] the care order won't happen in the next six months. You need more confidence, taking over [the child's] care yourself, [dealing with] arrears. You need new housing and there's the divorce.'

The parent did not reply. The social worker then talked about planning for a court hearing in four to five months' time in order to 'keep up momentum'. The chair's response was to speak about revocation of the order 'after the next review', which the social worker agreed. The parent again said nothing, and the review date was fixed for six months in the future.

This chair's assessment of the rehabilitation timescale was subtly framed by the administrative review cycle, while the parent simply deferred to the professionals' judgements.

The time interval for a review superimposed itself on the planning process in a similar case where a major step had to be taken at some time in the next reviewing interval.

> *Meeting 50.* There was a discussion about a plan to seek a new placement. The young person raised the issue of 'what to do when I leave?' In response, the chair made it clear that the review's purpose was 'to talk about the next six months', thus bringing the regulatory timescale into the discussion. The chair added that further discussion would take place between the voluntary agency and the child, but stated that the placement should continue 'as long as necessary'. The voluntary agency plan was to aim for a move in four months; this was agreed but the review date was still set for six months ahead, unless there was a need to meet beforehand.

Faced with a dilemma about holding a further meeting around the time of the new placement, the chair decided to fix the review at the latest date, rather than call it when the plan had been firmed up. Though not ruling out a possible meeting at an earlier date the decision honoured the review cycle, first and foremost.

Thinking about the next review tended to be focused only on the date. There was no evidence of forward planning to prepare for the tasks of the next review – consultation dates, assessment and report dates and so on.

Duration of meetings

Each of the meetings in the subsample was timed (when there was more than one child's case, the total meeting time was divided among the cases). Their duration was spread widely, from a minimum of 17 to a maximum of 120 minutes; the median duration of 57 minutes was the same as the mean duration (see Figure 5.3). These wide individual variations suggest there were few artificial time constraints; each case was given individual attention. This was not incompatible with careful planning beforehand: a chair who announced at the outset that she expected the meeting to take 80 minutes proved to be surprisingly accurate given the complex agenda. However, it is difficult to understand why the range was so large unless we appreciate that chairs and participants approached issues pragmatically. If there appeared good reason to extend the discussion, then it continued; otherwise the chairs were likely to move the agenda on.

By comparison with practice before the Children Act, the evidence shows that review meetings have become longer (Family Rights Group,

Figure 5.3 Duration of meetings

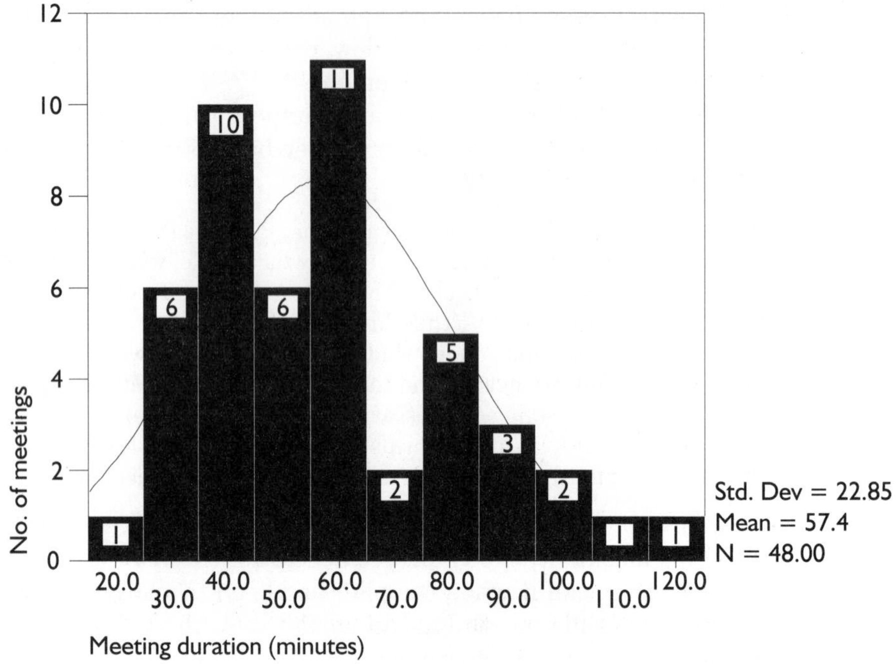

Meeting duration (minutes)

Std. Dev = 22.85
Mean = 57.4
N = 48.00

1985). In the past, meetings hardly ever lasted over 60 minutes yet the mean duration for the present sample was 57 minutes (Sinclair, 1984). For many cases, substantive discussion has markedly increased. The emphasis on holding a substantial meeting marks a significant change from the earlier period when 'paper' reviews were commonplace (Vernon and Fruin, 1986).

Conclusion

The review meetings were influenced by a practical social work approach, rather than by formalities. Social workers responding to the survey valued the following qualities of chairs: knowledge of the case; facilitation of discussion; a sensitivity to the child; agenda management; assessing the current situation; a positive approach and an ability to deal with anger and conflict. As key functions of a review chair, planning and decision making were mentioned less frequently than agenda management, knowledge of the case and facilitating discussion.

Reviewing was apparently conceived as discussing realistic adjustments of the plan in response to developments since the last review. Forward thinking was centred on predictable aspects of the current care plan. Reviews were only one of the settings in which plans were discussed, as the social work survey emphasised. 'Planning meetings' were regarded as significantly different from statutory reviews by a large majority (73 per cent). Again, a majority (64 per cent) agreed that 'most important decisions about the plan are taken as the issue arises: we can't wait for a review'. Actual planning was not the preserve of the review by any means.

While the survey evidence showed that social workers had clear ideas about the significance of planning and decision making, these functions were not crucial in their thoughts about chairing a review meeting. Chairs were mainly valued as mediators and facilitators based on their knowledge and understanding of the case.

This helps to explain why review meetings were generally conducted as exercises in communication rather than as formal inquiries or debates. The scope of actual planning was somewhat restricted because the current care plan was taken as a benchmark. Hence, where decisions were made, there was a concentration on means rather than ends. One possible reason for the ethos of the review meetings is to do with the roles of the chair: in two of the authorities, the chair also had a responsibility for the plan; in the third, the chair was independent but the review was not seen as a planning forum. The primacy of the existing plan was taken for granted by this independent chair.

> Chair, Northborough: 'It's not my role to materially alter the plan. I would make recommendations to be taken back to the line manager. I'd **review** the plan.' (emphasis added)

Hence, in none of the authorities was there any systematic reason for chairs to question the plan. Chairs who were line managers could claim that they had the advantage of knowing the case while not being involved in the day-to-day work.

> Chair, Westside: 'Is it a formal statutory review or is it about making a child's situation meaningful? You need a chair who knows the child. But from the statutory side you need to be more objective and distanced; some people see it as just another meeting. The team manager knows the case but is still objective.'

This remark acknowledged that in the choice of chair there was a dilemma between the chair being knowledgeable and being distanced. But it was argued that a line manager could be *both* objective and knowledgeable, if not necessarily distanced.

The organisation of meetings was therefore similar in some respects to earlier findings from the period before the Children Act 1989. For example, Vernon and Fruin (1986) comment on the extent to which reviews were seen as separate from decision making. Reviews reinforced the current plan rather than questioned it. Similarly, Sinclair (1984) found that nearly half the reviews maintained the status quo. At the residential reviews observed by the same author, the chairs were concerned to promote discussion around the general plan, rather than to hold social workers to account. As she remarks, the key issues may have previously been handled by supervisors in supervision sessions. The organisation of meetings was not in any sense forcing reviews into a rigid or mechanistic format.

Since the implementation of the Guidance and Regulations, however, the scope of the discussion has increased. Discussion of the substantive agenda was wide-ranging, consistently covering specific issues and making meetings much longer than in the past. Chairs showed skills in applying their knowledge and judgement to the handling of specific issues but decision making was often unspecific. Indeed participants needed to keep their wits about them in order to catch the flow of discussion.

These findings suggest that the main function of the review meetings was consultative, rather than to scrutinise or to sharpen up the care plan. Some questions must therefore be raised about the extent to which such meetings contribute to the consistently structured and coordinated approach to planning implied by the regulatory framework. There were few incentives to re-examine the fundamentals of the plan or its implementation and it was difficult to identify ways in which chairs – including the independent chairs in Northborough – were performing a comprehensive monitoring function on behalf of the local authority. In the next chapter we shall see how far the consultative focus of the meeting successfully encouraged participation by children and parents.

Key findings

- The list of attenders seemed to be influenced by practical social work perceptions of the meetings as occasions for people involved with the plan to consult together. Meetings were sometimes 'top heavy' even when children were present. The attendance list included a series of service providers but few supporters of children or parents.
- Meetings tended to occur at the placement but this practice also had disadvantages.
- The individual care plan was a major influence on the meetings. This meant that the minimum checklist of the Guidance and Regulations was drawn upon in order to concentrate on a substantive agenda considered relevant to the child's situation. The chair's role was to promote discussion rather than to chair a debate about the fundamentals of the plan or to initiate change.
- The centrality of discussion was emphasised by the fact that: preliminaries were brief; participants were assumed to know about the standing of the meeting and their roles in it; there was little time set aside for document reading.

- Monitoring of previous decisions tended to be brief and factual, rather than probing into the reasons for what had happened.
- Chairs assumed the responsibility for decision making which was usually conducted quickly once they had mentally assessed the progress of discussion. It was commonplace for decisions to be worded unspecifically. Chairs recorded the meeting as it proceeded and there were few cases of independent recording.
- Decisions about the next review were limited to setting a date, which was chosen generally at the furthest point in time permitted under the Regulations. Meetings have become much longer than they were before the Children Act 1989.

We must be careful, however, not to evaluate the meetings fully until evidence of the role played by children and parents is presented – a task for the next chapter.

6. The participation of young people and their parents at review meetings

It is a central principle of the Children Act that young people and their parents should be consulted before decisions are made about their care plans (S.22(4), 61 and 64, Children Act 1989). Their participation in a review meeting affirms this principle. This chapter builds on the evidence of the last by examining how far current experience of meetings matches up to the intentions of the Children Act.

Involvement by young people in review meetings is strongly supported by the Guidance and Regulations (RCC 7(2); Volume 3, Ch. 8.15–16). In the Guidance, the attendance of a young person for the whole of the meeting is taken to be the norm, though part-attendance should also be considered. A decision to exclude young people should be recorded, together with the reasons. It should be possible for someone to attend who can give the child friendly support. The general intention of the Guidance is to conduct meetings in the spirit of partnership embodied in the Children Act. The involvement of parents is discussed in very similar terms.

Attending meetings is therefore regarded as a significant element of involvement in the review. But being at a meeting is different from participating in one. How far did children and their parents make positive contributions to the meetings? There are also negative possibilities. For example, if the purpose of the meetings is to look at young people and their futures, how do young people cope with being placed in the spotlight among a group of adults? (Fletcher, 1993; Dolphin Project, 1993).

This chapter takes forward the study of meetings by looking more closely at the influences on the attendance of children and parents. Using observational data it then considers to what extent they may have participated in discussions. Next it draws on individual and group interviews with young people in order to gain some insight into their feelings. These findings are then used in order to show how observational data can be given a new significance. The perceptions of parents are then explored. Additional data from the social workers' survey and interviews with chairs provide further perspectives on the problem of facilitating participation. Finally, the implications of the findings for the study of participation are discussed.

Influences on children's attendance

The age distribution of children's attendances is set out in Table 6.1, indicating a rise which gathers momentum as children reach the age of eleven. The majority of 11- to 15-year-olds, and nearly all 16- to 18-year-olds, attended their meetings. Data on 166 cases was available from either the researcher's observations or from records.

Table 6.1 Children's attendance at meetings, by age group
(N=166)

	Present		Absent		Total	
Years of age	N	%	N	%	N	%
Less than 5	3	9	31	91	34	100
5–10	13	30	31	70	44	100
11–15	43	80	11	20	54	100
16–18	33	97	1	3	34	100
Total	92	55	74	45	166	100

The longer children had been looked after, the greater the frequency of their attendance (chi-square $p<.01$). Analysis of the relationship between age group and attendance also demonstrated a significant association ($p<.01$). A high attendance was found for young people accommodated under S.20, compared with somewhat lower attendance for those in care ($p<.05$). A higher attendance among young people from black and minority ethnic groups was accounted for by the refugees, who were largely an older group. There was no evidence of a link between attendance and a variety of other possible factors, such as the use of the Assessment and Action Record, the child having a disability nor with the ratings of consultation with children and parents, discussed in Chapter 4. Attendance by young people was a norm, rather than an exception. As the previous chapter revealed, this was reflected in social workers' views: children's attendance was given a very high priority rating. Indeed, the routine inclusion of children in meetings marks a substantial change from earlier practice (Stein and Ellis, 1983a; Sinclair, 1984; Vernon and Fruin, 1986).

Evidence of part-attendance was rare. According to the records, only seven children attended for just part of the meeting; four of these were five- to ten-year-olds. From observations, it seemed that some young people were guided out of the room by foster carers when difficult issues arose. In other cases, a child might hover within earshot or drift out occasionally.

Influences on parents' attendances

During the 1980s, researchers found, on the whole, very low rates of parental attendance at reviews (Sinclair, 1984; Family Rights Group, 1985; Vernon and Fruin, 1986). However, for children in particular situations, such as residential care, evidence of a higher rate of attendance began to emerge (Fox, 1988). Hence, analysis of the present data will focus on particular categories and circumstances. In a proportion of cases, notably refugees, parental attendance seemed to be impossible (13 per cent of mothers; 16 per cent of fathers) or information about it was lacking (6 per cent of mothers; 7 per cent of fathers).

When the attendance data was analysed, there was no evidence of any significant differences linked to the gender or ethnicity of the children. However, Table 6.2 shows how the pattern of parental attendance – like the pattern of consultation – was connected with the child's age. Parents of younger children attended review meetings significantly more frequently than parents of older ones (chi-square $p<.05$, $<.05$). The shorter the period that the children had been looked after, the more frequent were the attendances of mothers ($p<.01$).

Table 6.2   Parental attendance, by age group

	Mother				Father			
	Present		Total		Present		Total	
Years of age	N	%	N	%	N	%	N	%
Less than 5	23	68	34	100	11	36	31	100
5–10	18	42	43	100	9	21	42	100
11–15	15	34	44	100	8	19	42	100
16 and over	7	30	23	100	1	4	23	100
Total	63	44	144	100	29	21	138	100

As Table 6.3 shows, in cases where the child was placed on the child protection register, both parents attended significantly more frequently ($p<.01$, $<.01$). All the percentages represent the proportions of the relevant row in the table. Thus, the great majority (71 per cent) of mothers with a child on the child protection register attended the review. However, for fathers with registered children, the proportion who attended slipped below a majority. Similar differences apply to the parents of children on interim care orders. These relatively high levels of attendance can be compared with the lower levels (less than 40 per cent) now current at initial child protection conferences (Thoburn, Lewis and Shemmings, 1995).

Table 6.3 Attendance of parents at reviews, by CPR registration and legal status

	Mother				Father			
	Present		Total		Present		Total	
	N	%	N	%	N	%	N	%
CPR								
Registered	29	71	41	100	17	45	38	100
Not registered	30	31	96	100	11	12	93	100
Legal status								
ICO	15	68	22	100	11	50	22	100
CO	14	38	37	100	8	22	36	100
Deemed CO	6	19	31	100	3	10	29	100
S.20 (Short term)	11	85	13	100	3	23	13	100
S.20 (Other)	14	42	33	100	4	13	31	100
Other status	2	33	6	100	0	0	5	100
All	62	44	142	100	29	21	136	100

However, the transition to the full care order is associated with a decline in the attendance rate which was especially marked for 'deemed care orders' – those already in care when the Children Act 1989 was implemented in 1991. Hence, it appears that the passage of time may be a factor to consider in explaining the decline in attendance.

There were evident differences in the attendances of parents with children in S.20 accommodation: the highest attendances of all were for mothers of children in short-term placements (Macadam and Robinson, 1995); for those in other S.20 accommodation, parental attendances were much lower (even after the refugee cases with this legal status had been withdrawn). But there was no significant difference between the attendances of parents with children in care and those with children accommodated under S.20. There was a significantly higher attendance of fathers in Northborough ($p<.05$), a finding which seems to reflect its higher proportions of young children and of cases on the child protection register.

In conclusion, it appears that the child's age was again a significant feature associated with the rate of parental involvement. The formal and legal status of children was also a factor in the attendance of parents. What seemed to underlie this pattern was the degree to which parental responsibility remained active. It applies most obviously to cases on the child protection register but also to those in care and in different kinds of S.20 accommodation. But the most prevalent difference in all categories was the difference between mothers and fathers. This finding needs to be set in the context of lone parenthood which has been associated with children becoming looked after (Bebbington and Miles, 1989). However, it also suggests that the concentration of practical parental responsibility on mothers applies across the looked-after population and not only to new admissions. For example, the low attendance of fathers with children in short-term placements is a small but striking instance of the general pattern.

Further data on attendance will be examined in Chapter 9, where the pattern of attendance over time and instances of exclusion from meetings will be analysed.

Facilitating participation – language needs

The proportion of review meetings attended by foreign language interpreters was very small. In the main sample, interpreters were recorded as having attended on nine occasions (five per cent of the sample). Five of these attendances were mainly for the benefit of children, two for parents and one apparently for a foster carer. Given that the first languages of 27 children were recorded as being other than English, the attendances of interpreters appeared to be fairly infrequent. Children will often learn English rapidly, of course, but even young people who have learned to cope with everyday English may find a review discussion fairly exacting. For example, a young refugee who coped without an interpreter said in an interview that he was pleased the attenders spoke English slowly for his benefit.

Comments from parents give some insight into the diversity of interpreting needs. The first relates to a situation where the parent had major language needs, which had been insufficiently assessed. At interview she said she wanted questions and answers written down, because the interpreter appointed by social services had been too quick and she could not understand some words. She would have preferred someone she trusted as an interpreter. The second example concerns a woman with more limited needs who had attained competence in everyday English. But her daughter expressed a wish that her mother use an interpreter in order to cope with a review.

> Parent: 'I don't need anybody [to help me with English] but my daughter ... thinks I need it.'

Facilitating participation – supporters for children and parents

There was little evidence of independent supporters for children at the meetings observed. A young person with a disability and special language needs had a personal carer who also acted as translator. Only one other adult (who was also a manager of the independent placement) openly took on such a role with the agreement of the young person.

A number of the young people wanted some help from an adult they trusted; they identified carers or the social worker as the people they expected to help them. This support was not always forthcoming.

> 'I'd have liked some help from [foster] Mum and Dad and [the social worker].'

One young person was unable to identify anyone he trusted completely and so relied solely on himself.

There seemed to be a difficulty in defining a role for an independent supporter. Social workers and carers were supposed to give help and there seemed to be no means of assessing the need for a child's supporter. No one openly took on that role unless there was an obvious candidate, like a personal carer, or someone from the meeting, like the manager of the placement, volunteered.

Parents had supporters in attendance on few occasions. Support for parents was observed in five cases in the meetings sample. Formal support from a counsellor was given to two parents while the other three relied on adult relatives. None of the parents were supported by other social workers or health representatives. As the evidence about social workers' views has already indicated, additional support for parents was not regarded as a high priority. Indeed, there was some evidence to show that additional support for parents was seen as distracting from the main purpose of the review.

> *Meeting 152.* A parent with an addiction problem asked if the drugs support service had been invited to the review. The chair explained that they had not been invited, because the service was meant for the parents, not for the child, and their presence would have made the meeting even larger.

This argument that the meetings were for children helps to clarify the reason for the absence of parents' supporters, suggesting that their role was not regarded positively.

Assessing participation at meetings

The concept of a 'ladder of participation' was first proposed by Arnstein (1969). It has recently been applied to families in the child protection system (Thoburn, Lewis and Shemmings, 1995). It will be used in this chapter to assess the verbal contributions of young people and their parents at review meetings. The concept of a ladder implies a scale of steps rising from a complete lack of power to full control. Following Thoburn, Lewis and Shemmings, the steps were listed as follows (Figure 6.1).

Figure 6.1   Ladder of individual participation (from Thoburn, Lewis and Shemmings, 1995)

High power: Controls

Helps design service

Partner

Participant

Involved

Consulted

Informed

Placated

Manipulated

Low power: Powerless

Since the ladder of participation is an abstract concept, it is necessary to discuss the concrete way in which it was used in this research. The contributions of individuals were rated according to the **topmost** rung of the ladder which they reached during the meeting. The rating was of the highest level of participation achieved by an individual concerning at least one significant issue in the meeting. This means that the rating represents a clear highlight rather than a consistent performance across all issues. It also cannot be assumed that because individuals achieved a certain rating in discussion that the steps below were systematically ascended, for example, that participation was always backed by accurate and substantial information.

This approach to rating was preferred as a method of identifying children's positive contributions which can be more variable and sensitive than those of adults. It differs from the more complex cumulative assessment explained by Thoburn, Lewis and Shemmings. The rating does not therefore cover any 'low notes' in the performances of attenders. There were moments of silence and anguish such as the tears of a mother of three children in care proceedings. Though rated as a partner in aspects of the discussion she left the room for a while in order to give vent to her emotions. Even a 17-year-old young man was not necessarily a participant in discussions on every topic. He was consulted about issues such as aftercare, health, leisure and independence skills; he began to participate when he explained how he had turned down a job offer which involved starting work at 5.30 am.

These qualifications emphasise that the research focus was very much on identifying positive contributions within the ebb and flow of talk at meetings and that the individual scores represent a maximum achievement, even if only for a short time.

Table 6.4   Ratings of participation in discussion at meetings observed

	Child	%	Mother	%	Father	%
Informed	1	2	0	0	1	2
Consulted	5	10	0	0	0	0
Involved	7	14	3	6	3	6
Participant	12	25	10	21	6	13
Partner	6	12	7	15	4	8
Missing/Absent	17	35	28	58	34	71
Total	48	100	48	100	48	100

The distribution of ratings in Table 6.4 shows that a 'participant' rating was achieved by the largest number of young people while a similar number achieved lower ratings, being either 'involved', 'consulted' or 'informed'. There were fewer 'partners' among the children than in the 'participant' category. Parents, especially fathers, were less often in attendance than children. Just as for children, the largest category was composed of 'participants' but 'partners' were in a minority. To help account for these results, a number of possible factors were examined.

Though the numbers are relatively small, the data indicate a rise in the achievement of participation and partnership as young people become older. While only a quarter of those aged from five to ten years were rated as participants or partners, this proportion increased to over two fifths of 11- to 15-year-olds and to five out of six young people from 16 to 18 years old.

Another way of analysing the ratings was to compare them with the different reasons for being looked after, where these were clearly established. The figures in the different categories (see Table 6.5) are very small but they show something of the range of possibilities. There was a wide distribution of scores in the biggest category – abuse/neglect. The results for the other categories indicate that it was possible to achieve a 'participant' or 'partner' rating even when the reasons for being looked after might otherwise given cause for concern: for example, the scores of four young people in the 'at risk/own behaviour' category were encouraging in this respect.

Turning now to parents, their attitudes to the fundamental care plan were compared, in order to see how these affected their contributions (see Table 6.6).

Table 6.5   Participation ratings for children, by reasons for being looked after

	Parental health	At risk/ own behaviour	Abuse/ neglect	Refugee	Respite/ disabled child	Other
Informed	0	0	1	0	0	0
Consulted	1	0	3	0	0	1
Involved	0	0	3	1	1	2
Participant	3	2	2	1	0	4
Partner	0	2	1	1	1	1
Total	4	4	10	3	2	8

In a number of cases parental views were not an issue, for example, in relation to adoption placement. In each other case, the parental attitude to the plan was rated according to the degree of agreement with the social services' view. There was a broad distribution of attitudes along this scale. When the parental attitudes were compared to the ratings of participation at the meetings, there was a spread of results which suggested that disagreement with the plan was not a bar to participation: in eight out of ten cases where there was some parental opposition to the plan, mothers were rated as participants or partners; in six out of eight similar cases the fathers were also rated in these categories.

Table 6.6   Parental attitudes to child's plan

	N	%
Opposed	12	25
Partly opposed	5	10
Neutral/accepting or divided view	5	10
Mainly agreed	9	19
Fully agreed	3	6
Not an issue	12	25
Unknown	2	4
Total	48	100

The qualitative findings draw attention to the range of contributions made by young people and their parents. Young people's age was a significant factor and there were clearly some positive performances among the older groups. When reasons for being looked after were taken into account, there were a range of results which suggest that participation was possible in cases that might otherwise give cause for concern.

Similarly, a range of contributions was observed among parents even when their attitude to the plan was taken into account. However, in general, the rating method was geared to a relatively low criterion of participation and the evidence prompts further questions about how participation can be consolidated and deepened for all users.

The perceptions of young people

Now that the main observational findings have been presented, it is possible to look more closely at the perspectives of children themselves and to see how their perceptions relate to the observations. Data have been drawn mainly from 12 individual interviews conducted with young people after review meetings, supplemented by the results of two focus group sessions with a small number of young people who had experience of reviews. Those who gave their views were aged from 11 to 18 years. One focus group session took place in a fieldwork authority, while another was organised with the help of a voluntary agency. The results of the individual interviews will be considered first and then compared with the focus group findings. The examples are meant to illustrate the common themes which emerged from the interviews.

From the individual interviews, it seems that chairs took little part in preparing young people for meetings. It was very rare for young people to have any discussion with the chair before the meeting, even when they had never met the chair before. In fact, only one of the six chairs who had been a stranger to the young person had any prior discussion. Even after attending the meeting, some still did not know the chair's name. There were systematic reasons for this practice which are explored later in this section.

It was clear that the initial stages of the meeting left an impression on the minds of young people, as they had tried to cope with the scrutiny of adults. At the beginning, young people were strongly aware of the size of the meeting. The sight of a gathering of adults caused shock and nervousness in some.

'Bloody hell. So many people. Nervous.'

'Bit shocked. So many people.'

They were self-conscious and preoccupied with how they would be asked questions. As two separately put it, they were thinking,

'What are they going to ask me?'

Another summed up this sense of being exposed. 'You get nervous when a meeting is talking about your future. I didn't know what people would say.' At the forefront of one young person's mind was a particular incident for which he had been criticised – in his view, unfairly. Interestingly his forecast that the incident would be raised turned out to be accurate. For another young person the meeting was simply an object of dread.

'I thought it'd be horrible.'

Young people who felt they knew what would be discussed approached the meeting with greater calmness.

'No worries. It was a straightforward meeting.'

'Knowing the questions' in advance was a way of being prepared for what otherwise might be an ordeal.

In assessing the outcome of the meeting, young people expressed a range of views. However, more than half the young people interviewed individually felt that they had been asked to say what they wanted in their own words. Most of this group also gave a positive opinion about the fairness of the meeting and some added that they had said every-thing they wanted to say. One, however, complained of people 'butting in' – a point that deserves further exploration later.

Nonetheless, some had been reluctant to talk about sensitive personal and family issues: a young person was opposed to the plan for contact with his biological family but had not made plain his feelings; another had chosen not to raise his concern about having been sexually abused in his mother's home when a young child. Young people had therefore held back some issues from the discussion.

The informal way in which meetings were chaired encouraged a free flow of discussion. But some young people experienced this as a problem.

'[The chair] tried to find out what I thought. Sometimes I wasn't so sure. She's talking to the social worker one minute, then me.'

'I didn't get a chance [to say everything] because everyone was talking.'

Both of these young people had learning difficulties: although each had access to some support at the meeting, they remained disadvantaged. In contrast, a young person with special language needs had no difficulty in following the discussion and, thanks to her interpreter, made an active contribution.

The individual interviewees held divided views about whether making a plan had been discussed at the meeting but most clearly felt they had been consulted about the decisions and had been given a choice. More than half said they had been asked to do certain things in the future but only a few had any experience of signing plans. Formal rights did not figure strongly in their experience of the review. Few said they had been informed at the meeting about any rights of redress if they disagreed with the plan. But some had previously been given information. Taking these into account, just over half said they had knowledge of their rights. But less than half had been told of their rights to seek court orders. The failure to inform a young person in care about her rights in law meant that she was not enabled to pursue her wish to return to live with her mother.

'If a court let me live where I want, I'd live with my Mum.'

Review meetings were not therefore occasions when young people felt they were systematically informed of their rights.

There was a diversity of experience among this small number of interviewees but the main impression is that those young people who spoke of genuine consultation had benefited informally rather than by using any formal rights.

In general, rather more than half the young people felt their contribution had made a difference and looked back on the review positively rather than negatively. Nonetheless comments like 'fine' and 'positive' have to be balanced against critical remarks – 'crap' and 'boring, very boring'.

The data from the interviews are therefore reasonably consistent with the broad conclusions of the observational study on participation but they add another dimension by bringing out the feelings of stress experienced by some young people, especially at the beginning of meetings. Such emotions were not necessarily evident because, as one put it, 'I made loads of jokes'. Underneath, as he described, were feelings of confusion and nervousness.

Organising focus groups of three or more people allowed for a more free-ranging discussion than was possible in the individual interviews. Some of the issues emerging from focus groups reinforced messages from the individual interviews while others were more general, reflecting the accumulation of experience as young people go on to attend further reviews.

A message that echoed the individual interviews was about the sense of being put under the spotlight, especially when faced with intrusive questions from adults who appeared as strangers to the young people.

Group Two
Young person (1): 'You don't really want to sit and talk to a whole room about your problems, though, do you?'

Young person (2): 'There's, like, people you don't know who are going "How are you coping with your past experiences?" Well, it's none of your business!'

Focusing on the young person was also perceived as a way of deflecting attention from issues in the placement.

Young person (1) 'It's very like, "What has she been doing?" not "What's the family unit been doing?"'

A more constructive approach was to start by asking young people questions about their views.

Young person (2): 'Everyone's asking me if I've had any problems with carers or anything. That's [what it should be], them asking me.'

Being caught in the review spotlight led to a form of 'stage fright'.

Group One
Young person (1): 'They come into a review and just come straight out with all these questions . . . you're not really sure what to say, afterwards you think "You forgot to say so and so."'

Young person (2): 'Yeah . . . After the review I think "Why didn't I say this?" or "Why didn't I say that?"'

Lack of preparatory work before a review meant that young people felt pressurised to agree. A brief introduction to the agenda was not sufficient to allow space for reflection. Young people in the groups echoed the point that was made when considering consultation in Chapter 4.

Group One
Young person (1) 'I've only just started asking "What's the agenda?" I never really knew what they're talking about until I got in there.'

Young person (2): 'I don't know what they're going to talk about until we actually get there and they start reeling off this stuff.'

Group Two
Young person (1): 'When the meetings are about to start, they give you this paper. You know what they are going to talk about just before it begins. You're not ready for it. They give you a paper, talk about school, education and stuff like that right there. You don't have time to think about what you are going to do in there. They say "Is it OK? Is it OK?" and I go, "Yeah, that's fine."'

Young person (2) 'It's like what you . . . expected to say, you say it. It's, sort of, like pressurising you.'

Raising significant issues caused anxiety because the response of people in authority was felt to be potentially negative and frightening.

Group One
Young person (1): 'Some things I haven't even . . . something you want to hold back just in case, because they sort of twist your words and make you feel like you're doing something wrong.'

Interviewer: 'Do they?'

Young person (1): 'They say you can speak really freely in the review but it's not like that.'

Young person (2): 'I tell them that I want to move to another place then they bring, like **everyone** comes, [the social worker's] boss, [the fostering officer's] boss, [the fostering officer] comes then . . . gets scared, you know, first time . . . . They tell you to speak freely but still . . .' (emphasis in original)

Group One
Young person (1): 'They ask you before if you mind if another person comes. But you're already scared when the managers and staff are there but, the more people, you get scared. You get shy and try not to make a mistake in what you're saying.'

Young person (2): '. . . not too many people.'

Engagement in dialogue on a controversial issue was likely to be a risky affair.

Group One
Young person (1): '. . . they try to put words in your mouth, when you say something, they say "Is this what you mean?" and they contradict what you say.'

Young person (2): 'And they twist it.'

Young person (1): 'Yeah.'

A significant cause of irritation was the tendency for chairs to go over well-trodden ground; understandably, young people disliked ritualistic questions.

Group One
Young person (1): '"When was the last time you went for a medical?" They **know** when we last went for a medical, but they still ask you.' (emphasis in original)

Young person (2): 'When we go to a medical the doctors send them a medical report so they have to [know] . . . . Then they ask you, "How did your medical go?" They know more than us about most things.'

The feeling of being caught up in a mechanical ritual was mentioned in both groups.

Group One
Young person: 'I think they should have different reviews for different people because most of the questions in the review are totally irrelevant for me.'

Group Two
Young person (1): 'It's like they're going through a checklist on your CV. "So you're doing this . . . . Have you got anything to say?" and by the end of it you're like . . . [mimes sleepiness]'

Young person (2): 'That's exactly what they do.'

Ritualistic discussions were seen as a way of filling in time.

Group Two
Young person: '. . . it's "We'll go over health, education, foster placements and we've got nothing else to talk about" and it's really sort of "We've got nothing else to do now and we're just chatting."'

These comments give more substance to the complaint made by some individual interviewees that the meetings were 'boring'.

A rigid approach to agenda issues did not allow young people's development to be sufficiently acknowledged. For example, adolescents wanted to increase the practical scope of their responsibilities. Progress to independence was in their view too narrowly conceived in terms of domestic skills.

Group One
Young person (1): 'Sometimes they treat you like a little baby.'

Young person (2): 'What they're saying about independence is all about things in the house . . . washing up and . . . . They don't give us the independence outside the house, like the times you have to be in.'

Young person (3): 'They give you independent stuff inside your house but you're not very independent outside.'

How best to use adult support was a complicated question, as young people became aware that different adults have different degrees of power. To be really supportive, an advocate should be assertive, independent and have some influence.

Access to an independent person offering informed support would have been welcomed by young people who had been unhappy with their care plans.

Group Two
Young person (1): 'It would be a good idea when you first went into care that you had someone to back you up really.'

Young person (2): '. . . we had no one we could actually trust not to go back to our foster parents, or our social worker, people we didn't get on with that well.'

An effective supporter at a review would ideally be a powerful adult who could make a difference.

Group One
Young person: '. . . someone who can, like, who can influence your life.'

When requests were made that could not be fulfilled there was frustration at a lack of explanation.

Group One
Young person: 'When you ask them why they then just tell you "No, . . ." to stop the arguments. They don't tell you the reason why they're not doing it.'

Group Two
Young person: 'They said I could have my own bedroom . . . you know, for at least a year, but now they say "No". And they didn't even write a letter or apology or anything and my foster parent said it was in my best interest to have my own bedroom because I've never had one, never had my own space. Then . . . it all folds up and that's that.'

Fundamental disagreements between professionals and a young person bred cynicism about reviews as such. If preparation had taken place and professionals knew what young people wanted in advance, the professionals then had the advantage over young people.

Group One
Young person: ' . . . they're all ready for it, they're just there for the heck of it.'

So if young people felt locked into conflict with the local authority, the review itself was perceived as empty and mechanical.

Lack of systematic attention to informing young people about their rights was the subject of adverse comment from focus group attenders.

Group Two
Young person (1): ' . . . in my first foster placement I wasn't told about complaints.'

Young person (2): 'That is it, isn't it? You don't find out [till later].'

The observational data in the previous chapter showed that a significant proportion of review decisions were unspecific. Focus group attenders were aware of the ways in which unspecific review decisions reflected the uncertainties of bureaucratic organisations.

Group Two
Young person (1): 'It's all shared control, and you got no . . . . Nothing's certain. It's like "Well, I'll go and see."'

Young person (2): 'That's how things carry on till the next meeting. "We'll have to speak to so and so."'

Young person (3): 'There's so much red tape you've got to go through to get anything done.'

But they also felt that such issues needed to be questioned. Allocating responsibilities for a decision was a task that young people felt should be fairly approached so that their requests were given a proper share of attention.

Young person (1): 'They [name someone to do something] at my meetings,

if it's important to **them** . . . if it's something **they** need to have done.'
(emphases in original)

Professionals and young people in discussion

Knowing more about young people's perspectives makes it possible to analyse the discussions more insightfully. Observation of the meetings gave some clues about the ways in which opportunities for communication and participation were grasped or lost. There were occasions when communication was hindered by tactics that did not address young people's feelings and understanding.

Interrogation by several adults was a significant pitfall, as the intensity of the spotlight was focused upon young people.

Meeting 74.
The young person read out the contents of her consultation form which included a request for a change of social worker. She was then questioned.

Chair: 'You've fallen out with the social worker?'

Parent: 'Why?'

Chair: 'What can we do to make it better?'

Social worker: 'Is it to do with the problem over holidays?'

Young person: 'No [pause] I can't remember why.'

Chair: 'If you can remember, that'll be helpful.'

The issue of the social worker was sympathetically approached but the young person, when faced with a series of questions from different adults, including the social worker herself, could not 'remember' why she had asked for a change of social worker. With six adults present, the questioning clearly put this young person on the spot.

There were occasions during the meetings, when the emotions of young people came rushing to the surface. With skilful handling and patience it was possible for professionals to acknowledge these emotions and make progress. But failure to give sufficient priority and time to young people's views exacerbated the problems. The following vignettes illustrate these contrasting approaches.

A review in secure accommodation emphasised the problem of reviewing a case where the young person was opposed to the plan. At the outset he expressed his feelings by theatrically destroying his consultation forms.

Meeting 177.
Chair: 'Thanks for your issues.'

Young person: 'Don't read it out! Bullshit! Bollocks!' [The social worker handed the forms back to the young person]

> Young person: 'Where's the bin?' [He scrambled the forms into a ball, offering it to the residential worker beside him]
>
> Young person: 'Can you put it in the bin?' [The residential worker obliged]

Despite this anger, the professionals made a patient effort to continue the review on a positive note.

> Social worker: 'We've had useful conversations, talking about the placement.'
>
> Young person: 'So what? . . . . You can put me where you like but I'll still go back to London.'

Significantly, this review ended with the young person calmly negotiating about the storage of his property. A different outcome for the young person was observed at a meeting that seemed less sensitively handled.

> *Meeting 75.* After half an hour during which aspects of his behaviour, ranging from deceit to ineptitude, were subjected to criticism and speculative analysis by residential workers and by a teacher, the young person was invited to contribute. He indicated that the key worker should read out his consultation form, while he began to weep.
>
> The key worker duly read out his views, including the paraphrase, 'He'd like to stop pinching and lying'. This statement, which could have made a useful starting point, in fact closed the discussion. A psychologist, not present at the meeting, was to be asked to help.

Not allowing time to read reports meant that the child's views were not given attention until the pressure of criticism had reached crisis point. Recognising the warning signs was a skill that enabled chairs to defuse criticism before it could exert undue pressure.

These illustrations suggest how it is possible to make better sense of young people's behaviour at meetings, once their attitudes and emotions have been fully appreciated.

The perceptions of parents

The contributions of parents were more frequently observed than clarified through interviews. None of the parents approached for interview refused, though one was unable to make a further appointment. Just seven parents in six cases were interviewed after the meetings, and therefore we must be cautious in interpreting their views. Nonetheless, these opinions were largely positive.

The parents felt that the meetings had been fairly chaired and they had been able to express what they wished to say. They had also been able to follow what was said. A parent of a child in accommodation, however, did not feel she had been encouraged to participate.

> Parent: 'They don't **encourage** you. I intervened a few times. I felt it was my right.' (emphasis in original)

Some parents with children in accommodation felt that their contribution had made a difference to the decision making but this was not true of parents with children whose plans involved care. If decisions were not fully explained, this caused dissatisfaction. Asked if social services had explained their reasons for a decision, a parent replied:

> Parent: 'They never do. We just argue. I don't feel I've been given the reasons for their thinking.'

There were some gaps in parents' knowledge. Only one of the parents interviewed had received information about making a complaint. A parent who did not have parental responsibility had not been told how to acquire it.

> Father: 'I wasn't married when [the child] was born, so I don't think I have any rights legally. [Name] is the guardian [ad litem] – it seemed that I didn't really count.'
>
> Interviewer: 'Did anyone explain what you could do about that?'
>
> Father: 'No.'
>
> Interviewer: 'Did you ask about it?'
>
> Father: 'No.'

Similarly, lack of clarity about what parents were expected to pay for certain types of respite care was a source of complaint. It also led to suspicion when the chair appeared to relent, having previously asked parents to make a payment.

> Parent: '[The chair] seemed to change her mind, probably because you [the researcher] were there.'

The observational data indicated that there was a range of participation among parents; encouragingly, some parents who were opposed to the plan were able to participate in discussion. However, it must be questioned whether participation was soundly based if parents were inadequately informed, or the reasons for decisions were not sufficiently explained. According to the definitions of Thoburn, Lewis and Shemmings (1995), lack of understanding is an obstacle to real participation, as distinct from simple involvement.

Involving children and parents – the views of chairs and social workers

Professionals' perspectives on involvement were discovered by interviewing chairs and through the survey of social workers. The following section shows that these groups acknowledged the scale of the challenge in promoting involvement and participation. Children's attitudes to reviews, for example, were perceived as largely negative; the support and information they obtained was admitted to be sometimes inadequate.

A number of chairs saw children's involvement in meetings as a challenge. They acknowledged children's feelings of alienation and unease.

> Chair, Northborough: 'Children need help in understanding what a review is about. That's why they bow out. There's no leaflet. We are not geared to encouraging them to speak . . .'

> Chair, Westside: 'Children need to feel they know the people because it's boring. They hate it.'

> Chair, Northborough: 'Meetings seem to children quite alien.'

However, chairs were reluctant to take the initiative by talking to children and parents before the meeting. One explained how chairing child protection conferences gave more scope for talking with parents.

> Chair, Northborough: 'This preparation in this role is considerably less [than when I was chair of child protection meetings] . . . I'd meet parents at the initial conferences. [There'd be] preparation for the meeting, in terms of explaining it. I used to do a home visit and meet the family. Now that's not possible because of the work. One has to do that work in the confines of the meeting.'

It has been argued, from a practitioner's perspective, that the review works better if the chair meets family members before the review (Hughes, 1992). It was, nonetheless, very rare for chairs to meet children and parents immediately before a review. Though time constraints were mentioned, this practice was largely attributable to the chairs' conception of their role.

> Chair, Westside: '[Meeting the child was] not my task.'

> Chair, Westside: 'It would not be reasonable to see the family **before** the meeting . . . only if the social worker had not seen the child or parents would I see them before, and then not necessarily outside the meeting.'

> Chair, Midshire: 'There are clear roles – the fostering officer is there for the parents [in this case] and the social worker is [there] for the child.'

Familiarity with the chair was therefore normally possible only through repeated contact at a sequence of reviews. Yet these were separated by significant intervals. As we have already indicated, young people's attitudes to strangers at reviews were tinged with apprehension and dislike. Chairs who had not talked with young people outside meetings therefore faced a challenge in overcoming such barriers.

To add another perspective to the study of involvement, social workers were asked in the survey to assess the experiences and attitudes of young people at reviews. They had mixed views about the support and information provided for young people. Asked if children could ask for extra support to help express their views, a small majority (55 per cent) thought this was 'often true', while 30 per cent thought it was 'sometimes true' and 15 per cent that it was 'rarely true'. The least positive views were held by the Northborough social workers, more of whom considered this was 'rarely true' (43 per cent) than thought it was 'often true' (36 per cent).

But asked whether children were fully informed of their rights as a result of reviews, a smaller proportion (39 per cent) of the whole sample thought it was 'often true' while nearly half (48 per cent) thought it was 'sometimes true', and 12 per cent that it was 'rarely true'. The most positive answers to this question came from Westside (61 per cent 'often true').

Many social workers, while appreciating the efforts of chairs to involve children, also had reservations about the emotional effect of the review meetings upon children. Thus, asked if chairs put parents and children at ease, nearly half (48 per cent) thought that this was 'often true', 44 per cent that it was 'sometimes true' and only eight per cent that it was 'rarely true'. But asked to consider the statement that the review meeting did 'little to calm the fears of children who were nervous', half considered this was 'often true', 37 per cent that it was 'sometimes true' and 12 per cent that it was 'rarely true'.

More worryingly, asked if children had positive attitudes to reviews, only eight per cent of social workers thought this was 'often true', 31 per cent that it was 'sometimes true' and a significant majority (60 per cent) thought it was 'rarely true'. Most social workers therefore thought that the majority of young people had less than positive perceptions of reviews.

Social workers presented rather cautious views about the contributions of adults. A majority of social workers in the survey identified some problems in balancing the contributions of adults and young people at meetings. Asked whether parents and carers dominated the discussion to the detriment of children, few (only 15 per cent) considered this was 'often true', but a majority (60 per cent) regarded it as 'sometimes true' and 25 per cent as 'rarely true'. Social workers were moderately convinced that the review process reassured parents: about a fifth (22 per cent) thought this was 'often true', a majority (61 per cent) considered that it was 'sometimes true' and a few (16 per cent) that it was 'rarely true'. There were decidedly mixed views too about the information made available to parents. Asked if parents who disagreed with plans did not know how to register their point of view, about half (46 per cent) thought this was 'sometimes true' while the rest divided equally in their views (27 per cent 'rarely true; 27 per cent 'often true').

Discussion of findings

The final section of this chapter examines the evidence about participation in the light of what was said in the previous chapter about the organisation of meetings. It resumes some of the main findings and then tries to identify key difficulties that lie in the way of participation. These have to do with some assumptions about normal meetings which, it will be argued, do not apply to reviews attended by young people.

The observational and interview data show that a proportion of young people, especially the older group, were able to play some positive part in their meetings. But others did not participate in any realistic sense. Some appeared to have been disadvantaged by learning difficulties, feeling confused and unable to participate. More generally there were significant gaps in the knowledge of some young people which made it difficult for them to pursue their goals. The social workers' survey also indicates that professionals were aware of such gaps.

There were a number of ways in which the meetings as presently constructed jarred with the expectations of young people about what should happen. The evidence of the previous chapter indicated how agendas reflected the staple issues of the individual cases rather than fundamental questions about the care plans. Young people, however, saw much of the resulting agenda as tedious, unnecessary and disengaged from their own interests and development.

Young people were also unhappy about large meetings, feeling that adults could 'gang up' against them. The data on attendance in the previous chapter bears out the point about the frequency of attendance by professionals who do not belong to what the Guidance suggests are the 'core' group of attenders. There were few individuals offering young people support – a finding that repeats the results of earlier research (Gardner, 1985).

Young people typically felt self-conscious about 'their' meetings yet the meetings themselves were often not organised in ways that made them feel comfortable. Where difficult issues came up, they were prone to feelings of stress. Professionals varied in their sensitivity to young people's feelings and some were more adept than others in conveying their concern for young people's emotional well-being and sense of privacy. When particular requests were put forward by young people, the uncertain and unspecific response of professionals tended to lead to dissatisfaction, especially if the outcomes were not explained or were postponed to the next review.

The participation of parents was conditional on their attendance, which varied according to the parents' gender, the child's age and the legal status of the case. At the meeting itself, however, their attitudes to the plan did not significantly affect their participation. Hence, though there were some background influences on parental attendance, it was still possible for parents who opposed the local authority plan to make positive contributions at review meetings. The small sample of parents interviewed gave largely positive views about the meetings, though they did not all have sufficient knowledge to become informed participants. Social workers acknowledged the review process did not satisfactorily inform parents of their rights. The evidence suggests that parental involvement was first of all a function of attendance, which in turn is likely to depend on a broader relationship with professionals. Once at the meeting, parents need information if they are to play a full part in the process.

These issues allow us to identify what lies at the heart of some of the problems. The review process seems governed by the assumption that, with some exceptions, attenders approach meetings on a reasonably equal footing and that fair and open discussion can be generated with little prompting. The avoidance of undue formality in discussions seems to be intended to support that approach. But it is one thing to remove artificial barriers to communication; it is quite another to promote discussion in ways that maximise calm and knowledgeable participation by children and parents.

Meetings, as presently organised, conform to a model of consultative discussion in which all those involved in the plan have a role to play but the chair has the last word. The focus of the meeting is on facilitating this discussion around an agenda which is related to the current care plan. Young people and parents have been introduced into this model late in the day. To young people, the routines of the agenda often seem mechanical, as the items deal with issues familiar to them, if not to all present.

They are also uncomfortable about being in the spotlight. As the meetings are about individual young people, those individuals cannot be equated with the others present at the meetings. For young people the meeting can never be simply a business-like discussion about 'what to do', no matter how informally this is discussed. To them, it is often more about the underlying question of 'What kind of person am I?' or 'What kind of person do others think I am?' Meetings are successful only if they find ways of recognising the unique position of young people who attend (Blaug, 1995).

For parents, too, there are fundamental questions at stake. While parents achieved certain levels of participation, the analysis of their attendance suggests that a similar question is posed for them – 'What kind of parent am I?' or 'What kind of parent does the local authority see me as?' Issues connected with parental gender and the child's legal status may influence the ways in which parents respond to these questions. Further research comparing different types of 'family welfare' meetings, such as child protection conferences and family group conferences, would pay dividends (Thoburn, Lewis and Shemmings, 1995; Swain, 1995; Morris and Tunnard, 1996).

Above all, the position of young people requires further attention if they are to benefit to the maximum. The evidence of the study strongly suggests that the Guidance has influenced social work practice in the direction of including young people in meetings (Kendrick and Mapstone, 1991). However, the routine fact of their attendance should not in itself be taken as a sign of participation. There is a sense in which their attendance has become an administrative norm rather than something that has itself led to changes in the meeting format. The substantial increase in attendance by young people since the Children Act has transformed the context of reviewing. Whereas it might have been treated as an administrative routine or a forum for professional case management, the review meeting has taken on new responsibilities to promote participation and partnership. Further thought needs to be given to new ways in which young people can be given a more central, informed and comfortable role in the review process. A practitioner's comment underlines the point.

Chair, Westside: 'It's not a boardroom. It's about families and feelings and dynamics. That's important.'

Key findings

- The majority of 11- to 15-year-olds, and nearly all 16- to 18-year-olds, attended their review meetings – a substantial change from practice ten years ago.
- Support for language needs was provided on nine occasions in the main sample, a third of those cases in which the child's first language was not English. Support for children and parents was rarely observed.
- Some young people were able to achieve a level of participation in meetings. These tended to be older and better prepared. A minority were rated as partners. Those who were less able to participate suffered from disadvantages such as learning difficulties. A free flow of discussion at the review meeting did not assist them to participate.
- In general, young people had to overcome the emotional strain of being placed in a spotlight, especially at large meetings attended by strangers. If young people disagreed with the local authority plan, they experienced the discussions as unproductive rather than as helpful. They expressed criticism of mechanical approaches to the review agenda, which included issues irrelevant to their circumstances. Adolescents wanted to raise issues about the growth of their personal responsibility.
- Young people were aware of the unspecific formulas used in decisions. They felt that such decisions reflected the fact that no one in an organisation could take an important decision alone. They

preferred to have advocates who were powerful and could make a difference to their lives.

- Parental attendance at review meetings has climbed significantly since the early 1980s. Parents' attendances were more frequent for younger children, those on the child protection register and those on interim care orders (compared with children subject to full care orders). Their attendance was more frequent for children in short-term placements than in other S.20 accommodation. No difference was found in the attendances of parents with white children compared with other ethnic groups. Mothers' attendances were more frequent than fathers'.

- By rating observed participation, it was found that the largest category of parents was composed of participants, but a minority of parents performed more successfully than this, as partners. Parents who were interviewed expressed largely positive views about the meetings but had not systematically received important information.

- Largely because of the way they perceived the chair's role, chairs did not meet children and parents before reviews. Both chairs and social workers considered that children had negative views about reviews. Nearly half the social workers thought it was 'sometimes true' that children were fully informed about their rights as a result of reviews, and a similar number considered it was 'sometimes true' that parents who disagreed with plans knew how to register their point of view.

7.   The arrangements for chairing review meetings

Introduction

The fieldwork study has presented some direct observational evidence about the chairing of review meetings in the three different areas. In two of them, supervising team managers normally took the chair while, in the third, the task was carried out by an 'independent' non-supervising team manager, once the first review had taken place. Such variations were permissible under the current Guidance which refers to the identity of chairs in the following neutral terms:

> 8.13 A meeting to review a child's case should be chaired by an officer of the responsible authority at a more senior level than the case social worker.

This chapter begins by tracing the origins of this guidance and the policy background behind the widespread introduction of 'independent' chairs. As a result of these developments, it has become apparent that the identities of review chairs vary substantially across local authorities. But very little evidence has so far emerged about the working of these different arrangements. Hence it was decided, after the fieldwork research had been completed, to conduct a sample survey of English local authorities, in order to map these variations and to ascertain how successful they were perceived to be. In addition we shall look at three comparable forums for child care decision making – Family Group Conferences, Child Protection Case Conferences and Reviews, and Children's Hearings and Reviews in Scotland.

Policy background

The drafting of the Guidance

When the Guidance was being prepared, the original proposals of the Department of Health gave a clear lead about the most appropriate system of chairing reviews: the chair was to be taken by a powerful and independent officer of the local authority. However, in the final version, this proposal came to be modified. The initial consultation document on review arrangements specifically supported the principle of chairing by an officer senior to the supervising team manager, without any direct line management responsibility for the case (Department of Health, 1990). This high level chair was very clearly to carry out a monitoring function, providing 'independent oversight'.

However, the final version of the Guidance dropped this specific proposal and allowed chairing by any practitioner senior to the case social worker. It seems that such senior personnel were too few to be able to chair the likely number of reviews. The term 'independent oversight' was replaced by a reference to 'a degree of oversight and objectivity', introducing the idea of 'objectivity' for the first time.

The rather cautious stance of the Guidance permitted a variety of local arrangements to flourish. While some authorities have appointed chairs with a degree of 'independence', others have been content to let team managers chair reviews. The next section examines the reasons for the changes that have taken place.

The case for 'independent' reviewing

The history of the draft Guidance suggests the existence of a philosophical and practical dilemma. It seems that, where practicable, 'independent' chairing is favoured on philosophical grounds. But where does the idea of independent chairing come from and why does it have this support?

As a rule, review meetings in the 1980s were chaired by managers who had a significant line management responsibility (Sinclair, 1984; Vernon and Fruin, 1986). But were they sufficiently independent to give a proper evaluation of the social worker's care planning or to monitor the implementation of decisions? Hence an argument was put forward for the appointment of independent chairs with sufficient seniority to question line managers and ensure that children's rights were safeguarded (BASW, 1983; Children's Legal Centre, 1984). The case for 'independent' reviewing was further supported by reference to various judicial monitoring arrangements, both in Scotland and the United States (Sinclair, 1984; McDonnell and Aldgate, 1984b). However, contrary evidence about 'neutral' chairing suggested some problems in these arrangements (Vernon and Fruin, 1986; Smith and May, 1980).

In child protection too, there were very similar arguments in favour of chairing by specialist coordinators, rather than by line managers. Certainly, research had concluded that objectivity about child abuse was deficient (Dingwall, Eekelaar and Murray, 1995). Moreover, the dangers of poor decisions were graphically driven home by successive inquiries into the deaths of children, which, in the case of Jasmine Beckford, led to a call for the case conference to embody 'an objectivity that *cannot be obtained* by those directly involved in the management of a child abuse case' (emphasis added) (London Borough of Brent, 1985, p.250). Hence the movement towards independent chairing of reviews has followed a parallel change in the arrangements for child protection conferences. Nonetheless, as for 'looked-after' reviews, local authorities have undergone a transitional period in which many conferences continued to be chaired by supervising team managers (Lewis, 1994; Hallett, 1995).

The apparent consensus formed in the 1980s therefore helped to shape opinion in favour of new systems of chairing reviews, even though the research evidence on chairing did not necessarily point the same way. Nonetheless, various developments have led to a strong tide of support for innovations, provided that any practical obstacles and limitations could be overcome. The next section uses data from a survey of English local authorities in order to shed light on what has happened.

The survey of chairing arrangements

Methods

An opportunity to carry out the survey was presented at the dissemination phase of the fieldwork research, during which three regional seminars were organised. A sample of 15 local authorities in each of three broad regions (the North, the Midlands, and the South) was systematically selected, in order to represent a balance of county, borough and unitary authorities from all over England. As well as making it possible to invite a representative sample of authorities to the seminars, this exercise produced for the survey an original target sample of 45 authorities, with up to two respondents from each. Where it seemed that an individual authority was unlikely to become involved, another was contacted.

The perspectives of local authority policy makers and those chiefly responsible for implementing policy were sought by dispatching individual questionnaires to the contacts identified in the local authorities. In several cases, more than one copy of the questionnaire was returned from the authority contacted, reflecting various perspectives from particular districts or managerial levels.

At least one response was received from each of 45 local authorities and the total number of responses was 66 – a highly satisfactory rate of return. The standard regional sample size of 15 authorities meant that nearly all the Midlands authorities were represented, compared with almost a third of those in the North and just a fifth of the Southern region (including London). Evidently a higher representation of the Southern group, in particular, would have told us more about any specific regional differences. However, this was not a major purpose of the survey. Rather, the focus should be on the range of systems identified across the regions. Hence, in the following section, a regional breakdown will be given for the systems, so as to make clear how far the evidence spans more than one region.

The questionnaire focused on the nature of the chairing systems in these authorities and asked for opinions about their advantages and disadvantages.

The first question asked respondents to confirm whether particular kinds of manager chaired a 'significant proportion of reviews'. The types mentioned in the question were as follows:

- supervising team managers – the ones responsible for supervising the social worker allocated the case (STM);
- non-supervising team managers (NSTM);
- non-supervising Reviewing Officers specialising in reviews (SRO);
- other managers, with specific expertise (SM).

The responses indicated that, while some authorities had simple systems, using only one of the options above, other authorities made use of a mixture of arrangements. Respondents were also asked to indicate which type of manager chaired reviews most frequently.

The main evaluative question asked respondents to describe, in their own words, up to three advantages and up to three disadvantages of their arrangements. This formulation was designed to encourage respondents to present a balanced view of the arguments and to prioritise the key issues as they perceived them. The data do not therefore make it possible to come to definitive conclusions about the value of particular arrangements, but rather to identify the perceived issues, and to map how they were seen within each system. Further questions were asked about young people's views of the systems and the frequency of specific training for review chairs.

The identification of systems

Because of district variations within authority boundaries and minor disagreements among respondents from the same authority about how to characterise their system, the identification of systems from the questionnaires is not definitive. The analysis does allow us, however, to work out how respondents perceived their local systems and what their opinions were.

The evidence of the survey showed such an extent of diversity in the arrangements that it was decided to divide the authorities, as far as possible, into two categories: those with simple systems, and those with mixed ones. The category of simple systems – employing only one significant type of chair – comprised four distinct systems, as suggested by the survey question. Respondents identified a total of 23 authorities within this category. Mixed systems – identified as utilising more than one of the options to a significant extent – were found within 25 authorities.

The mixed systems were more numerous: in fact, there were eight different combinations of the original four options. As will be explained later, these were then divided again into two broad categories: those using the supervising team manager in some combination with other managers, and the remainder which used a combination of other managers but not the supervising team manager. The data about perceptions of the systems demonstrates that the Guidance has licensed a considerable variation in practice which presents some complications for the evaluation. Hence it was decided to organise the analysis into stages, beginning with the simple systems.

The evaluation of simple systems

Four simple systems were identified, in the sense that a single type of chairing was in operation across the local authority. The simple systems, together covering 23 of the local authorities, were distributed as set out in Table 7.1.

Table 7.1   Simple systems of chairing

System	Authorities
Supervising team managers only	9
Non-supervising team managers only	3
Specialist reviewing officers only	9
Specific managers only	2

The findings for each system are discussed below.

Supervising team managers only

There were nine respondents from nine authorities. The authority locations were: North, 3; Midlands, 2; South, 4.

The most frequently mentioned advantage of chairing by supervisors was their knowledge of the case (four responses) and, in particular, knowing children and parents (three responses). Continuity of chairing was seen as another advantage, enabling supervisors to take responsibility for decisions and to see the outcome of plans.

However, there was an equal recognition that the objectivity of decisions could suffer and, that the review could become too 'cosy'; in fact, four of this group were in favour of using independent chairs to a greater or lesser extent.

> [With supervising team managers] there could be a tendency to chair reviews 'routinely', without a critical eye upon plans, social workers' performance, etc. (Professional Practice Officer, Unitary Authority)

Although the simplicity of the chairing system was regarded as a virtue, there were some indications of practical problems, such as difficulties in working with resource providers.

> [The] planning/reviewing system is not central to social work practice, between commissioners/providers. Providers feel the system to be 'loaded' and unbalanced. (Assistant Director, Borough Authority)

Non-supervising team managers only

There were seven respondents from three authorities. The authority locations were: North, 2; Midlands, nil; South, 1.

The most commonly identified advantage of this system was the chair's independence from the line management of the case (six responses); only one respondent suggested that continuing in this role over time would mean a decline in independence. Three responses associated objectivity with having a non-line manager in the chair.

The main disadvantages were described in practical terms, especially the amount of extra time required from both the supervising and non-supervising managers.

Specialist reviewing officers only

There were 15 respondents from nine authorities. The authority locations were: North, 5; Midlands, 3; South, 1.

The most frequently mentioned advantage was the chair's independence from line management responsibility (two thirds of responses). Offering a consistent, focused or objective viewpoint was cited by just over half the group. Maintaining continuity of reviews was mentioned by almost a third, reflecting the way that specialist chairs kept on reviewing the same cases. Being able to monitor practice was identified as an advantage by a third. A similar proportion valued the chairs' experience of conducting reviews in different areas across the local authority.

The most common disadvantage lay in working out effective relationships with line managers – the reverse of the independence model. Almost half the respondents, spread across six of the nine authorities, mentioned this problem.

> . . . can have a split in opinion between case managers and reviewing officers which need(s) resolution. (Service Manager, Borough Authority)

Happily, only one respondent was conscious of an inflexibility, in having to stick to a rigid timetable of reviews. Though a minority of responses identified practical advantages (in achieving targets for punctual reviews, for example), a majority referred to practical problems, such as costly postponements and the pressures of travelling across the area covered by the local authority. Problems of this nature were reported in five of the nine authorities.

Specific managers only

There were three respondents from two authorities. The authority locations were: North, 1; Midlands, 1; South, nil.

The remaining option identified as significant was to call on the chairing skills of managers with other specific duties, such as area managers or child protection specialists. In just two authorities, such managers were the sole chairs of reviews. Their ability to monitor cases was the only advantage mentioned in both authorities. But a lack of managers' time, seemingly a result of their specific responsibilities, was a shared problem. Questions about the executive responsibility for decisions were raised in each case.

It should be remembered that any simple system is expected to deal with all types of case. For simple systems, the results of the analysis reveal some of the most evident differences in the way chairing systems are perceived to affect the handling of a wide range of children's cases. Hence it is useful to attempt a sketch of these advantages and disadvantages (see Table 7.2).

Table 7.2 A balance sheet for simple systems

	Advantages
STM	Knowledge of the case; continuity of chairing and responsibility.
NSTM	Independence from line management and objectivity.
SRO	Independence from line management; objectivity; continuity of chairing; monitoring; and cross-departmental consistency.
SM	Monitoring.
	Disadvantages
STM	Problems with resource providers; lack of objectivity.
NSTM	Additional time commitments from managers.
SRO	Problematic relationships with line managers; inefficiency.
SM	Lack of managers' time.

The resulting picture suggests that it is not easy to identify a balance of advantages and disadvantages favouring one system over another. A crucial problem seems to lie in reconciling the different advantages enjoyed by line managers and the independent chairs. The line managers' knowledge of cases was offset by their alleged lack of objectivity. In the case of the specialist reviewing officers, their relationships with line managers were said to lead to problems; many specialist chairs continuously review the same cases and therefore must try to establish agreed ways of working. The relationships between non-supervising team manager chairs and their line manager colleagues were less often fraught but, even so, working together required additional time from both sets of managers.

The evaluation of mixed systems

As was earlier explained, a mixed system was identified wherever more than one of our original options was perceived to account for a significant number of reviews. A mixed system might utilise from two to four types of chair. Because of such variations, the mixed systems were less easy to evaluate, a point implicit in some responses which concentrated on parts of their system, rather than the whole. In order to focus on the theme of independence in chairing, they were divided into two main categories: those including supervising team managers to some extent; and those using a combination of independent chairs. The responses identified mixed systems within a total of 25 authorities, as set out in Table 7.3.

Table 7.3   Mixed systems of chairing

Mixed system	Authorities
Supervising team managers and others	12
Independent and other chairs (not supervising team managers)	13

The evaluations of these mixed systems are given below.

Supervising team managers and others

There were 17 responses from 12 authorities. The authority locations were: North, 4; Midlands, 3; South, 5.

Table 7.4   Mixed systems: supervising team managers and others

System	Authorities
STM + NSTM	4
STM + SRO	3
STM + SM	3
STM + NSTM + SRO	1
STM + NSTM + SRO + SM	1

The responses clearly indicated that in all these systems the supervising team manager was the most frequent chair of reviews, though there were variations in the reasons for this, some of which were pragmatic. In the following two examples, the role of non-supervising first line managers was circumscribed, in the first case, for principled reasons, and, in the second case, for pragmatic reasons.

> Non-supervising first line managers chair the second review always [at four months]. Otherwise, supervising line managers do it. (Principal Officer, County Authority)

> In principle, the two care planning team managers have been asked to 'cross over' – chairing each others' reviews to give some independence. In practice because of [the] sick leave of one manager this hasn't happened very often. (Team Manager, Borough Authority)

The prominent role of supervising team managers was therefore a considerable factor in the operation of these systems.

The main advantages, mentioned by about half the respondents, were those typically associated with chairing by line managers – clarity of responsibility, knowledge of the case, and so on; the principal disadvantages were again those associated with line managers – collusion with social workers, lack of objectivity and lack of independence. The largest category of all the responses for this group concerned practical problems and demands. For example, the three authorities which used a combination of specialist reviewing officers and line managers commonly complained of a lack of reviewing officers.

Despite the complications and variations in these systems, most reviews were still chaired by the line managers and the evaluations reflected the predominance of their chairing role.

Independent and other chairs (not supervising team managers)

There were 15 responses from 13 authorities. The authority locations were: North, 2; Midlands, 6; South, 5.

Table 7.5 Mixed systems: independent and other chairs (not supervising team managers)

System	Authorities
NSTM + SRO	5
NSTM + SM	3
NSTM + SRO + SM	3
SRO + SM	2

Where the system featured non-supervisory review managers, these typically chaired the majority of reviews; in only three authorities did specialist reviewing officers play a predominant role.

Predictably enough, the main advantage of systems without any significant line manager role in chairing was felt to lie in the chairs' independence (just over half the responses). A third of respondents mentioned the monitoring role of the chairs as an advantage. In all, seven responses identified practical advantages, such as the reliability of the system, and its capacity to feed information into the policy process.

> Independence of review chair carries some power in enabling policy [and] research changes. (Team Manager, Borough Authority)

The most frequently mentioned disadvantages of these systems were practical – a significant total of 14 problems distributed across all four variant systems. The highest number of problems (five) was associated with three of the five authorities where non-supervising team managers and specialist reviewing officers chaired reviews. The difficulties were identified as administrative or operational, owing to large workloads or lack of time.

> Some inefficiency due to the numbers of chairs involved; other work takes priority for operational managers. (Principal Officer, Borough Authority)

One of these authorities was undergoing a transition towards a system using specialist reviewing officers and had problems in organising its work. But this did not apply to the other two, suggesting that the problems were more deep-seated. Despite the level of support given to the idea of independence, three respondents questioned how independent the chairs really were, for example, if they belonged to the same area management group.

From the evidence of the survey, it is clear that the advantages and disadvantages associated with mixed systems were linked to the concepts that we have already discussed in relation to simple systems. What was less expected was the frequency of practical problems associated with mixed systems (see Table 7.6).

Table 7.6   A balance sheet for mixed systems

Advantages	
STMs and others	Clarity of responsibility, knowledge of case.
Independent and other chairs (excluding STMs)	Independent of line management, monitoring.
Disadvantages	
STMs and others	Practical problems, collusion with social workers, lack of objectivity, lack of independence.
Independent and other chairs (excluding STMs)	Practical problems.

The evaluative agenda of local authority respondents

In this section, we look at evidence about respondents' evaluative agendas, based on the issues identified in their comments. As was explained earlier, all respondents were asked to cite up to three advantages and disadvantages of the systems in their authorities. As far as possible, the responses were classified into 18 categories for advantages and the same number of categories for disadvantages – a total of 36 categories.

For both advantages and disadvantages, the rankings point to a clear agenda in the respondents' evaluations of chairing systems. When the four most frequently mentioned advantages and disadvantages were examined, these were found to be familiar issues about independence from line management, objectivity, executive responsibility and so on. In the same category, there were high numbers of responses concerning practical issues.

However, it also became apparent that there were other issues ranked as much less significant. For example, there were low rankings for: knowledge of the child and parents (ranked tenth as an advantage, and a lack of knowledge never mentioned as a disadvantage); sensitivity (never mentioned); promoting openness and sharing (ranked eighth as an advantage, and failure to do so ranked seventh as a disadvantage); producing an integrated plan with other agencies (never mentioned); and flexibility (ranked tenth as an advantage, and lack of flexibility ranked eleventh as a disadvantage).

The balance of evidence strongly suggests that the responses were mainly concerned with chairing as a role within rational bureaucratic organisations, rather than as a means of facilitating an open, shared, sensitive or flexible planning process.

Young people's views

Only a minority of respondents possessed any evidence of young people's views about plans and reviews in general, or chairing review meetings in particular. Those with evidence of views on chairing represented little more than a quarter of respondents, compared with just two fifths who had evidence of young people's views on plans and reviews in general.

Six items of evidence including reports and studies were enclosed by respondents originating from authorities with the systems shown in Table 7.7. In the reports, there were a number of findings that indicated positive practice, such as regular attendance by young people at meetings, their views being taken into account, and so on. However, there were also some commonly reported difficulties – complaints about overlarge meetings, in particular. Two reports, for example, referred to young people's feelings of being intruded upon or put on the spot. There were also echoes of other findings from the fieldwork study, such as the boredom felt at some meetings, feelings of vulnerability and of being undervalued. Though the evidence is limited and small-scale, it tends to confirm the impression that, despite the evidence of consultation with young people, meetings can be rather difficult experiences for them to cope with. Moreover, it is not at all clear that the system of chairing made much difference to this experience. The fact that only a minority of respondents could claim to have any evidence about young people's views suggests that thinking about the practice of chairing has not been substantially influenced by knowledge of their perceptions and experiences.

Table 7.7   Evidence of young people's views, by system of chairing (N=6)

System	Authorities
STM only	2
STM + SRO	2
NSTM only	1
STM + SRO +SM	1

The training of review chairs

In almost two thirds of authorities, there was evidence that chairs had received training for their task. The lowest proportion of authorities with trained chairs was found in those where only supervising team managers chaired reviews. This finding indicates that chairing was perceived as a normal part of the supervising team manager's work. However, in other systems, including the mixed systems involving the supervising team manager, there were more frequent reports that chairs had been trained for their task. It was therefore rather surprising to find a few authorities which had provided no training for their specialist reviewing officers.

Implications of the survey

The survey confirms that, under the rubric of the current Guidance, systems of chairing have diversified and sometimes become complex.

In evaluating their systems, respondents working in simple systems identified a similar set of advantages and disadvantages to those identified within complex systems. The main advantages of chairing by supervising team managers were that they possessed knowledge of the case, were continuously involved and held overall responsibility for decisions and their implementation. However, in not being independent from the management of the case, they were felt to lack objectivity. The most obvious advantage of independent chairs was perceived precisely in terms of supplying objectivity. However, this meant establishing a good basis of cooperation with supervising team managers, and addressing the practical problems of covering a relatively high number of cases in an efficient manner.

A broad analysis of the advantages and disadvantages cited by respondents demonstrated that their focus was upon a particular set of issues associated with a rational bureaucratic organisation of tasks. Issues of participation were much less prominent in their evaluation: evidence of young people's views was scanty.

Evidence from other forums of decision making

In this section we look beyond the framework of the specific Guidance and Regulations to see if other, rather different forums of decision making can help to clarify the issues that have been raised so far. We review the evidence about chairing and decision making in forums where the care and protection of children are considered:

- Family Group Conferences, particularly the role of the independent coordinator;
- Child Protection Conferences and Reviews, especially the role of chairs;
- Children's Hearings and Reviews in Scotland, and the role of their lay panels.

The purpose of the comparison is to see if these different structures and approaches offer any lessons for the organisation of meetings under the current Guidance and Regulations for planning and reviewing.

Enhancing partnership – the Family Group Conference

In this country, the Family Group Conference (FGC) has attracted increasing attention as a forum for decision making, following its incorporation within New Zealand's child welfare legislation. The concept marks a substantial departure from the review meeting described in the Guidance and Regulations. Instead of including the family within a conventional meeting dominated by professionals, the conference creates a space for the family to come up with its own solutions.

The organisation of the conference is placed in the hands of an 'independent' coordinator. 'Independent means that the person has no casework or management involvement with the family' (Morris, 1996). In consultation with the child and the parents, the coordinator identifies the 'family network' (in the broad sense of that term), issues invitations and subsequently chairs the first general meeting of the conference. Then the professionals withdraw, allowing the family to consider a plan of action in private, but the coordinator remains available to give help if the family requests it. At the final stage, the coordinator chairs a second general meeting which decides on the way forward, using the family's plan unless this is inconsistent with the principles of legislation.

Sympathisers with the FGC concept have welcomed it as a buffer against the 'bureaucratisation' of child welfare planning (Marsh, 1996). However, giving 'the family' a measure of control over decision making may not always ensure that the interests of the child are maintained as paramount (Lupton, Barnard and Swall-Yarrington, 1995). Evidence about young people's participation in FGCs is not very substantial but one recent study in England indicates that they have some mixed feelings – embarrassment, nervousness, but also relief that a decision was being made (Lupton, Barnard and Swall-Yarrington, 1995). The legislation in New Zealand makes provision for the attendance of supporters who can help the child participate effectively (Marsh, 1994).

Another advantage claimed for the FGC stems from its roots in New Zealand, where it was designed to fit comfortably with the social structures of Maori or Pacific Island communities. Practitioners in the UK are currently using the model in work with minority ethnic groups in this country (Kohar, 1994). On the other hand, some doubts have been expressed about how the boundaries of 'the family' can be determined especially among the majority white ethnic group (Lupton, Barnard and Swall-Yarrington, 1995).

Good coordination is vital if the FGC is to work well (Swain, 1995). In New Zealand, there is no effective provision for standardising the practice of coordinators. Hence their approaches to work with families are known to be very different. It has been argued that the whole functioning of the FGC is so dependent on the qualities of the coordinator that this dependence may be a source of weakness in practice (Hamill, 1996).

Though the conference presents a framework for planning, New Zealand legislation does not specify very clearly a structure for reviews. The coordinator is expected to ensure that this happens 'regularly' (Hamill, 1996). However, some progress in strengthening the review function is now underway (Lupton, Barnard and Swall-Yarrington, 1995). Unfortunately, there is a lack of evidence about the long-term outcomes for children in New Zealand (Swain, 1995). Until such evidence is forthcoming, it will be difficult to judge how far the FGC can become a model for successful planning and reviewing systems.

There are still many questions surrounding the FGC, particularly around the participation of young people, the role of the independent coordinator, and the structure of reviews. Nonetheless, the enthusiastic implementation of FGCs in this country suggests a potential contribution which should not be minimised.

Implications for chairing reviews

The major attraction of the FGC is its capability to enhance partnerships between professionals and families – in the wide sense of that term. However, it has not been developed to the point where it can be regarded as an all-purpose mechanism for planning and reviewing. In sum, the FGC's main lesson for current chairing practice is its emphasis on a participative process which cannot be compressed into a single meeting and therefore demands more in the way of coordination than simply the conventional skills of chairing.

Chairing Child Protection Conferences and Reviews

In looking at the lessons of research on child protection, it is clear that the scene is changing, particularly as young people and their parents begin to take a stronger role in the process of decision making (Lewis, 1994). However, recent research does have some definite things to say about practice in chairing, in particular about the problem of achieving objectivity in decision making – the principal issue that will be discussed in this section.

There are two major challenges for chairs of child protection conferences and reviews: the management of risk and uncertainty in the case itself; and the management of emotional and 'political' processes at the meetings. As exercises in decision making, conferences and reviews call for objectivity and detachment. Yet the evidence discussed in this section will show that the practice of chairing has often been unequal to these challenges and that the use of independent specialists does not offer a panacea. The research on child protection commissioned by the Department of Health forms a particularly valuable source of evidence about the responses made to such challenges (Gibbons, Conroy and Bell, 1995; Farmer and Owen, 1995).

The defining feature of a child protection conference is its focus on identifying the risk of significant harm to the child and making a plan that takes account of future uncertainties. It is not hard to see why there have been calls for 'objective' chairing in order to tackle the problem of how exactly this can be successfully done. It has also been widely noted that case conferences play a role in managing the emotional strains associated with child protection work. These are exacerbated by the power differentials among the agencies and professions (Valentine, 1994; Hallett and Birchall, 1992). In practice, the shared anxieties around child abuse tend to encourage the development of professional consensus and to marginalise dissent (Farmer and Owen, 1995).

Hence some means of achieving greater objectivity and emotional detachment is called for, not only in initial decision making but at reviews. The perspectives from which chairs actually approach their task have been illuminated by the detailed ethnographic study carried out by Lewis (1994). How they might improve on their performance has been suggested by the critical analysis of Kelly and Milner (1996).

Focusing on objective considerations is difficult in a setting to which participants bring subjective and partial information. The chairs of conferences in Lewis's study tended to adopt a 'pseudo-court' model, though members of the conference presented biased and incomplete views. Not surprisingly, the task of chairing in these circumstances was burdened by problems. The skill of applying objective criteria to information seems poorly developed. Though Lewis argues that non-line managers have an advantage over line managers in preserving objectivity, it seems that their apparent advantage lay more in not being so ready to defend the social services agency.

The meaning of objectivity in child protection decision making has been concretely analysed by Kelly and Milner (1996) who draw attention to common pitfalls in risk assessment. They argue that, in practice, the framing of risk in terms of future losses without considering gains often leads to irrational conclusions. Indeed, the psychological effects of 'group polarisation' mean that a group decision goes further than an individual might contemplate. Moreover, if errors are made at the initial stage, these are not necessarily corrected later; the group processes at reviews tend to accentuate initial perceptions of a case.

The quest for objectivity has certainly led to the spread of new chairing systems in which 'independent' specialists are featured. But do independent chairs actually operate more successfully than, say, area managers? Two longitudinal examinations of decision making and reviewing cast more light on the practical performance of different models.

The first recent study was focused on child protection registrations and their outcomes (Gibbons, Conroy and Bell, 1995). Though this study did not go into great detail, it does seem that the different chairing arrangements in local authorities did not affect the likelihood of registration. Nor did particular local authority practices appear to affect the outcome in terms of repeated abuse or neglect. However, the second study presents a more rounded and comprehensive picture. This research by Farmer and Owen (1995) is particularly relevant because it looked at practice in two authorities, one of which used area managers as chairs while the other had appointed specialist coordinators for this purpose.

Chairs were typically found to be influential in shaping the final decisions of case conferences. However, the methods by which decisions were reached were considered by the researchers to be unsatisfactory.

> The methods of assessing risk which we have identified tend to be atheoretical and pragmatic. (Farmer and Owen, 1995, p.156)

Moreover, the assessments were insufficiently focused on the needs of the child, failing therefore to build a foundation for subsequent planning, a point that echoes Lewis (1994).

The styles of the respective chairs were not greatly different, independent coordinators being somewhat more concerned to weigh evidence 'judicially'. More significant was the finding that social workers regarded the conference decisions as less authoritative when independent coordinators had been in the chair. Moreover, the functioning of subsequent reviews was questionable, especially so when independent coordinators failed in their attempts to influence the line management of the case. A separation between operational planning and child protection reviewing made their task significantly more difficult to accomplish. Reviews also failed to correct poor decisions made in the past.

> . . . once a pattern of case management had been established it was usually endorsed at subsequent reviews . . . even then it was deficient . . . . However, there were a few occasions when review chairs actively sought to bring about a reconsideration of the management of the case. **These attempts met with little success when the chairs were not line managers** since their authority was limited and most of the key decisions about entry to care and day-to-day case management took place in the context of discussions with team leaders or in **quite separate care planning meetings**. (emphases added) (Farmer and Owen, 1995, p.258–259)

As a whole, the lessons of the research indicate how difficult it is for decision makers to attain an objective viewpoint. They also suggest that we must beware of the danger of conflating independence with objectivity, as if one automatically accompanies the other. Effective chairing seems to depend primarily on two things: achieving emotional detachment and considering evidence systematically. Clear decisions must then be acted upon.

Implications for chairing reviews

Chairing child protection meetings represents a strong test of the capacity of a system to provide 'objective oversight'. The challenge lies in overcoming the emotional stresses and group pressures that detract from an objective approach. Whatever the system, research suggests that chairs encounter some difficulties in supplying that objectivity. The crucial requirement highlighted by the child protection research is a methodical approach to evidence which clearly entails some thought and preparation before a meeting takes place. Though statutory reviews will often be less concerned with risk, their planning will involve a balanced consideration of future possibilities which should be equally rigorous. Independent specialists, in particular, need to find ways of influencing the implementation of decisions – a clear parallel with the present survey findings.

Independent reviewing by a lay panel – the case of Scotland

The Children's Hearing system in Scotland represents an alternative method of making independent judgements about the care and protection of children without necessarily going to the lengths of a formal judicial hearing. In cases where 'compulsory measures of supervision' may be required, an official known as the Reporter brings the cases to a Hearing (Kelly, 1996). The hearing concentrates on the future welfare of the child, rather than fact-finding. Responsibility for making decisions is given to a lay panel, one of whom acts as chair. For our purposes, this is its most significant feature since the power of decision making is given to a truly independent body drawn from the community, rather than yet another local authority official. However, the current arrangements raise questions about the participation of children and parents and the extent to which the panel operates as part of a coordinated system of reviewing.

In principle, the chair is expected to break down any barriers by welcoming the child and parents. Nonetheless the difficulties of participation in the Children's Hearings sound similar to children's experiences in England and Wales. The discomfort of attending a Hearing and the feeling of being undervalued are symbolised by the imposing sight of the 'big desk' behind which panel members sit (Omond, 1995). The introduction of 'safeguarders' who can advocate the best interests of the child is seen as one way of ensuring that children's rights are not forgotten. However there are still a number of constraints on the participation of children and parents that have not been satisfactorily removed (Black, 1992; Veitch, 1995).

The second major issue has been the coordination of subsequent reviews. Once a measure of supervision had been decided, the local authority had a responsibility to review the case under its own procedures (Kendrick and Mapstone, 1991). But there were also a number of ways in which the case could return to the Hearing for review and its role in reviewing cases is likely to be strengthened in future, raising issues about the borderline between professional and judicial responsibilities (Kendrick and Mapstone, 1989; Veitch, 1995).

The changing role of the Hearings is only one factor in the equation. Until recently, children in some legal categories, such as those on place of safety orders, were not subject to local authority reviews. Under the recently legislated provisions of its Children Act, Scotland is now wrestling with the task of introducing a comprehensive statutory system of reviews (Jamieson, 1995).

It is too soon to say with any certainty whether Scotland offers clear lessons for the future of reviewing practice. Nonetheless, the system illustrates how the quest for a 'truly independent' view brings with it a number of challenges, especially in promoting participation and in clarifying the different roles of the panel and the local authority.

Implications for chairing reviews

The Scottish system embodies a more radical concept of independent oversight than any found within England and Wales. In principle, the thinking of the lay panel should be detached from the assumptions of child care professionals and it may be seen as more capable of listening to the views of parents and children. However, this apparent advantage seems to be neutralised by both formal and informal constraints on their participation. The 'big desk' symbolises the panel's authority, no matter how much its independence from professionals is emphasised.

Implications of the findings for the chairing of reviews

The findings of this chapter carry implications for the possible roles of senior professionals in reviewing. First of all, they suggest that coordination of the review process is a more inclusive role than just chairing a meeting. Secondly, they imply that the coordinating role must be related to the functions of a review.

The idea of a planning process based on inquiry, consultation and assessment is intended to highlight the importance of preparation for making a decision at a meeting. Before assessing decision options at a meeting these need to be formulated carefully, if necessary in advance. There seem to be lessons too from the experience of Family Group Conferences, which give careful attention to coordinating a process involving a sequence of meetings. Thus chairing a final meeting is not the same thing as coordinating a good review. The qualities of a coordinator should be defined in terms of an ability to oversee the fulfilment of the central functions of a review: enhancing the participation of children and parents; achieving a structured process; and monitoring (Volume 3, Ch. 8.8).

> *Key point*: A priority for practice in the future should be to focus on the coordinating functions of a senior person, rather than chairing per se.

In terms of participation, it is clear, not only from the evidence in the fieldwork study but from other local authorities, that children, in particular, feel hamstrung by conference-style meetings. This calls for a change of emphasis. The process itself should be planned, on the basis of consultation with young people and parents about their knowledge of the issues and their attitudes towards decision making. If this means managers taking part in 'getting to know you' exercises, or wearing badges, for example, then so be it!

> *Key point*: Rather than simply introducing the child and the parents to a conventional meeting, an attempt should be made to apply sensitive communication skills to the organisation and conduct of the whole process.

In terms of enhancing the structure of a review, there should be consideration given to the particular means by which the coordinator can achieve both an objective and informed view, rather than seeing the issue as an 'either/or'. It is not simply a choice between the 'objective' independent chair and the 'subjective' line manager. As the research on child protection has illustrated, ways need to be found by which managers can detach themselves from subjective influences. Objectivity is not something inherent, by virtue of coming fresh to a situation, not knowing the history; it has to be acquired by the application of a method.

> *Key point:* The priorities here are twofold:
> - rather than independence, to emphasise a capacity for detachment;
> - rather than assuming that an alternative viewpoint will by itself bring objectivity, to highlight the need for a systematic method of considering evidence.

The final function of reviews, though not the least important, is that of monitoring. This means looking at the outcomes of past decisions and their relation to current needs. In general terms, it is not at all clear how far this task should occupy a meeting, and how far it should be accomplished beforehand, in consultation with the child and the parents. In particular, it is crucial that the viability of the plan as a whole is evaluated at the review stage. Hence monitoring should never be regarded as a simple check on past actions; it must assume an evaluative dimension. Unfortunately there seems little new to be learnt from experience in other forums of decision making, where issues of monitoring remain problematic or unresolved.

In reflecting on the evidence of this chapter, it appears that much more thought should be given to the various processes that need to occur if the functions of a planning and reviewing system are to be fulfilled. Coordinating processes successfully involves more than chairing a discussion and then taking a decision. Objectivity, for example, can only be attained by systematic work and preparation in the face of complex, sometimes insidious pressures. Opportunities for participation by children and parents are likely to be significantly enhanced if they have a space of their own and access to support, so that they can develop their ideas and communicate more effectively. 'Who chairs?' is only a preliminary question in what should be a much more comprehensive debate about the future coordination of planning and reviewing.

Key findings

- A survey of arrangements for chairing reviews showed that in some systems line managers took the chair while, in others, various

officers without direct line management responsibility were given that role. The chairs were divided into four categories:
- supervising team managers – the ones responsible for supervising the social worker allocated the case;
- non-supervising team managers;
- non-supervising Reviewing Officers specialising in reviews;
- other managers, with specific expertise.

Twenty-three authorities had set up a simple system involving one category of chair, compared with no less than 25 that had mixed systems.

- The comments of senior managers suggested that the different systems had a variety of advantages and disadvantages. For example, line managers' knowledge of cases was offset by an alleged lack of objectivity; specialist reviewing officers, considered more objective, had to find effective ways of working with line managers.

- These opinions were based on an evaluative agenda that reflected the role of chairing within rational bureaucracies. Only two fifths of respondents had any evidence of young people's views on plans and reviews.

- A comparison of three forums of decision making identified messages about the coordination and organisation of a decision making process. Family Group Conferences demonstrate how families can be given an enhanced participative role. Studies of Child Protection Conferences and Reviews indicate that the task of 'objective' chairing is complex and challenging. In Scotland, Children's Hearings and Reviews, which utilise the judgements of a lay panel, form part of a complex system incorporating local authority reviews which is currently undergoing change.

8. Evaluating child care plans

So far, we have looked at aspects of the process which leads eventually to the conclusion of the review. In this chapter, the aim is to answer major questions about the output of reviews. How comprehensive and specific were the plans that emerged from reviews? How often did they involve parents and children in carrying out tasks? How often were the records of reviews shared with them?

The main task of the chapter is to consider how far the content of the recorded decisions of reviews matched up to the criteria set by the Guidance and Regulations. The chapter will use evidence from the case files but it will also consider data from the survey of social workers and from interviews, in order to set these findings in a broader context.

Comprehensive and specific plans

The Guidance and Regulations prescribe the topics to be considered in plans and reviews. They also state that timescales for implementation should be set and responsibility for carrying out decisions should be allocated. An evaluation of the review decisions was therefore undertaken, covering these three aspects: comprehensiveness of plans, allocation of responsibility and attention to timescales. Data was also collected about several detailed aspects, such as the number of decisions and any follow-up arrangements. A profile of the overall care plans is presented, showing how they need to be considered not as static entities but as evolving within the dynamics of planning and reviewing over periods of time.

Comprehensiveness

The rating of comprehensiveness was based on the minimum checklist of issues in the Guidance and Regulations (Volume 3, Ch. 8.19). The specific issues were decisions about:

- the child's legal status;
- placement;
- contact and the role of parents in the child's care;
- disability and special needs;

- health and education;
- culture; language; ethnic origin and religion;
- placing the child in a new family;
- after care.

When a specific issue relevant to the individual child was omitted, the decisions were rated as 'limited'.

The rating applied not to the discussion at the review meeting but to the review record completed by the chair. This is an important methodological distinction, since it recognises that decisions which were dealt with cursorily during a busy meeting could be clearly and formally recorded afterwards. The following plan received a positive rating for its comprehensiveness.

> *Case 99.* This three-year-old white girl had entered care because of abuse and neglect. The care order was to continue, along with the foster placement. The child's nursery placement was to be maintained for five days per week. As before, one weekend in four was to be spent with a respite foster carer. Preparations for adoption, including identifying adopters and applying for a freeing order, were to go ahead.
>
> Contact with the child's mother was to take place once a month, subject to the local authority's right to refuse it. Social work supervision was to take place in accordance with the regulations.
>
> The child's name was to be removed from the child protection register and an application was to be made on her behalf to the Criminal Injuries Compensation Board.
>
> Her health would continue to be monitored by the health visitor and other health professionals. Referral of the case to a child psychiatrist was to be progressed.

By contrast, a set of planning decisions could be flawed by not paying attention to significant issues such as health or education, as in the next example.

> *Case 2.* A 13-year-old young white woman had been placed with the same foster carer for some years. Various legal options to secure her future had been explored and a legal guardian had more recently been appointed for this purpose.
>
> The planning decisions at the review were: for the young person to remain in this permanent placement; to update the life story work; to arrange for a change of surname; to discuss social services' involvement in the future and, in particular, services under S.24 of the Children Act 1989; and that an independent visitor should not be appointed.

Where specific cultural needs were indicated by the case records, a plan that omitted any reference to them appeared to be 'limited'.

> *Case 180.* A 16-year-old Eritrean Catholic refugee was currently living in a hostel. It was decided that this would continue until a placement with other Eritreans was arranged.

Although the young man had had previous contact with the Eritrean Catholic Church and with other expatriates at the hostel, the plan did not mention the young person's present cultural or religious needs.

Figure 8.1 presents the ratings for each local authority sample. In general, the largest proportion of the cases (37 per cent) was rated as 'adequate', while just less than a third were rated as 'limited' and another third as 'positive' or 'excellent'. The results indicate some differences among the local authority samples: Westside achieved the highest proportion of 'positive' or 'excellent' ratings (57 per cent), followed by the Northborough sample and, finally, by the Midshire sample. Westside also achieved the lowest proportion of 'limited' ratings (14 per cent) compared with nearly a third of the Northborough cases and almost a half of Midshire's cases. 'Positive' or 'excellent' ratings were significantly associated with the use of the Assessment and Action Record ($p<.01$).

Number of decisions

The comprehensive list of issues which should be considered in care plans is likely to have some indirect influence on the number of points covered in each individual care plan. The decisions identified at each review were therefore counted. The mean number of decisions was almost ten and the maximum was 22.

The number of identified decisions varied significantly among the local authority samples, with the highest mean figure to be found in Westside (12.7), followed by Northborough (9.1), and, finally, by Midshire (6.5). In cases where an Assessment and Action Record had been used, the mean number of decisions was 12, compared with nine in the rest of the sample (Kruskal-Wallis $p<.01$, $<.01$). The layout of other forms sometimes appeared as a constraint on the number of decisions made.

In order to get round such obstacles it was necessary to write appendices on separate pieces of paper. In Northborough, space on the review forms was 'freed up' by some review chairs who were using word-processed versions. These had greater flexibility and could therefore include more decisions.

There was no difference in the number of decisions for children in care, compared with those accommodated under S.20. But children with placements in the parental home or a community setting were the subject of fewer decisions (mean 6.2) than those in other types of placement. There was also some evidence that a greater number of decisions was made for children in black and minority ethnic groups (mean 11.9) compared with white children (mean 8.2) (Kruskal-Wallis $p<.01$).

These findings suggest that substantive issues in the cases, such as the ethnicity of a child, exerted some influence on the number of

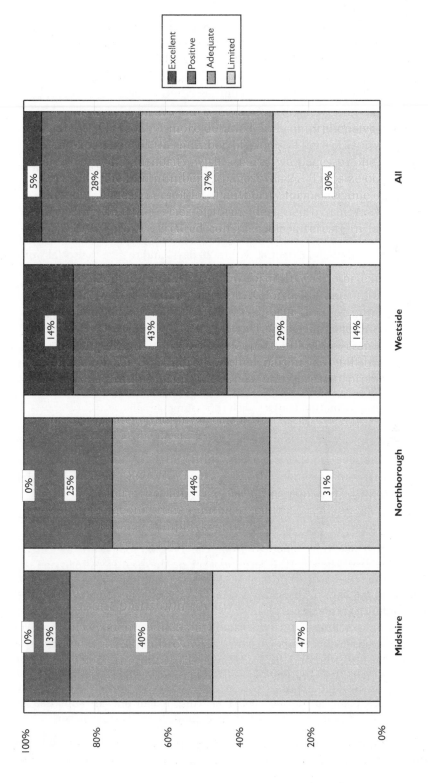

Figure 8.1   Comprehensiveness of plan, by local authority sample

decisions; however, procedures and paperwork, like the Assessment and Action Record, should not be discounted as influences. It is likely that the practice-related and procedure-related factors interact, once practitioners routinely perceive relevant issues listed on the forms they use. They are then more likely to recognise when a decision needs to be made.

Allocating responsibility

Making plans should also involve assigning responsibilities for carrying out tasks, according to the Guidance and Regulations (Volume 3, Ch. 8.21). The following case illustrates a positive approach to the allocation of responsibility (as well as to implementation timescales).

> *Case 149.* The young person was a 13-year-old refugee recently arrived in the UK. The foster carer was to register the young person with a GP within six days and a dentist within 20 days, and to give the social worker the GP's name within that timescale.
>
> The foster carer was to be responsible for the pocket money arrangements specified in the plan.
>
> The foster carer would seek interviews with a school so that the young person would begin attending within 11 days.
>
> The social worker and the foster carer would ensure that the young person visited the Home Office and saw a solicitor within the following week.
>
> There was to be no independent visitor; no further legal decisions were noted. The social worker would arrange extra language tuition and go through information leaflets with the young person.
>
> Work would continue in order to encourage the development of the young person's skills and to integrate him into the local community and support network.

In contrast, the next case illustrates a 'limited' approach, in which too many significant responsibilities were left unallocated.

> *Case 113.* A two-year-old boy had recently been made subject of an interim care order and was placed in foster care.
>
> Twelve decisions emerged from the review: four were allocated to specific professionals (the social worker or the health visitor); one (that the foster placement continue) was ongoing; one (that the child should not be reunited with his parents) entailed no action.
>
> Significant remaining tasks were not allocated: for example, responsibility for arranging a medical examination was not assigned to anyone specifically, even though the health visitor was supposed to be responsible for 'routine health oversight'. Nor was it clear who exactly was to carry out an assessment of the parents' supervision of their children, to consider whether the child's contact with parents should be supervised, or to carry out work prior to the next court hearing. It can only be supposed that responsibility for these tasks fell, by default, to the social worker.

Only four per cent of the plans failed to pay any attention to responsibilities. Figure 8.2 shows the ratings given to the plans which did pay them attention. In all, almost a fifth of cases that dealt with this issue did so to a 'limited' extent; over a third were rated as 'adequate'; encouragingly, over two fifths were rated as 'positive' or 'excellent'. There were significant differences, however, among the local authority samples (p<.01): in Westside, almost seven out of ten cases were rated as 'positive' or 'excellent', compared with a third of Midshire cases and only a quarter of those in Northborough.

In three out of ten cases, children were allocated some responsibility for carrying out the decisions. These were mainly young people over 15 years old, who were given an average of nearly three responsibilities compared with an average of almost one for the whole sample. The number of responsibilities was higher in Westside than elsewhere, and was higher, on average, among refugees and members of black and minority ethnic groups. Children who were living in semi-independent placements had a greater average number of responsibilities than those in foster or residential placements (Kruskal-Wallis p<.01, .01, .01, .05, .01).

The findings for this older group support the evidence presented in Chapter 5 about the building of partnerships with young people approaching adulthood.

Parents were allocated some responsibility for implementation as frequently as children were. Most of these were assigned one or two responsibilities and the maximum number was five. In examining whether or not parents were given some responsibility, it was not possible to discern any difference between those cases where the child was accommodated under S.20 or was in care, but the great majority of cases where parents had responsibilities related to children looked after for less than one year (p<.01).

Parents of younger children were also more frequently given responsibilities: half the parents who had children under five years old acquired responsibilities, compared with only a fifth of the parents who had children aged from 11 to 15 years. Almost a third of the parents in Westside and Northborough were allocated responsibilities compared with only an eighth of the Midshire parents (p<.01, <.01).

Parents therefore were accorded formal responsibilities for carrying out parts of the plan when the child was young and had recently entered the system. The child's legal status was not a significant factor. The following example clearly illustrates the general pattern.

> *Case 152.* This two-year-old girl was in care. The care plan decided at the review was that she be rehabilitated to her parents within six months.
>
> In the plan, her parents were expected to discuss further changes in contact and to help with arrangements for a pre-school play group placement.

The first year of being looked after appeared to be a crucial time in which the possibilities of partnership were explored.

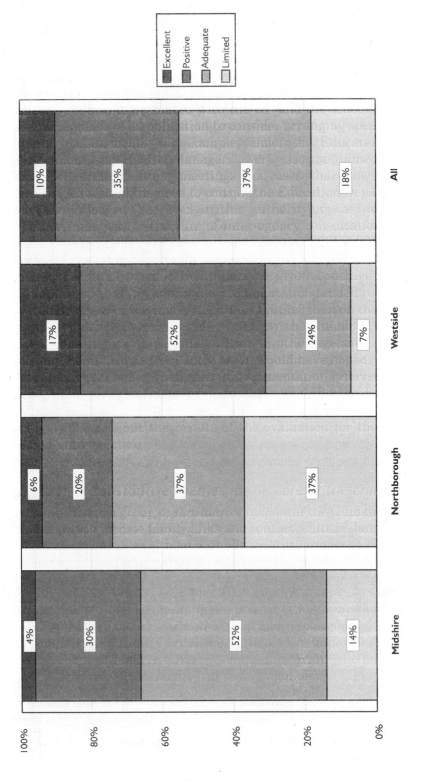

Figure 8.2   Evidence of allocation of responsibility, by local authority sample

Another indicator of participation is the frequency with which plans are signed by children and parents (Volume 3, Ch. 2.64). In order to see if practitioners had extended this practice to decisions emerging from reviews, a check was made on review records. Despite the number of occasions on which children and parents were allocated responsibilities, there was little evidence of their signatures (only two by children, and five from parents).

The Guidance supports a further aspect of participation by advising that any dissent from the plan should be recorded (Volume 3, Ch. 8.21). A record of dissent was found in less than a fifth of cases. Unsurprisingly, nearly all these instances concerned children in care. For example, dissent was recorded in three quarters of those cases in which the child was subject to an interim care order and when the mother had also attended the review meeting. It is clearly important that the process of reviewing is capable of registering the actual views of parents in this way so that the potential for dialogue and contact is maximised.

There was a significant difference among the local authority samples ($p < .05$): dissent was recorded in about a quarter of Northborough and Westside cases, compared with only a twentieth of those in Midshire. The very low figure for Midshire suggests that practice in recording dissent was only partly a function of the composition of cases in the fieldwork areas.

Setting timescales

If plans are to be put into practice, it is helpful to include timescales for implementation (Volume 3, Ch. 8.23). Examination of the cases revealed more problems in meeting this criterion than in meeting the other criteria. Indeed, one eighth of the plans made no reference to timescales at all. The following example illustrates a plan with 'limited' timescales.

> *Case 62*. A four-year-old disabled white girl was subject to a care order and placed with family foster carers.
> There were six decisions made at the review: the first was ongoing, relating to social work support; the second set out a broad timescale for respite care – 40 days per year; the remainder involved preparing a report for the adoption panel, making representations about transport, a possible application for funding conductive education, and completing a placement agreement. None of these four decisions had been allocated a timescale.

Figure 8.3 gives the ratings for the plans which referred to timescales. Almost half of the cases that dealt with this issue did so to a 'limited' extent, while almost a third were rated as 'adequate' and a quarter as 'positive' or 'excellent'. Again, there were indications of differences among the local authority samples: two fifths of cases in Westside were rated as 'positive' or 'excellent', compared with less than a fifth in Midshire and less than a tenth in Northborough.

At a general level, these findings were reflected in the views of social workers, who, for example, were sceptical that timescales for placement plans could always be set. Only a quarter regarded the statement that 'it is impossible to set timescales for placement plans' as 'rarely true'. Almost three fifths considered that the statement was 'sometimes true'.

When all the three plan ratings are taken into account, the Westside sample therefore achieved higher ratings than cases in the other samples. There was no evidence that the distributions of the three plan ratings were linked to the child's gender, age group, ethnic category, the type of placement or whether the child was in care. Procedure and practice in the local authorities seemed to be a more significant influence.

Other forward planning and follow-up

Plans should include additional specific features, such as arrangements for changing or ending them, and contingency plans (Volume 3: ACPG 4(1); Ch. 2.62). In only 44 per cent of cases was there a statement about how a plan could be changed and this was usually little more than a reference to the next review date, usually six months ahead. On this limited basis, there were some differences among the local authority samples, with Westside's forms presenting a clearer picture than those of Midshire and Northborough. How plans might be ended was unclear in the great majority of cases; only 15 per cent contained this information.

Contingency plans were identified in only 14 per cent of cases. They were most common for residential placements (25 per cent of these placements had contingency plans compared with 16 per cent of foster placements), but they did not exist for semi-independent and other types of placement.

Lack of attention to arrangements for changing, ending or switching plans when necessary was therefore widespread. If this reflected a well-founded confidence in the plan then it might be welcomed. But if there is no forward thinking and the plan later needs adjustment, this may mean a reduction in the continuity of the planning and reviewing process. It is also important that children and parents understand how future arrangements will work and how they can influence future decision making.

Unfortunately, young people interviewed in a focus group setting were not aware of the possibility of asking for an early review, though this would have been a helpful option.

Interviewer: 'Is that something you would have wanted?'

Young person: 'I think so. I've been worrying so much about my career, it's unbelievable. Once I have actually made my decisions I have to wait until the next review . . . I should put it down on paper.'

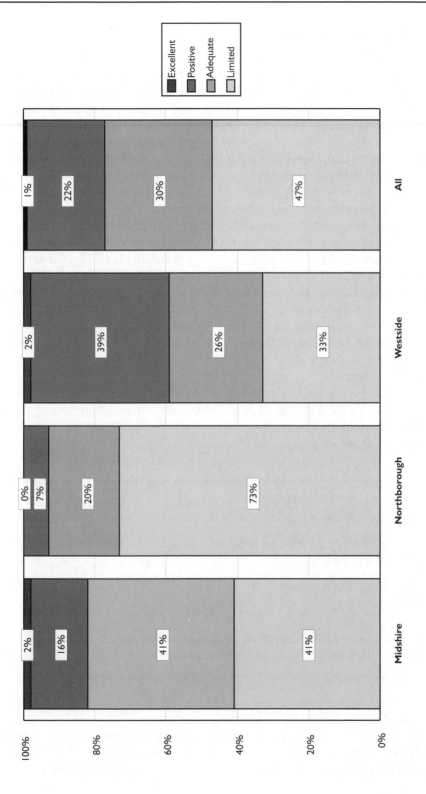

Figure 8.3 Evidence of planning timescales, by local authority sample

Sharing the record of reviews

Sending a record or summary of the review to children and parents is an integral part of maintaining their participation (Volume 3: RCC 7; Ch. 8.22). Yet it was often difficult to find any evidence that this had been done. One authority, Westside, had designed a monitoring form which was supposed to contain such information. But the form was frequently not to be found. In some cases the only evidence on the record was a handwritten mark opposite the name of a child or parent. Anyone unfamiliar with an individual team's practice would have missed this evidence. Even with the benefit of such knowledge, no evidence of this was found in virtually two thirds of all cases.

As expected, a major consideration in sending a record or summary to children was the child's age. Half the young people at least 16 years old were sent a document, compared with a third of 11- to 15-year-olds and less than a fifth of children aged 10 years and under. Though there was an understandable link between the child's age and the likelihood of being sent a document ($p < .01$), this was not sufficient to explain the shortfall from expectations based on the Guidance and Regulations. In fact, only 38 per cent of those children at least five years old who attended the meeting were sent a record or summary, according to the available records.

When asked, after their reviews, whether they expected to receive a copy of the meeting record, only three out of a dozen young people clearly thought so. Focus group interviewees emphasised the importance of receiving records.

Group Two
Young person (1): 'I think we should have a copy of it as well, what everybody said. Not just major points.'

Young person (2): 'Yeah.'

Young person (3): 'Well, at least get the plans actually sent home, like they're supposed to.'

They experienced a lack of control over the records that were made of meetings.

Group One
Young person (1): 'We don't see what they are writing . . . . You can see it's handwritten but you don't know what's written.'

Young person (2): 'You don't know what's going down on paper.'

Making sure that records are shared therefore increases young people's sense of ownership of the decisions.

At first sight, sending a record to a parent seemed to be an equally arbitrary practice: in about 45 per cent of cases, a parent who attended a meeting was found to have been sent a copy. In about two fifths of cases, a parent who had been consulted during the review process received a copy. However, it was expected that the partnership principle for cases accommodated under S.20 would be sustained by sharing review records with parents. Indeed records were more frequently sent if the children were accommodated under S.20 (42 per cent) than if they were in care (29 per cent) though this difference failed to reach statistical significance. Significant differences were not found among cases in different types of placement (though parents of children placed at home or in community settings were the most likely to be sent a record).

The frequencies of sending records to children and parents were significantly different among the local authority samples (p<.01): the lowest frequency of sending records was found in Northborough (11 per cent for children; 20 per cent for parents) compared with higher rates in Midshire (35 per cent for children; 50 per cent for parents) and in Westside (37 per cent for children; 32 per cent for parents). In Westside it was virtually impossible to contact parents of refugees. In other respects the differences among the local authority samples are consistent both for parents and for children, suggesting that they are not sufficiently explained by social work practice considerations. Instead it seems that administrative practice in the local authorities was a factor influencing the process of sharing records with children and parents.

Sharing records with children and parents is a significant expression of the partnership principle. Sending such a summary of the points may require some care from social workers on occasions, but it is difficult to explain the research findings without concluding that too little attention was paid to this aspect of the Guidance and Regulations.

Care plans and the courts

One of the questions explored in the study was whether the care plans associated with reviews were significantly affected by the specific decision-making processes in the courts. Information about the submission of plans to the courts was therefore systematically collected. The care plan was defined as the plan identified at the review.

In practice, out of 166 cases where information was found, only 36 had been submitted to the courts, representing just over a fifth. Fourteen of these (39 per cent) were children currently on interim care orders, compared with 20 (56 per cent) currently subject to a full care order.

It emerged that in very few cases had the care plans been materially changed as a result of the process of going to court. The following example was exceptional:

> Case 116. After being appointed, a Guardian ad Litem had recommended an application be made for a Care Order and the social worker subsequently agreed.

The courts had, on the whole, ratified the care plans presented to them. There were 11 such cases, compared with only four where something new had come out of the court process; the evidence was unclear in the remaining five cases. The role of the courts in care planning seemed to be 'adjudicative' (concerned with the grounds of the order), rather than 'participative', a finding which is consistent with legal trends since the implementation of the Children Act 1989 (Dewar, 1995).

These findings, albeit small-scale, tend to emphasise the significance of the planning and reviewing process within the local authority. There was little evidence to suggest that matters were being taken to court with an open agenda and left for the court to decide. Nor were the courts intervening to alter the substance of the care plan. Rather, the care plan emerging from the planning and reviewing process acquired considerable practical and legal importance.

Overall care plans and the passage of time

We now consider again the care plans that were identified at the review stage. In order to perform an analysis of a large group of plans, we will follow a categorisation of overall plans suggested by the LAC plan form:

- remain with the family
- restore to birth family
- restore to other family
- time limited fostering
- long-term foster placement
- special residential placement
- adoption
- progress to independence
- independence
- assessment
- court resolution

In this section, the overall care plans will be examined from a dynamic perspective, showing, as far as possible, which planning options were favoured at different ages and stages in children's careers within the system.

Before this is done, a note of methodological caution needs to be sounded. A cross-sectional sample does not present comprehensive information about child care careers. A cohort of admissions is more illuminating (Rowe, Hundleby and Garnett, 1989; Bullock, Little and Millham, 1993). However, a cross-sectional sample can help pick out any differences in the current plans of children who are at particular stages of their careers.

Again it must be emphasised that the definition of an overall care plan was linked to the review rather than to a formal document called a Care Plan. Using information in the review document gave a much clearer and more up-to-date picture of the current plan than simply relying on a planning document. According to this definition, evidence of an overall plan was found in over nine out of ten cases, though it was easier to discern overall plans in Westside, where, of course, early versions of the LAC materials were used.

Clearly, the child's age was a factor in the choice of overall plan: over eight out of ten adoption plans were for children less than 11 years old; conversely, eight out of ten long term fostering plans were for young people at least 11 years old; virtually all the independence plans concerned young people who were at least 16 years old.

Children's careers within the system are another factor to be considered, as Table 8.1 shows. As a child's experience of being looked after lengthens, certain planning options rise and fall as proportions of the plans that are made. In the first year of being looked after, assessment was a key activity. The planning options at this stage were more likely to involve the birth family. After a year, remaining with the family became unrealistic. The overall proportion of care plans aimed at restoration of the child to the birth family was slightly higher than found in previous research (12 per cent, compared with nine per cent in Vernon and Fruin, 1986). As the years passed, their significance continued at a steady level, until declining sharply after five years. As a proportion of plans, adoption increased up to the fourth year, before dropping sharply. Long term foster placement was the most frequent option for those looked after for at least five years.

Interpretation of findings

The findings in this chapter have something to tell us about how frequently comprehensive plans are produced. But they also raise serious questions about how successfully the continuity of planning is maintained.

The evaluation of child care plans suggested that the use of paper forms was associated with differences in the ratings of plans. While data indicate that use of the LAC forms was associated with better results on the evaluation, it would be a mistake to conclude that somehow the forms themselves were solely responsible for the results. We can assume that the results were also influenced by the commitment of the time and effort on the part of practitioners. More generally, the fact that Westside was a pilot authority for the LAC project created a significant impetus to perform well.

It should also be remembered that, during the fieldwork, staff from the LAC project were helping Westside to implement the materials. Hence the findings relate to a major 'start-up' period for a new planning and reviewing system. It will be important to see how far this progress is sustained in the future.

There was evidence that the forward planning and follow-up to the review did not fully satisfy the requirements of the Guidance and Regulations. Lack of consideration to future planning arrangements was found in a significant proportion of cases. The evidence also suggested that written records of the review were not routinely shared with children and parents who had attended reviews. If these follow-up activities are not satisfactorily completed, it is clear that the possibilities of participation by children and parents are likely to be reduced.

Overall plans seem to have a 'shelf-life' which the planning system needs to reflect. Such findings lead us to focus on planning sequences unfolding over time. These are the subject of the next chapter.

Key findings

- In terms of comprehensiveness, over a third of the plans emerging from reviews were rated as adequate, just less than a third as limited, and another third as positive or excellent. In terms of allocating responsibility for carrying out tasks, over a third were rated as adequate, almost a fifth as limited and over two fifths as positive or excellent. In terms of setting timescales, almost a third were rated as adequate, almost half as limited and a quarter as positive or excellent.
- The Westside sample for which early LAC materials were in use achieved higher ratings on the three rating scales than the cases in the other local authority samples.
- Young people over 15 years old were given an average of nearly three responsibilities compared with an average of just under one for the whole sample. The frequency of allocating responsibility to parents was similar to that for children. Parents with young children and with children who had been looked after for less than a year were more likely to be given responsibilities. There was little evidence of children or parents attaching their signatures to review records.
- Less than half the reviews contained any indication of how a plan could be changed. Only 14 per cent referred to contingency arrangements.
- Only 38 per cent of those young people who attended a review meeting were found to have been sent a record or summary of it; the equivalent proportion of parents was 45 per cent.
- When the role of the courts in care planning was examined, it was found that the courts ratified a majority of the plans presented to them.
- In the first year of being looked after, the overall care plan involved remaining with or returning to the birth family in over a third of cases. Over a fifth of these early plans were focused on assessment. In the next two years, long term foster placement was the most

frequently chosen option. Adoption was ranked second in frequency, followed by return to the birth family. In the subsequent two years, adoption was the most frequently chosen option, matched closely by independence. After five years of being looked after, a clear majority of plans involved long term foster care, while plans for adoption or return to the birth family all but disappeared.

Table 8.1   General care plan, by years looked after (rank order of percentages)

Less than 1 year (N=63)	%	1 to 3 years (N=36)	%	3 to 4 years (N=24)	%	5 years and over (N=29)	%
1 Assessment	22	1 Long term foster placement	33	1 Adoption	26	1 Long term foster placement	59
2 Remain with family	21	2= Adoption	17	2 Independence	25	2 Independence	24
3 Restore to birth family	14	2= Restore to birth family	17	3= Restore to birth family	12	3 Adoption	7
4 Adoption	11	4 Independence	14	3= Special residential placement	12	4= Restore to birth family	3
5= Long term foster placement	8	5 Special residential placement	11	5 Restore to other family	8	4= Special residential placement	3
5= Progress to independence	8	6= Remain with family	3	6= Assessment	4		
7= Restore to other family	6	6= Progress to independence	3	6= Long term foster placement	4		
7= Court resolution	6	6= Assessment	3	6= Progress to independence	4		
9 Time limited fostering	3						

9. Continuity and effectiveness of planning and reviewing

The purpose of this chapter is to examine planning and reviewing as part of the dynamic flow of child care decision making and activity.

Focusing on the main sample, the chapter examines a range of data about a sample period which runs up to the time of the principal review that has been studied so far in this report. This is in order to identify sequential evidence of care planning and implementation as well as unplanned changes. Because some children were not looked after when the sample period began, some of this data refers to a period before these children became looked after. Therefore, case conferences, child protection reviews, network meetings and legal planning meetings were all included in this part of the data collection.

The frequency and continuity of planning meetings

The number and frequency of planning meetings will be analysed next, as well as the number of chairs in each case. The extent to which reviewing took place within the intervals laid down by the Regulations will be examined. Evidence about the attendances of children and parents over this sample period of time will be discussed, together with any evidence of their exclusions from reviews.

The study of meetings was intended to include all types of planning meeting, including any convened before the children began their current episode of being looked after. Meetings were to be identified for up to a year prior to the main review. In some cases this meant going backwards further than a year in order to find a meeting that had produced the plan current a year ago. In two cases, for example, it was necessary to go back over two years in order to find such a meeting. In other cases, contact with social services had begun very recently. However, the average period of monitoring turned out to be 11 months. Table 9.1 compares data about the meetings for the whole sample.

The comparison of mean data, relating to an average period of over 11 months, highlights a number of important findings, though it must be emphasised that the figures below represent averages.

- On average, there were four planning or reviewing meetings in almost a year.
- There was at least one significant planning meeting in addition to the reviews which took place.
- The number of actual reviews fell somewhat below the number expected under the Regulations.
- There was a good chance that the review venue would change (though this information was not always recorded).
- In general there were two different chairs for the meetings that took place on each case over the sample period.

A clear implication of the data is that it is not sufficient to look at statutory reviews on their own; other meetings also played an important role. Another conclusion is that typically both the venue and the chair were likely to change. For these reasons maintaining the continuity of the process was not a straightforward business.

Table 9.1 Planning meetings (comparison of summed and mean data)

	Summed	Mean	Standard Deviation	N=
Meetings	709	3.98	2.20	178
Months	1954	11.29	6.19	173
Venues	226	1.69	0.85	134
Chairs	362	2.07	1.08	175
Expected reviews	467	2.65	1.08	176
Actual reviews	424	2.38	1.06	178

Further analysis highlighted differences in the frequency of meetings. First of all, there appeared to be some differences in the average number of meetings, depending on the child's age (Table 9.2). For children less than five years old, planning meetings were more frequently held over a shorter period: an average of nearly five meetings in almost eight months, compared with only three meetings a year for those aged 16 years and over.

There was a high frequency of planning meetings for children who had been granted interim care orders during the past year. On average, such children had been the subject of over five meetings during a period of eight months.

A greater number of meetings was held in cases where, in the past year, the children had experienced more than one placement – almost five meetings in a period of ten months compared with only three meetings in 12 months for other children.

Table 9.2   Planning meetings, by age group (comparison of mean data)

Mean data	Less than 5 years	5 to 10 years	11 to 15 years	16 years and over	All
Meetings	4.92	4.33	3.63	3.17	3.98
Months	7.93	12.08	11.68	12.85	11.29

When the period of being looked after was examined, there was some evidence of a 'planning curve' (Table 9.3). The frequency of planning meetings dropped as the child's experience of being looked after increased. For children in their first year of being looked after, virtually four meetings were held during an average period of seven months. This rate dropped after a year. After three years, it had begun to decline below the average for the whole sample.

Table 9.3   Planning meetings, by time looked after (comparison of mean data)

Mean data	Less than 1 year	1 to 2 years	2 to 3 years	3 to 4 years	4 to 5 years	5 years and over	All
Meetings	3.99	4.57	4.92	4.00	3.69	3.20	3.98
Months	6.99	12.37	14.24	13.55	13.77	16.93	11.29

The second line of Table 9.3 illustrates how the period of research monitoring was extended backwards in time in order to identify a planning meeting that could be said to have produced the plan current a year ago. Children looked after for a long period were more likely to have these long-distant reviews.

These apparent trends raise important questions about the planning process: how far is the reduction of planning frequency linked to the easing, over time, of the legal and administrative demands of child protection, and how much is it related to the child's needs?

Table 9.4 compares data for the local authority samples. The Midshire sample had the lowest average number of meetings (3.31) over the longest average period – over 12 months. But a three-month industrial dispute over car usage made holding meetings difficult. This hit social work in rural areas particularly hard and affected most Midshire cases. To estimate its impact, we might assume that no meetings at all could take place in that time. If we then reduce the planning period proportionately for the relevant cases, the average number of planning months for the Midshire sample consequently falls to just over a year (12.05 months). This still exceeds the average periods for the other two areas (both approximately ten months) and implies only a small rise in the frequency of meetings. The impact of the dispute was not sufficient to account for the differences in the frequency of meetings among the fieldwork areas. As Table 9.4 also shows, Midshire's ratio of expected to actual reviews was lower than in the other areas, and it had the lowest rate of change of venue.

Table 9.4   Planning meetings, by local authority sample (comparison of mean data)

Mean data	Midshire	Northborough	Westside	All
Meetings	3.31	4.08	4.53	3.98
Months	13.85	10.17	9.91	11.29
Venues	1.47	1.74	1.76	1.69
Chairs	1.81	2.54	1.84	2.07
Expected reviews	3.18	2.52	2.30	2.65
Actual reviews	2.47	2.32	2.37	2.38

The Northborough sample again looks like an intermediate case in terms of the frequency of meetings. It had the highest rate of change in chairs – an average of well over two chairs, during an average period of ten months. A system with independent chairing was therefore found to have a higher rate of change than if supervisors normally took the chair. However, bearing in mind that two fifths of the children were on the child protection register, another factor to be considered was the frequency of child protection review meetings, chaired by specialist officers appointed for that purpose.

The frequency of meetings in Westside was high: over four meetings during the average period of monitoring of almost ten months. In fact, there were more reviews, on average, than would have been expected under the Regulations. These findings clearly demonstrate the practical importance accorded to reviewing in Westside.

The punctuality of reviews

In this study, the definition of a punctual review has been that the review meeting took place within the timescales set by the Regulations (RCC 3). In all, less than half the reviews in the main sample were performed on time (see Figure 9.1). The range was from 36 per cent (Midshire) to 55 per cent (Northborough). As stated earlier, the low proportion in Midshire was partly explained by the disruption caused by the three-month industrial dispute over car usage. Barely a seventh of the reviews completed in the ten weeks after the end of the dispute were punctual. Over a further ten months this proportion increased to a level almost identical with Westside's. Despite its managers' awareness of slippage, Northborough's proportion of punctual reviews was the

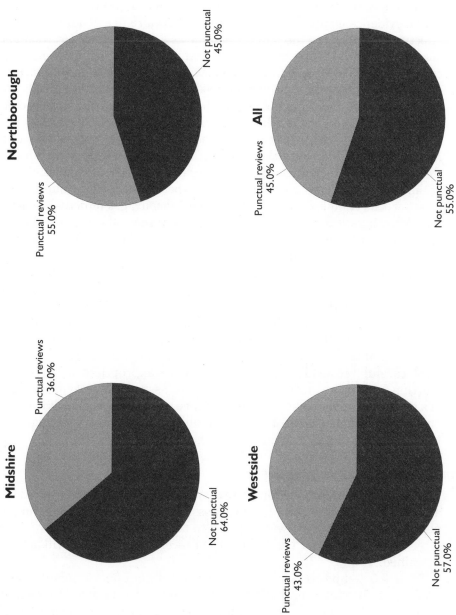

Figure 9.1   Punctual reviews, by local authority sample

highest in the three fieldwork samples, though the differences among them were not found to be statistically significant. Other possible factors, such as child's age, legal status, or placement on the child protection register, were also not found to have a significant influence.

The evidence about late reviews points therefore to a general problem affecting over half the cases in the sample as a whole. However, we must also look again at the data for the sample period of planning and reviewing in Table 9.4. Those data showed that the frequency of formal reviews was somewhat below what was expected, but not drastically so. It appears that over a significant period a high proportion of expected reviews typically took place but they were often late.

A further implication of the data about the meetings should also be noted. It was found that other types of meetings took place within the timescale of the formal statutory reviews chaired by the relevant officer of the local authority. From a practice perspective, it must be questioned whether this complex pattern of meetings encourages punctual reviewing. After a relevant planning meeting has taken place, practitioners may sometimes ask themselves why they should organise a formal review by a particular date.

Punctuality is also influenced by the dates set at previous reviews. It was normal practice at review meetings to fix the date for the next review at the furthest point in time compatible with the administrative cycle of the Guidance and Regulations. Hence there was often no leeway for contingencies that might mean the meeting had to be delayed.

These points suggest that the relationship between types of meeting need careful reconsideration so that where appropriate a particular meeting within the statutory timescale can assume the responsibilities of a statutory review. Though the Guidance supports this principle there has been too little practical discussion about how various meetings can be managed in order to achieve such a goal.

Attendances by children and parents

In Chapter 6, the proportion of review meetings attended by children and parents was discussed. It is also possible to look back at each sample period of planning and reviewing and to consider the frequency of such attendances over time. The frequency of recorded exclusions will also be examined.

Table 9.5 compares the summed and mean data on attendances and exclusions, for children, mothers and fathers; the columns on the right again show the numbers of meetings which took place and the periods of planning and reviewing to which these data relate.

Table 9.5   Attendances and exclusions of children and parents

	Child		Mother		Father		Meetings		Months of planning/ reviewing	
	Sum	Mean	Sum	Mean	Sum	Mean	Sum	Mean	Sum	Mean
Attendances	200	1.28	242	1.59	91	0.62	709	3.98	1954	11.29
Exclusions	11	0.07	64	0.42	63	0.43				

The data in the table emphasise that over the sample periods many more meetings took place than were attended by children or parents. In all, the most frequent family attenders – mothers – were present at little more than a third of all possible meetings. Exclusion accounted for only a small proportion of the absences and they will be discussed in more detail shortly.

Table 9.6 analyses the attendances of children and parents according to the child's age. The table shows how, on average, the older children attended more meetings than the younger ones, though even the oldest group did not, on average, attend more than two thirds of meetings. Attendances of mothers declined steadily across the age range; the attendances of fathers were very low and declined less consistently. There seemed to be few differences between the attendances of white parents and those from black and minority ethnic groups.

Table 9.6   Attendances by children and parents, by age of child (comparison of mean data)

Mean data	Less than 5 years	5 to 10 years old	11 to 15 years old	16 years old and over	All
Meetings	4.92	4.33	3.63	3.17	3.98
Months	7.93	12.08	11.68	12.85	11.29
Attendance					
Child	0.53	0.49	1.67	2.36	1.28
Mother	2.86	1.53	1.00	0.92	1.59
Father	0.97	0.55	0.61	0.24	0.62

Table 9.7 compares attendances according to the length of time that the child had been looked after. Here the average figures again show a steady decline in the frequencies of attendance by mothers. There was an upward trend in children's attendances apart from the fifth year. From a very low base, the average figures for fathers' attendance peaked in the third year and then declined, again revealing an inconsistent pattern.

Table 9.7   Attendances by children and parents, by time looked after (comparison of mean data)

Mean data	Less than one year	1 to 2 years	2 to 3 years	3 to 4 years	4 to 5 years	5 years and over	All
Meetings	3.99	4.57	4.92	4.00	3.69	3.20	3.98
Months	6.99	12.37	14.24	13.55	13.77	16.93	11.29
Attendance							
Child	0.94	1.33	1.62	1.88	1.00	1.70	1.28
Mother	2.40	1.76	1.50	1.00	0.90	0.28	1.60
Father	0.67	0.61	1.78	0.46	0.90	0.20	0.79

Whether the child was in care or accommodated under S.20 seemed to make no difference to the frequency of parental attendance. However, mothers attended, on average, over half the very frequent meetings about children who had been placed on interim care orders during the past year.

When the local authority samples were compared, the average attendances of children and of mothers were highest in Westside (1.81 and 2.33, respectively) while the average attendance of fathers was highest in Northborough (0.94).

Exclusions of children

It was not always possible to determine reasons for exclusions, though, where available, this information was noted. The children who were clearly excluded from meetings numbered only eleven. Exclusion of a child was never recorded for more than one meeting, though it would be difficult to draw precise conclusions from this. In several cases, for example, a single exclusion was attributed to the child's age. It would have been more logical to exclude young children from a series of meetings. Age was also widely defined. Five- and six-year-olds, for example, were likely to be excluded for this reason. But the same judgement was also made about an eight-year-old. By recording their judgements, chairs were fulfilling at least one of the principles set forth in the Guidance. But there would seem to be many cases when such decisions were not clearly recorded.

In further cases, where age was not an issue, no formal note was made of the reason for an exclusion but other information about the case suggested that the young person's behaviour was regarded as unpredictable.

In all, it seems that chairs sometimes recorded the reasons for their decisions to exclude a child but this was not a consistent practice.

Exclusions of parents

As Table 9.5 revealed, mothers and fathers were, respectively, excluded on over 60 occasions. The number of individuals concerned was rather lower in each case: 32 mothers, compared with 26 fathers. Clearly, these constitute a significant proportion of the sample: over a fifth of parents (taking into account those who it seemed impossible to consult). When fathers' exclusions were examined, most were excluded jointly with mothers (18, out of 26 excluded fathers). Uncertainties about the family situation were apparently not a major cause of exclusion: only a tenth of parental exclusions happened in cases where the plan was to conduct an assessment. Even so, a parent was excluded because of a current police investigation.

A fundamental reason was the virtual exclusion of parents from the plan, as in adoption cases.

> Case 16. The care plan for a one-year-old boy was to find a suitable adoption placement, involving limited contact with parents, who were excluded from six meetings during the period of planning and reviewing.

In fact, the existence of an adoption plan accounted for a third of the parental exclusions.

In some cases, the children's wishes were the principal reason for exclusion.

> Case 28. A 15-year-old girl did not wish to have contact with her parents so they were excluded from three reviews during the period of planning and reviewing.

In other cases, parents were said to have had created a 'scene' at a previous review.

> Case 31. A 14-year-old boy was placed in foster care. The mother was excluded from a review because there was too much animosity between the mother, the paternal grandfather and the foster mother.

In general, however, the reasons for parental exclusion seemed to be that the plan had evolved in ways that marginalised parents. It is interesting that over eight out of ten parental exclusions were for children in foster or community settings.

Effectiveness of planning

This section examines data about the planning decisions over the sample period and compares these with evidence of implementation. It looks specifically at certain types of decision and asks whether they were implemented, whether implementation took place within a timescale, and whether any unplanned changes occurred. Evidence was collected about each successive plan and its subsequent period of implementation during a sample period of, on average, about eight months. Thus, data has been compiled about the total number of planning decisions and their outcomes over the sample period. The decisions considered in this section were classified as follows: legal, placement, educational, health, contact with parents, and miscellaneous items. One question to be considered is whether there were any differences in the rates of implementation and unplanned change for particular kinds of decisions.

This section raises important issues about the relevance of reviews to practical decision making. Were they closely integrated into practical decision making, or were they periodic attempts to bring purposefulness and order to a more variable and contingent style of decision making?

Methodological considerations

The implementation of planned decisions is a significant evaluative criterion for the planning and reviewing process, but not a completely satisfactory one. There are several reasons for being cautious about the value of implementation as a criterion for success. For example, circumstances may change and make the plan irrelevant, or implementation may sometimes be counter-productive (Sinclair, Garnett and Berridge, 1995). However, one of the benefits of a flexible and continuous process of planning and reviewing is that the results of decision making can be regularly monitored and fresh meetings can be held at which plans are appropriately adjusted. Hence the duration of planning cycles can vary as circumstances change. Even so, there will be some unplanned changes.

Studying decision implementation in child care is therefore complex but by examining these planning cycles over a significant period it is possible to maximise the relevance of the study to practice. Hence, where possible, each sequence of planning and reviewing over a given period was examined. After the planning meeting had occurred, the implementation of the resulting decisions was followed up.

The examination of planning and reviewing sequences was intended to build directly on the study of meetings prior to the main review. The initial target was therefore to record the planning and implementation of decisions over a period of up to a year. Given the number of plans and decisions it became apparent that the task was too complex to accomplish in every case. Thus, it was decided to record the 'planning year' for half the cases; for the remainder, only the last plan and its implementation was to be recorded. As a result the findings include 'single-plan' cases and 'multiple-plan' cases. Table 9.8 gives a breakdown of these, indicating that the maximum number of plans studied in an individual case was nine. Even with the adjustment of the data collection target, the planning data alone was of a formidable size – a grand total of 345 recorded plans, comprising 2,915 decisions.

Table 9.8   Cases, by number of recorded plans

Number of recorded plans			
One	2 to 4	5 to 9	Total cases
95	59	16	170

To follow up the outcome of almost 3,000 decisions would have been an enormous task. The only available source of information was the individual case files, which varied in the clarity and continuity of their records. Information was often contained in reports attached to reviews, but frequently these were not comprehensive. As Chapter 5 revealed, the focus of discussion at review meetings was rarely on monitoring; instead it was very much on summarising the current situation so as to move forward. Where the researcher found that information was missing from reports, it was possible sometimes to scan through running records in order to locate it. However, flicking through pages of daily items was time-consuming and sometimes fruitless. As Chapter 5 also suggested, monitoring of plans was made more difficult by patchily written reports.

The problem of monitoring implementation was not simply a methodological issue for this research. Anyone with an interest in following up the outcome of previous decisions would have experienced the same obstacles. Most crucially, this applies to a review chair perhaps coming to the case for the first time.

The thinness of the information in reports was reflected in this comment by a newly appointed independent chair.

> Chair: 'I'm not happy with the amount of hard-core information about what's happened between reviews, in terms of significant events. It's too sketchy. It's like Tardis touchdowns!'

Hence it was decided to concentrate on major planning issues that were likely to be consistently recorded. These major topics were legal status, placement, health, education and contact issues together with miscellaneous services relevant to the case. The miscellaneous services included the provision of services to parents, such as arranging accommodation, parenting skills advice, or clinical help. It was evident that it would be impossible to systematically trace the outcome of other decisions (say, about children's religious attendances) on the basis of the case records. Table 9.9 shows how often plans on these major topics were made.

The most frequent topic of decision making was the child's placement, followed by legal issues. Health, education and contact were the topics of

Table 9.9   Cases in which plans were made, by topic of decision

	Legal		Placement		Health		Education		Contact		Miscellaneous	
	N	%	N	%	N	%	N	%	N	%	N	%
Yes	135	75	164	91	118	66	119	66	113	63	160	89
No	35	19	4	2	50	27	39	22	50	28	9	5
Not applicable	0	0	2	1	2	1	12	7	7	4	0	0
Missing	10	5	10	5	10	5	10	5	10	5	11	6
Total	180	100	180	100	180	100	180	100	180	100	180	100

decisions in around two thirds of cases. These findings are interesting because they related to significant periods of decision making, not just to a 'one-off' review meeting. They add a different perspective on the previous findings of this chapter about the adequacy of plans emerging from reviews. The data sets are not completely equivalent because, unlike the main sample reviews, these include meetings held before some of the children became looked after. Nonetheless, they illustrate the near-universal focus of plans on placement and the less frequent attention given to health and education.

Table 9.10 shows, in each category, the number of planning decisions that were followed up by a search of the available records. Hence the follow-up applied to about half the total of identified decisions (1,572 out of 2,915), focusing on these major categories.

Table 9.10   Planning decisions followed up, by category of decision

Legal	258
Placement	322
Health	240
Education	219
Contact	177
Miscellaneous services	356
All decisions	1572

The analysis of outcomes

The data on outcomes seeks to answer three main questions:

- How many decisions were implemented substantially or fully?
- How many were implemented within a planned timescale?
- How many unplanned changes took place?

The period of follow-up varied for the methodological reasons explained. Table 9.11 presents information about these periods.

Table 9.11   Period of follow-up for planning decisions

	Minimum	Maximum	Mean	Total
Months	0.13	31.90	8.26	1362.90

The mean period of follow-up was more than eight months, but there was a wide range, including two cases that were monitored for over two years. It is reasonable to ask whether these differences preclude valid comparisons. Hence this study of outcomes begins with a comparison of the patterns of implementation in cases for which different periods of planning and reviewing were followed up. Table 9.12 categorises cases by reference to these sample periods and makes it possible to see how they differ from the pattern in the sample as a whole. This indicates hardly any differences in the pattern of outcomes for these periods of planning and reviewing. This finding makes it possible to carry out further comparisons with greater confidence. In the following tables (Tables 9.12 to 9.14), the data are presented as percentages of the number of plan items: the middle two rows represent the proportions of items 'im- plemented' and 'implemented within a set time scale'; the unplanned changes are calculated as a ratio of the plan items, in order to illustrate their relative frequency.

Table 9.12 Implementation of plans, by period of planning and reviewing

	Less than 6 months		6 to 12 months		12 months and over		All	
	N	%	N	%	N	%	N	%
All plan items	449	100	632	100	491	100	1572	100
Implemented	299	67	426	67	340	67	1065	68
Implemented within timescale	67	15	74	12	88	18	229	15
Unplanned changes	123	27	155	25	162	33	440	28

Figure 9.2 sets out the outcomes for the major topics of decisions. In all, over six out of ten decisions were implemented. The categories of decision most successfully implemented were legal and placement plans: over eight out of ten were put into practice. The least successful category included the plans for contact. Plans concerned with health, education and other services achieved moderate success.

Attaining planned goals within set timescales was far more challenging and occurred in little more than an eighth of cases. On this particular outcome, legal decisions failed the test more often than any other type of decisions. At the higher end of the scale, health and education plans achieved virtually the same results as placement plans.

The number of unplanned changes was relatively high. It measured more than a quarter of the size of the total number of decisions. There were about four unplanned changes for every ten implemented decisions. Health was the category where such changes were most frequent; by contrast, unplanned legal changes were the least likely to take place.

It can be suggested that the outcomes of planning for older and younger children are likely to be rather different. For example, there was some evidence that social workers saw planning for adolescents as particularly challenging because their volatility quickly put plans out of date. Almost six out of ten thought this was 'sometimes true' and a quarter considered it 'often true'.

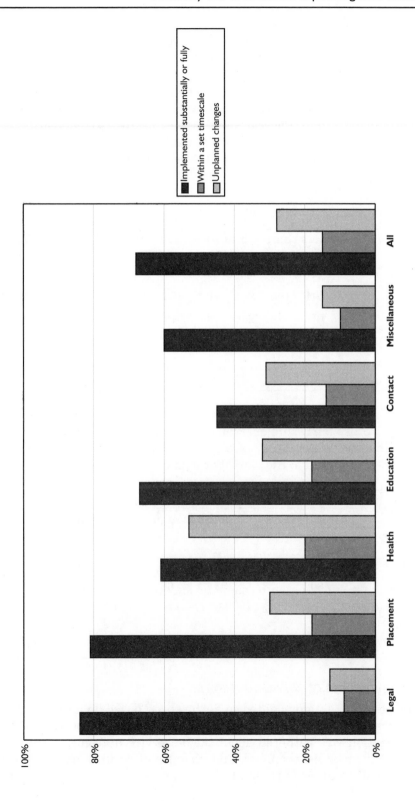

Figure 9.2   Outcomes of plans, by category of decisions. All decisions N = 1572

Table 9.13 compares the outcomes data for different age groups. The table reveals few clear differences in the outcomes of plans for the various age groups. One notable difference is between the slightly higher rates of implementation for those aged up to ten years and the slightly lower rates for young people over that age. In addition, the implementation of plans within timescales was highest for five- to ten-year-olds. Nor was there any substantial difference between the outcomes for children in different ethnic categories or between children in care or accommodated under S.20.

Table 9.13   Outcomes of plans, by age group

	Less than 5 years		5 to 10 years		11 to 15 years		16 years and over		Total	
	N	%	N	%	N	%	N	%	N	%
All plan items	404	100	361	100	496	100	311	100	1572	100
Implemented	291	72	266	74	317	64	191	61	1065	68
Implemented within timescale	53	13	87	24	54	11	35	11	229	15
Unplanned changes	110	27	120	33	135	27	75	24	440	28

As Table 9.14 shows, the outcomes of plans in the local authority samples were also fairly similar. Plans were implemented most often in Midshire but the differences were small. The highest rate of unplanned changes was found in the Northborough cases.

Table 9.14   Outcomes of plans, by local authority

	Midshire		Northborough		Westside		Total	
	N	%	N	%	N	%	N	%
All plan items	414	100	502	100	656	100	1572	100
Implemented	302	73	333	66	430	65	1065	68
Implemented within time scale	49	12	89	18	91	14	229	15
Unplanned changes	95	22	180	36	165	25	440	28

Additional measures of service outcome

The planning data presented so far has been based on a varied range of timescales. In order to obtain another perspective in specific outcomes, information was gathered about major service outcomes – care placements, medical assessments, and changes of educational placement – which had occurred in the year leading up to the main review. It should be remembered that the children had been looked after for various periods during that year.

Care placements

The total number of separate care placements (rather than of moves) over the previous year was counted. Out of 176 cases, 85 (48 per cent) had experienced more than one placement during the year (range: one to six). So almost half the sample had in fact experienced more than one placement. This proportion looks rather higher than would have been expected on the basis of the large study of placements carried out some years ago (Rowe, Hundleby and Garnett, 1989).

The number of care placements was compared with the number of months that the children had been looked after in the previous year. The number of placements was significantly higher for those children who had been looked after for two to nine months in the previous year (Kruskal-Wallis p<.01), suggesting that the number of placements is at risk of increasing once a short 'honeymoon' phase is over but this risk is later reduced.

Unlike the findings of Rowe and her colleagues, the ages of children seemed not to mark any significant difference. Nor did their gender or ethnic category. It was, however, possible to discern a significantly higher number of placements among young people currently in residential and less dependent placements (Kruskal-Wallis p<.05). The number of placements was also significantly higher for children in Northborough, and for children in care (Kruskal-Wallis p<.05, p<.01). The findings do not necessarily lead to a simple set of conclusions but they do indicate some transitional points, such as the 'post-honeymoon' phase at which the number of placements increases. The findings add some further data to the consideration of planning outcomes, in particular, by pointing to problematic outcomes for children in Northborough and for children in care. It will be remembered that in the previous section these were the categories showing higher rates of unplanned change.

Medical assessments

Data was collected from the files on the frequency of medical assessments during the previous year. In this case, the focus of the data collection was on assessments by medical practitioners. Because the Regulations are somewhat different for younger children these will be considered first of all.

The Regulations state that children under two years of age should receive two medical examinations each year (RCC 6). There were 26 children who were less that two years old. Only one of these children had received no medical assessment at all and this child had been looked after for less than a month in the previous year. Of the 12 children who had been looked after for six to 12 months, seven had been given just one assessment and the remaining five had received from two to five. These small-scale findings indicate a high rate of medical surveillance for the youngest children in the sample.

If we now turn to older children, for whom one examination a year should take place, a clear majority of these had received at least one assessment: out of 140 cases, only 37 (or 27 per cent) had undergone no assessment at all in the previous year. Less than a tenth of that group had been looked after for under a month, suggesting that delays were not the main reason for non-assessment. The young person's age was a more significant indicator: almost three quarters of the non-assessed cases were over ten years old (chi-square p<.01).

The data revealed further indications of a lower rate of assessment among adolescent girls: almost half the 11- to 15-year-old girls received no assessment, compared with less than a fifth of the equivalent category of boys (chi-square p<.05). This finding was apparently not due to any difference in the proportion of the year that the girls and boys had been looked after, since there was no significant difference of this kind.

The number of medical assessments was significantly higher for young people on the child protection register (Kruskal-Wallis p<.01). There was no significant difference connected with the broad ethnic category of the young person, the type of placement, or whether the young person was in care.

The findings indicate that a majority of the cases had received at least one medical assessment in an annual period. Confirming the conclusions of Chapter 4, the main specific area of difficulties seems to lie in the lack of an appropriate service response to the needs of adolescent girls.

Changes of educational placement

Another perspective on educational outcomes was gained by collecting data on any changes of educational placement (other than normal age-related transitions) which occurred in the previous year. A major aim was to discover whether the number of placements was associated with instability in schooling – a danger specifically identified in the Regulations (APC(G) 4(1), Sch. 3). Other recent research, using a community sample, has shown that changes of school and changes of address are associated with educational difficulties (Ward, 1995). Hence this was an important topic to explore. Because the schooling transitions of young people with disabilities may be influenced by their special needs, they were left out of the analysis.

The analysis concentrated on young people of compulsory school age, many of whom had been looked after for most of the previous year. Of 84 children of compulsory school age (excluding those looked after for reasons connected with their disabilities), 54 (or almost two thirds) had been looked after for between six and 12 months in the previous year.

Just over half (56 per cent) of the children had experienced more than one care placement; for this age group, there was no significant link between the number of care placements and the type of current placement (such as foster or residential care); nor did the differences among the local authorities reach statistical significance; but those children in care and those on the child protection register had more care placements than their counterparts (Kruskal-Wallis $p<.05$, $p<.05$).

Just under half (45 per cent) had experienced a change of school not due to age. The period of months looked after during the year was not associated with changing school. There was a small positive correlation between care placements and changes of school not due to age ($r=0.22$, $p<.05$). The present study therefore suggests that a higher number of care placements is part of a pattern of instability, but that it does not explain the whole story. For this group, changes of school not attributable to age were also associated with being placed on the child protection register at the time of the main review (Kruskal-Wallis $p<.05$). Hence, child protection concerns may have influenced the location of placements and of schools. These findings put into sharp relief the complexity of the considerations underlying the plans of particular groups of children.

So far, the focus has been on young people of compulsory school age. For those over that age, an additional degree of educational choice is likely to be available. When young people at least 16 years old were included in the analysis, there was in fact a very small increase in the correlation between changes in educational placement and the number of care placements ($r=0.24$, $p<.05$), suggesting, at the very least, that members of the older group were undergoing transitions at a similar rate to their younger counterparts, though in a rather different context with wider choices.

Social workers' perspectives

The outcomes of planning and reviewing are indeed complex, making it harder to arrive at a blanket conclusion about the operational value of the current system. But it is possible to throw further light on the system by comparing the opinions of those professionals who are perhaps most closely in touch with those outcomes – social workers. There were 33 social workers with experience of reviews before the Children Act 1989: only three considered that currently reviews were less effective than they had been; 13 regarded them as being similarly effective; and 17, or more than half the group, identified an improvement. Let us now return to the detailed findings themselves in order to identify more closely the operational strengths and weaknesses of the planning and reviewing system.

Discussion of findings

Looking backwards at planning histories opened up a perspective on a shifting, dynamic scene. However, the potential complexities of child care planning processes are not a new discovery. For example, the number of different meetings held before a child becomes looked after has been noted in other research.

> It is possible for all these meetings to be running together at staggered intervals, so that the social worker is kept busy moving from one to the other. (Owen, 1992, p.78)

Owen questions the continuity of a process in which different personnel appear at different meetings and too little occurs between meetings to warrant follow-up. The evidence of the present study indicates that there was some flexibility and responsiveness in the holding of meetings to meet the contingencies and circumstances of particular cases. This was most obvious in dealing with the young, the vulnerable, and those undergoing changes of placement.

The problems seemed to lie in maintaining continuity and involvement as different types of meeting with different chairs followed one another. In relation to all these types of meeting, the average attendances of children and parents over the sample periods were comparatively low, raising questions about their effective involvement. This seemed to be an issue with implications for the long term, as well as the short term. While the attendances of children seemed to rise according to their age, the attendances of mothers declined and this decline also occurred as the period of being looked after increased. The formal exclusion of parents from meetings was linked to the evolution of plans that marginalised their role. The reduction in the frequency of meetings also raises a further question about the responsiveness of the system to the needs of those in long-term placements. The care plans for this group were varied enough to suggest that they require consistent individual attention. It is not enough to rely on the apparent security of a longstanding placement.

The issue of continuity is also raised by the findings on planning outcomes. A major conclusion of the follow-up study is that a large number of planning decisions were made whose outcomes never became clear. In some cases this is because the planning decisions were not specific enough for their outcomes to be assessed. In others, it is because the information about outcomes was not collated and reported. This suggests that planning and reviewing are seen as discrete activities.

In general, the findings demonstrate a rate of decision implementation above 60 per cent. But the rate of implementation within a planned timescale was much lower. In some cases, this was because the timescale had not elapsed before the next meeting. But the most common reason for not meeting this criterion was not having set a timescale in the first place. Unplanned changes were more frequent than plans implemented on time. In the light of this general picture, there were some variations in the patterns for major decision topics which deserve comment because they seem to tell us something about the priorities of current planning for looked-after children.

Legal planning is one field where purposeful planning seems to be feasible. The local authority can hold a meeting at any time in order to discuss alterations to a child's legal status. By holding legal planning meetings in emergencies, it can turn even these situations into opportunities for planning. It is also capable of ensuring that a given legal status is maintained.

A high rate of implementation of legal decisions has been found in other studies (Sinclair, Garnett and Berridge, 1995). However, legal timescales are complex and depend on the operation of both legal administrators and the courts.

> *Case 142.* The mother of this three-year-old had been diagnosed as a paranoid schizophrenic. After assessment, it was decided to place the child for adoption. Before this happened the plan was to seek a care order within the next two months.
>
> The outcome was a care order granted in the third month.

As in this case, few legal plans were implemented within set timescales. Placement decisions were also often implemented but infrequently within timescales. As was previously noted, social workers were significantly sceptical about placement timescales.

The data on care placements in the previous section show that many children had multiple placements, some of which were presumably planned and others not. The higher rate of unplanned changes for particular categories, such as children in care, was confirmed by the data on multiple placements.

For other issues, practitioners seemed to exert less control over the outcomes. By comparison with legal and placement decisions, the patterns for health and education outcomes displayed only moderate rates of implementation and, in the case of health, a greater level of unplanned changes.

These plans are, of course, dependent on inter-agency cooperation. Yet education and health professionals have their own planning processes. In some cases, for example, it emerged that regular medical surveillance took place which was not incorporated in the local authority's plan. In other cases, health practitioners had their own assumptions about planning, for example, setting preconditions, such as settling the child in a stable care placement, before undertaking complex mental health work. The data on the rate of children receiving medical assessments suggests that practice frequently came up to the expectations set by the

Regulations. Yet these represent minimum baselines for health assessment and substantive planning will entail more than this.

Working with educational agencies could also present challenges. Special educational placements were sometimes the subject of complex procedural negotiations. Among social workers, there was a degree of doubt about the commitment of educational professionals to plans: almost six out of ten considered that such commitment was 'sometimes' missing and one in five thought this was 'often true'. Changes of educational placement seemed to be significantly correlated with multiple care placements but only to a comparatively small extent. There are a range of issues in this particular interdisciplinary relationship, and multiple placements constitute only one of them.

Most social workers perceived the commitment of other agencies to plans as 'sometimes' problematic. They took a similar view about the reliability of other agencies in implementing their part in plans.

Contact plans were least frequently carried out as intended. Unlike other plans, these depend very substantially on successful work with carers, children and parents. Timescales for contact plans were rarely specific and detailed. Contact plans typically contained a clause about the frequency of contact but it was assumed that plans would come into effect immediately and the arrangements were open-ended. Hence, by definition, implementation within given timescales was relatively infrequent.

The issues around contact draw attention to the plans made for future social work input. Miscellaneous service plans sometimes referred to future social work contacts or to tasks that the social worker would carry out. Some included specific commitments to provide a level of social work service but this was comparatively rare. Formulas such as 'continuing social work support' were routinely employed. Among the social workers who responded to the survey, there was a very lukewarm response to the idea that the frequency of social work visits could be laid down in a plan and revised only at a review. Little more than a quarter of respondents judged this proposal to be practical. The planning of operational social work services seems to be unsystematic. Even for child protection cases, recent research has found that the existence of social work plans and progress summaries is still very variable (Gibbons, Conroy and Bell, 1995).

In all, the data on implementation indicate that priority has been given to securing legal and placement outcomes. The outcomes of work with other agencies were less predictable and less likely to be related to the child care plan. Work with families on issues such as contact is less susceptible to straightforward implementation and requires not only careful assessment but also a good deal of work. A lack of specificity in plans for social work input raises questions about how such tasks are to be addressed.

Key findings

- Examination of a sample period for each case produced the following average findings: there were about four planning and reviewing meetings in over 11 months; there was at least one significant planning meeting in addition to the reviews which took place; the number of actual reviews fell somewhat below the number expected; there were two different chairs for the meetings that took place over the sample period.

- On average, the older children attended more meetings than the younger ones, though even the oldest group did not, on average, attend more than two thirds of meetings. Attendances of mothers declined steadily across the age range; the attendances of fathers were very low and also tended to decline.

- Over a fifth of parents were excluded from meetings, mainly because the care plan seemed not to involve them any further.

- The outcomes of 1,572 planning decisions were investigated.

- The highest rates of implementation were for legal and placement decisions (over 80 per cent); moderate rates were found for education (67 per cent) followed by health and miscellaneous services (61 and 60 per cent respectively); the lowest rate was for contact decisions (45 per cent).

- Implementation within set timescales was much less frequent, ranging from 9 per cent (legal) to 20 per cent (health).

- When the numbers of original decisions were compared with the proportions of subsequent unplanned changes, it was found that unplanned change was nearly as frequent as implementation within set timescales, ranging from a ratio of 13 per cent (legal) to 53 per cent (health).

10. The regulatory strategy and the future of planning to care

Introduction

We now return to the starting point for the whole project – the Children Act 1989 and its Guidance and Regulations on planning and reviewing (Volume 3, Ch. 2, Ch. 8). Before drawing final conclusions about their implementation it is time to look at them again and to ask why they appear in a particular form.

Chapter 2 gave an account of the evaluative methodology applied to the documentation. We identified no less than 13 substantive topics and under each heading listed specific and detailed considerations mentioned in the paragraphs of Guidance and Regulations. Looking at that evaluative scheme again, it is clear that the planning and reviewing requirements are both complex and diverse. For example, the very first of our key topics was the connection between plans and reviews: despite the fact that they were treated in separate Guidance and Regulations, did local authorities understand their essential continuity? Similar questions were posed by the variety of subjects to be covered by a plan, the challenge of producing a clear procedural framework, taking a cohesive approach to the different categories of children being looked after, and so on. The requirements of partnership (with children, parents and other significant people) and co-working (with other agencies) added new aspects to the process. The detailed assessment and planning prescriptions for substantive topics, such as health and education, underlined the intensive nature of the planning and review requirements.

Why are the Guidance and Regulations so comprehensive and detailed? Earlier, in Chapter 1, we noted that the knowledge base was deemed sufficient to justify the prescription of a detailed regulatory framework, the purpose of which was to promote good practice and to regulate out poor practice. All this was designed to be translated into local procedures which in turn would enhance social work practice and ultimately affect outcomes for young people. In other words, the complexity was part and parcel of a specific regulatory strategy.

In some ways, the regulatory strategy appeared risky and ambitious precisely because it packed in so much detail that had to be transmitted down the ladder, from procedure to practice, and finally to children themselves. It rested on the supposition that local authorities would pick up complex messages without any specific process of education or information-sharing. The survey of local authority documentation was an important initial test of the strategy. The findings suggested that the strategy had surmounted its first hurdle: about 70 per cent of the rating scores rose to the mark of 'adequate' or better, suggesting that many of the key messages had been absorbed by local authorities. Though the survey raised some questions about a relative lack of emphasis on informing users and working with other agencies, these were deficiencies that could be remedied by greater attention to guiding principles, such as open and shared ownership of procedures.

In looking at the next step in the regulatory strategy – the level of practice – we have presented so far a series of separate findings on particular elements of the process. In order to evaluate the whole, we need now to concentrate on fundamental issues and this means going back again to the functions of planning and reviewing. After an analysis of how the regulatory strategy has been translated into practice, there follows a discussion of how it might be refurbished and, finally, an outline of the steps that could be taken to clarify and enhance current systems.

The functions of planning and reviewing

The Guidance and Regulations appear to be the product of a long history of reflection which addressed directly or indirectly the functions of reviews. Previous research identified three major functions which reviews were thought to be capable of fulfilling. These functions were summarised by Sinclair (1984), as follows:

- supervision and monitoring of practice
- facilitating an effective planning process
- promoting participation by children and parents.

In evaluating their findings the researchers gave various emphases to the functions of reviews: Gardner (1985) and Fox (1988) focused on the participation of children and parents respectively, while McDonnell and Aldgate (1984b) proposed an external review system dedicated to monitoring. How the particular functions were to be related and balanced seemed open to a variety of definitions.

By the time of the Children Act there was evidence of an active planning culture in local authorities though the quality of planning was patchy (Robbins, 1990; Department of Health, 1991a). The time seemed ripe to give expression to the full range of planning considerations that had emerged over the previous period. We have already seen how many of the research conclusions absorbed into the Children Act referred to detailed considerations, such as taking into account a child's culture, language, ethnic origin, and religion. However, many of these specific messages were concerned with the substance of planning rather than with the concept of the review. Hence in the Guidance and Regulations there is a welter of specific messages which may detract from a thorough appreciation of what it is saying about the basic functions of reviews.

At the beginning of the Guidance, there is a very firm statement about the continuity of planning and reviewing.

> 8.3   The concept of review as governed by the Reviews of Children Cases Regulations and discussed in this Guidance is a continuous process of planning and reconsideration of the plan for the child.

It makes clear that the review is not a response to a complaint or part of a line management supervision of a decision. Nor is it a case conference. The Guidance is very insistent that *planning* is at the heart of a review.

> . . . A review of an individual child's case is held solely to make plans in the interests of safeguarding and promoting that child's welfare. (para. 8.4)

The review includes any such meeting regardless of its title; in this sense, planning meetings count as reviews, or parts of reviews. The Guidance puts this point as follows:

> Any meeting that is convened for the purpose of considering the child's case in connection with any aspect of the review of that case falls within the scope of these Regulations. Whether such a meeting is called a planning meeting or a review or review meeting will not determine whether it is in fact part of a review. This will depend on the purpose for which the meeting is convened. (para. 8.3)

From our discussion with many local authority representatives, it is evident that these statements about a review's functions are not well understood. The last extract is seen as particularly obscure. What it seems to be saying is that the review is not only fundamentally about planning, it is also the primary locus of planning: other meetings are part of the review. However, this second point is hardly transparent.

Of the possible functions identified by previous research it is the planning function which is given primary attention by the Guidance and Regulations. Reviewing becomes virtually identical with planning.

> The first review meeting is the occasion on which the planning process is most clearly illustrated as being inseparable from the review process. (para. 8.10)

Nonetheless, other functions are acknowledged:

> . . . In revising existing arrangements or establishing new procedures, responsible authorities should ensure that their review system provides for:
> - the full participation of both children and parents in the decision-making process;

- a structured coordinated approach to the planning of child care work in individual cases; and
- a monitoring system for checking the operation of the review process. (para. 8.8)

This statement is reminiscent of the threefold list of functions identified by Sinclair (1984). However, it is clear from what has been cited earlier that the supervisory component, in the sense of line management, has been relegated to a back seat. Rather, the intention of monitoring is more general than supervision; it is 'to afford an overview of effectiveness in decision-making and social work practice' (para. 8.26). There is also an important reference to 'structure' in the approach to planning, which deserves to be noted.

In the next section, we look at what the evidence of the fieldwork study tells us about these functions in practice.

Evidence of the functions in practice

The first question to ask is whether there is evidence that each of these functions have been fulfilled adequately. Were children and parents fully participating in decision making? Was there a structured and coordinated process of planning? Did this involve proper attention to the individual components of planning, such as inquiry, assessment and decision making? Were there appropriate multi-agency contributions? What were the outputs of reviews? How effectively were plans put into practice? And, not least, how were these processes monitored?

Participation by children and parents

The research has produced a cluster of evidence about forms of participation by children and parents, including consultation, attendance at review meetings and involvement in decision making. By comparison with practice in the 1980s, there are signs of a more systematic approach to promoting participation: most children were consulted about their wishes and feelings and their attendance at review meetings was normal; again, most mothers, and a significant proportion of fathers, were consulted and many, if not most, parents attended review meetings. In terms of attendance at meetings, there were encouraging findings on participation by teenagers, by parents of children in short-term accommodation under S.20, and by parents of children on the child protection register and those subject to interim care orders. However, particular categories of children and adults were much less frequently consulted: children under eight years of age; parents of older children; and those with children on full care orders. Patterns of attendance at review meetings showed similar variations.

Once the whole sequence of planning and reviewing meetings was examined, there was evidence of a much lower level of attendance at planning meetings other than reviews, the reasons for which deserve further discussion. It seemed that the standards applied to planning meetings were less clear and rigorous, compared with those applied to reviews. It was disappointing that information about the results of the review was not shared more frequently with children and parents.

Though trends in attendance at meetings were positive, the evidence of interviews with young people and their parents showed the other side of the coin; their experience of trying to participate appeared uncomfortable and frustrating. We shall reflect later on what this tells us about the functioning of reviews.

Structured and coordinated planning processes

In addition to consultation, the Guidance refers to three other components of the planning process: inquiry, assessment and decision making. Moving further down the line, the output and effectiveness of the planning process over time are the focus of concern.

The initial stages of planning

The Guidance does not specify a general format for undertaking the components of planning. Hence, it has been left to local authorities to consider how they should encourage and facilitate good practice by their staff. However, there has been official support for a structured approach (Department of Health, 1991a). In this context, we have seen the development and dissemination of the *Looking After Children* (LAC) materials. These are becoming part of local authority systems, alongside the routine forms which they partly displace. Among the fieldwork authorities, Westside was the only user of the early LAC forms at the time of the research.

Evidence of inquiry was found in the great majority of cases. However, its quality was varied: only a quarter of the cases were rated as 'positive' or 'excellent'. Better results were associated with the Basic Facts Sheet (predecessor of the LAC Essential Information Record), which followed a structured approach.

A central focus of the preparation for a review is an assessment of the child's needs as a whole, bearing in mind that the Guidance and Regulations specifies a series of topics to be considered at a review. The Assessment and Action Record is part of a structured system designed to fulfil these requirements, though it is directed at long term cases, rather than new admissions. In this study, the Record proved to be the most common structured assessment format used at reviews. There was no evidence of other materials like those appended to the *Patterns and Outcomes* study (Department of Health, 1991a). Even at critical stages of transition, formal assessments were relatively infrequent: formal parenting assessments, including 'Orange Book' assessments, were found in less than a quarter of those cases where the child was on the child protection register and had been looked after for up to a year; only one child in this category received a psychological or psychiatric assessment. Even in such circumstances, therefore, most of the main assessments for reviews were completed on routine forms. Similarly, in Westside, Records were found to apply to less than half the reviews.

The research evidence raises questions about the function of assessments in relation to the specific needs and circumstances of children over time (Sinclair, Garnett and Berridge, 1995). If the Guidance calls for regular consideration of certain topics, does this mean going through similar assessment processes each time? Or should there be some guidelines or expectations about the kinds of assessment appropriate to particular circumstances or needs?

One of the general conclusions was that good paper forms appeared to enhance the quality of inquiry, consultation and plans. This was partly associated with the use of LAC forms but other instruments (in particular, consultation forms for children and parents) seemed to have a positive effect. If the forms are poorly designed, practitioners do not transcend these weaknesses but they do respond to the strengths of better forms. The forms can also influence the whole process: for example, good consultation forms can refocus attention on preparations for a meeting, rather than leaving matters till the last moment. In such ways, paper forms can function as means of organising and facilitating a better planning process.

Work with education and health agencies

The Guidance and Regulations establish clear expectations about a structured, coordinated approach to health and education issues. The evidence about the frequency of educational assessment is encouraging: the great majority of children in mainstream schools were assessed, as were nearly all those in special education. However, young people in further education were the least likely to receive an assessment. The general quality of educational assessment was rather more disappointing: four out of ten were rated as 'limited'.

Health assessments were identified for three quarters of the cases, but there were significant differences among the local areas in this proportion. Adolescent young women were less likely to be involved than other categories of young people. In the great majority of cases, the assessment fell within the intervals set by the Regulations. There were some problems in meeting specific regulatory requirements, such as references to health histories. Just over a quarter of the assessments were rated as 'limited'. Additional data on assessments over the period of a year again revealed a lower frequency of assessment for adolescent young women.

A wide range of practitioners in education and health agencies were responsible for assessments, from specialists to frontline workers. Hence, good coordination was necessary but evidence of it was limited, particularly in education. Further data on changes of school placement highlighted the importance of integrated planning for educational and care placements.

A major means of involving these agencies in decision making seemed to be to invite them to review meetings. Indeed, representatives from education were the most frequently represented of the agencies: they attended a quarter of review meetings. However, this meant that, for many children, liaison had to occur through other contacts. Clearly attendance at meetings was not a sufficient, nor necessarily the best, way to create a common purpose and commitment.

In just two thirds of the sample, education and health plans were identified. When outcomes were examined, it became apparent that by comparison with other aspects of the plans there was moderate success in implementing health and education decisions; unplanned changes were particularly noticeable in delivering services for health. Questions must be raised about the extent to which the system promoted coordinated planning in conjunction with these agencies.

Decision making

In Chapter 5, the process of decision making for a review was found to be centred on a single review meeting typically lasting for about an hour.

The status and identity of meeting chairs conformed with local procedures. Reviews were therefore taken seriously as an aspect of the local authority's decision making for children. The concentration of attention on the meeting, however, frequently appeared to involve a wider circle of attenders than the Guidance seemed to envisage. Hence, a significant proportion of meetings became general forums for people with a range of involvements in the plan, rather than being sharply focused on a core group.

The conduct of business appeared fairly relaxed without much attention to preliminaries or formalities. In some respects, scrutiny of the care plan was selective rather than rigorous and searching, but this left plenty of room for discussion of significant issues. In keeping with the informal atmosphere, decisions were quickly announced and sometimes couched in vague or unspecific terms. The meetings could be described as primarily exercises in communication. The emphasis on substantive discussion meant that the framework for decision making, the role of the chairs in this and the rationale of the decisions all tended to be taken for granted.

The strengths of the decision-making process lay in opening up topics for general discussion by a fairly wide group involved in the care plan. Its weaknesses seemed to be associated with the restricted scope of scrutiny, the lack of attention to the context of decision making, and the tendency to avoid specifics. In terms of the general functions of reviews, the findings prompt queries about the extent of the preparatory consultative work, in that participants were occupied with exchanging views that might have been crystallised earlier. This focus permitted attenders to gloss over the 'tough' issues: how good is the overall care plan? Who takes decisions? What should actually be done?

Output and effectiveness

When the plans emerging from reviews were examined in Chapter 8, it was found that the strongest positive feature was their attention to allocating responsibility for carrying out the plan: eight out of ten cases met this criterion to an acceptable extent. In terms of comprehensiveness, two thirds of the plans were rated as adequate or better. The weakest area was the setting of timescales: almost half the plans that referred to timescales gave them limited attention. The social work survey indicated that practitioners were indeed sceptical about planning timescales. Forward planning for the next review was often confined to fixing a date at the maximum interval permissible under the Regulations.

The links between planning and reviewing were examined closely in Chapter 9, which showed the dynamism of the process over time. Though reviews were typically late, an average of over two statutory reviews occurred within an average interval of 11 months. However, the idea of bringing forward a review, where necessary, did not seem to be accepted in practice; instead, a variety of planning meetings were held. Most social workers thought that planning meetings were significantly different from reviews and could be used to make decisions about the plan. The consensus was: 'We can't wait for a review.' Indeed, meetings were most frequently held for younger children, those undergoing changes of placement, and those in the first year of being looked after.

This separation of planning from reviewing was associated with several difficulties: children and parents attended a limited proportion of all the meetings which occurred; timescales for implementing planned decisions were often indefinite; and monitoring of previous decisions was fairly cursory. Once again, the evidence pointed to a lack of consistent standards.

When the outcomes of some 1,500 decisions were examined, over six tenths were found to have been implemented. Legal and placement decisions were the categories that were most successfully implemented. The least successful were decisions about contact with parents, while decisions concerned with health, education and other services achieved moderate success.

Attaining planned goals within set timescales could only be said to occur in little more than an eighth of cases, partly due to the failure to fix timescales. Unplanned changes were more frequent than implementing decisions on time. There was little evidence that the pattern of outcomes differed significantly among categories of children or among the local authority samples.

In Chapter 7, the survey of arrangements for chairing underlined the problem of ensuring that decisions were not only objective but also carried out. Whereas line managers were well placed to carry out decisions, they were perceived as lacking objectivity. Independent chairs were perceived as objective but did not possess sufficient executive power.

Monitoring

The findings of the fieldwork study revealed significant gaps in the actual arrangements for monitoring: in Rural Midshire, for example, there was no oversight of reviews by senior management, while in Northborough and Westside there was somewhat greater management oversight. Authority-wide information about reviews was rudimentary.

The role of chairs in case monitoring tended to be limited; even the independent chairs did not seem to have the information to check thoroughly on what had happened since the last review and their style of chairing was not very dissimilar from supervising team managers. The chairing survey in Chapter 7 seemed to indicate that better monitoring of cases was possible when the chair was taken by specialist reviewing officers or other managers with specific responsibilities.

In seeking to answer our first major question, we can conclude that each of the main functions was fulfilled to a different degree. It is clear that they are also complex, in different ways, and it is important to assess how they interact.

The compatibility of functions

The second major question which the study should help to resolve is how far these broad functions are compatible in practice. The following problems were identified, many of which are to do with the problem of reconciling participation with coordination. There is always a danger that a complex process will be reduced to a series of separate mechanisms. As will be seen, too often these difficulties appeared to stem from an over-mechanical approach to what are fundamentally aspects of a process.

Partnership with parents was constrained by factors associated with the planning process. There is evidence that the progress of plans can in itself lead to the effective marginalisation and exclusion of parents from participation (most obviously, for parents in adoption cases). Contact decisions were implemented on a less frequent basis than other decisions.

One of the principal mechanisms for coordinating planning – the review meeting – was found to be a difficult experience for young people, raising questions about how this could be improved, while ensuring effective coordination with a range of service providers. Lack of preparation was compounded by exposure to insensitive questions and substantial groups of adults.

This problem highlighted the question of the role and function of chairs. Should the priority be to maximise participation or to ensure an optimum level of coordination? The priority given to coordination, compared with participation, was illustrated by the finding that service providers attended review meetings far more systematically than people who might offer support to children or their parents. Nor did participation rate as a key issue for respondents to the national survey when evaluating their chairing systems.

Just as 'the meeting' caused discomfort to young people, a similar question mark must be set against the 'medical examination' which may have deterred some young women from involvement in health matters.

Another sign of rigidity was the separation of planning from reviewing. This seemed to detract from the overall frequency of participation, because there were no clear standards or rules governing participation at planning meetings as distinct from reviews.

Participation was diminished because young people and their parents received insufficient information that might have clarified the planning process as a whole. The priority seemed to be picking up information from them rather than engaging in a process of dialogue.

The weaknesses of monitoring prevented managers and practitioners from identifying and reflecting on these problems. For example, they lacked significant information by which they could evaluate the participation of children or parents; nor were they helped to examine the effectiveness of plans comprehensively.

There is some way to go before the functions of reviews are properly fulfilled in practice and tensions between these functions need to be resolved. A greater willingness to conceive reviewing as a process may help to ease these tensions. The next step in the argument is to consider how these functions can be related more coherently and systematically. For the remainder of this chapter, the implications of these findings will be our concern.

Orchestrating the functions of planning and reviewing

This section seeks to identify the key dimensions of a coherent approach to planning and reviewing. In order to relate the major functions of reviews coherently, the fundamental elements of planning should be clearly identified and then linked to the idea of reviewing as a process.

The point of departure for planning is a cogent assessment of the child's individual needs which involves the consideration of objectives, both long term and short term, and the specification of means by which these can be achieved. Alongside this, an open process of consultation and decision making should reflect in a sensitive manner the relative contributions of all the participants, who will vary in number, function and organisational role as the care plan requires. The more extensive the care plan, the greater the priority that must be given to integrating all its aspects.

By their nature, children's needs change over time, as do the circumstances of their parents and carers. A good planning and reviewing process should be designed to address these issues of development and change positively over time.

Reviewing is not therefore simply stocktaking; it must be a process, rather than an event occurring at some fixed administrative point. Bringing together information and views from the child and members of the care network, it draws upon these to create executive plans which are at a later stage subject to further review and amendment. The process requires active and sensitive coordination, typically involving a social worker and supervisory staff.

As children attain an increasing self-awareness and a capacity to express their views, their role becomes more central. The research has shown that planning and reviewing has not taken account sufficiently of this self-awareness and of the emotional significance which attaches to being the subjects of reviews. It is not child-centred practice to put the child 'on stage' at a meeting. Instead young people should be encouraged to develop their sense of responsibility and ownership of the whole planning process, by encouraging their involvement in setting the agenda, asking questions, and expecting follow-up.

The same considerations apply to parents. There is evidence that they are positively involved if it is clear that they have a role in the child's future. Even those parents of children on the child protection register or subject to interim care orders are frequent attenders at reviews. It is when orders are confirmed and sustained that their practical participation declines.

The particular plans of children differ in the nature of their objectives and in the mechanisms and timescales which these entail. Protecting vulnerable infants is a very different activity from supporting the parents of disabled children through short-term placements. In many cases this means that care planning has to confront a whole set of diverse uncertainties. Often it must engage with a complex world of powerful influences, some of which are outside the control of those involved in the immediate care network: these include legal decision making, school policies, health service administration and so on. By the same token it would be quite inappropriate for the full panoply of administrative decision making to fall on cases where the objectives of the care plan did not justify it.

It is important that the process has the capacity to be responsive and flexible so that, if plans run off course, new paths can be identified quickly and action can be taken effectively. Hence there will be differences in the rhythm of planning and reviewing, depending on the objectives of the plan and the practical steps necessary to keep the process on track. These differences make it more difficult to defend a rigid administrative timetable for reviews, based on fixed intervals. If reviews are to function as a mechanism for planning, they must reflect the actual timescales of planning.

To make review arrangements more consistent, it seems advisable to establish key principles and standards that are readily translated into practice. These should express the main functions of reviews in terms that make possible a flexible response to new needs and circumstances. The guiding principles for reviewing discussed in Chapter 2 form a useful set of criteria. Those responsible for case coordination periodically need to ask themselves systematic questions, such as the following:

- What have been the outcomes of the last review?
- Is a new assessment of need called for?
- Has the care plan been called into question by developments?
- Do its objectives need to be reformulated?
- Or is it a question of choosing new means to achieve the same ends?
- How integrated does the care plan now appear?
- How is the principle of sensitive, open and shared planning being upheld?
- How cogent is the planning process?
- How is the current planning process being recorded so that it can be monitored as part of a flexible but continuous long term process?

These questions should help practitioners to consider how to update the planning process and to decide how to begin its next stage.

However, the task of coordination does not stop there. One role of senior management is to ensure that the actual provision to meet need fully reflects the potential available. It should also ensure those responsible at case level are aware of a wider environment and make good use of the organisation's resources as a whole. Senior managers can help to improve the continuity of decision making by devising ways of mediating between the different stages of the planning sequence. The research has shown how the care network at the centre of the review process has to engage with a diverse set of decision making bodies, such as panels and conferences. Typically, review decisions take account of these problems by formulating certain decisions as recommendations rather than as action plans. They are also likely to be uncertain about the timescales that implementing such decisions might involve. Systems that clarify such options can help to knit these decision making processes together.

There is unlikely to be a way of simplifying decision making into some single model using a particular type of chair: no chairing system in the fieldwork study seemed to offer clear advantages, and the evidence of the national survey shows how the advantages and disadvantages of types of chairing were finely balanced. All chairs will have to confront a complex decision making environment. It is possible that one of the most useful roles of specialist reviewing officers might be to act as the linking and enabling agents in this environment.

The operation of a higher level coordinating function should go hand in hand with an effective monitoring system that looks at reviewing from a broad perspective, combining attention to issues of process and participation as well as output and effectiveness. There is a case for uniting the monitoring and the aggregate coordinating functions by insisting that information is not only collected but regularly scrutinised by those responsible for strategy development, so that procedures and services are constantly updated to meet new needs.

Planning and reviewing is a process that combines a range of different functions that need to be orchestrated. It should be possible to devise more effective ways of fulfilling those functions which forestall or at least minimise the risk of serious incompatibilities between them.

In the next section the policy implications of the research will be examined so that the main issues can be identified and taken forward in new initiatives.

Refocusing the fundamentals

As we saw earlier, the detail of the Guidance and Regulations was not a major obstacle to their translation into local policies and procedures. But the critical test of the strategy lay in the realm of practice. What is our final assessment of current practice? There is evidence that points to a greater degree of participatory planning than in the past. There are signs too that the importance of good coordination is being acknowledged. Some monitoring was thoughtful and assiduous. However, in considering the evidence as a whole, there is, using the old school report cliche, room for improvement.

The next crucial question concerns the source of these particular problems. How far do they derive from weaknesses in the Guidance and Regulations or from misinterpretations, or failures of implementation? In the next section we concentrate on the subject matter of the Guidance and Regulations, first and foremost because it is essential to identify any root problems, especially any that might make the regulatory framework unworkable, as distinct from being simply unacknowledged. These inherent problems are likely to be found in the areas where functional conflicts and dilemmas have been identified. However, the task of thoroughly renovating the regulatory framework, section by section, is not straightforward. Unless there is a clear focus, any revision carries the risk of further complicating a subject that, above all, needs illumination and clarification. Hence, we propose a new statement of fundamentals which may serve as a point of departure designed to give new clarity to key concepts and standards. This must take account of new practical developments, especially the wider adoption of the LAC materials.

Improving upon the current regulatory framework

So what are the core problems in the Guidance and Regulations and what would help to resolve them? There are a number of key issues which require greater clarification:

- the care plan
- the planning process
- reviewing
- concepts of participation
- the scope and timing of statutory reviews.

Care plan

Any new statement of fundamentals should make clear what is meant by a care plan. The basic concept of a care plan must be forward-looking, focusing on objectives and how to achieve them. A definition must also allow people to identify how the plan is progressing and whether it needs to be reconsidered. Too general a definition and almost any change will be seen as consistent with the plan; too specific a definition and the first hiccup will be perceived as a signal to re-examine it.

As previous chapters have made abundantly clear, the care plan defined by the Guidance contains a number of very specific elements and considerations (Ch. 2.62). The LAC Care Plan reflects these, but, in addition, has introduced the more general concept of an 'overall care plan'. We shall argue that this approach is not yet wholly satisfactory, giving insufficient emphasis to the developmental objectives of the Assessment and Action Records.

Part of the problem addressed by the LAC definition is that in the regulatory framework the plan is formally defined in terms of 'arrangements for placement'. But does this mean that the care plan ceases as soon as the placement ends? Must a fresh one be produced? Or are we really talking about a placement plan which is specific and applies only during the period of placement?

The solution adopted by the LAC system is to define what is called an 'overall care plan'. This contains several classified options, which are rather different in kind. Some, such as a plan for rehabilitation or adoption, refer to how parental responsibility is to be exercised; others, such as 'special residential placement', refer to a type of placement. The overall care plan remains valid even if the actual placement changes. In this way a placement agreement serves as a subsidiary planning document. The consequence is that a statutory review is supposed to happen whenever the overall plan is to be reconsidered. Indeed only a review can change the overall care plan.

This approach has obvious advantages over a narrow focus on a single placement. It also gives due weight to issues like health or contact that transcend the details of an individual placement. However, it must be clearly and consistently followed through, continually returning to the question of objectives. The long term objectives for young people will need to be adjusted as they grow and their circumstances change. It is true that Assessment and Action Records are designed to focus on developmental objectives and how these are to be achieved. Yet currently the LAC overall plans include some, like rehabilitation, that clearly represent future objectives and some, like special residential placement, that represent means of fulfilling long-term objectives. It is therefore possible for misunderstandings to arise. It would be better if the primacy of objectives was to be made absolutely clear throughout.

The main point here is that the consideration of future objectives is an ongoing process and it is important that the care plan contains developmental objectives regardless of the stability of the relationship between parent and child or of the placement. There is evidence from the study that the frequency of planning and reviewing decreases markedly the longer a child remains looked after. Sometimes this seems to be due to the feeling that there is little to review provided the placement remains stable. Yet this would be a recipe for long-term drift. The consistent use of Assessment and Action Records should make clear how new developmental targets can be defined and incorporated in the plan.

The overall care plan should contain a set of objectives that reflects an assessment of the child's developing needs in the long term. For example, an objective might be 'with appropriate support, to take increasing responsibility for looking after his or her own needs, over the next two years'. That might mean thinking about a sequence of types of placement, such as foster care, then supported living in the community, followed by 'independence' or eventually living with relatives.

In addition to the overall plan, the complete care plan will contain a description of the steps envisaged to be necessary for achieving the main objectives. These steps are likely to be more in the nature of executive arrangements about tasks, responsibilities, and specific timescales. In the present system they are one part of the business of a statutory re-view as the LAC form entitled 'Review of arrangements' correctly points out. The other main part is a review of the overall care plan. If it is clear that the overall plan is about objectives, the rest of the plan should fall into perspective. The complete care plan is a combination of objectives and the steps that are judged to be necessary to achieve them.

> *Key point*: The complete care plan should consist of objectives (the overall plan) and the steps that should be taken to achieve them (the executive arrangements).

A dynamic planning process

The Guidance makes clear that planning is a process, which consists of no less than four components: inquiry, consultation, assessment and decision making. The challenge for professionals is that the process is rarely a one-off exercise. It has to be repeated in some form at each review if there is to be a continuous and responsive development of the plan. First of all, the recorded facts of a case require regular updating so that the relevance of the plan can be compared with any significant developments. Similarly, consultations at a subsequent review will help to gauge the success of the plan's implementation and how the plan is currently perceived. It will be necessary to recognise that feelings about the plan may evolve in new directions and will need to be sensitively taken into account.

Assessment too should be conceived as a progression. At first sight, it may appear difficult to determine the kind of assessment which is appropriate at a particular point in time, especially when a substantial amount of assessment has been completed at some previous stage. However, decisions may have altered a child's circumstances significantly, presenting a new situation to be assessed. The main requirement is a clear agreement about the aims and objectives of the next assessment in the light of the progress of the plan and the current needs of the child.

Particular instruments will become useful only when the purpose of an assessment has been clearly determined. For those children who have significant long term needs, the great advantage of the LAC materials is that, as time passes, they guide social workers in asking the right questions, focusing on objectives for the child. Use of the materials should make it possible to consider when to conduct more specific assessments of options such as rehabilitation or adoption (Bullock, Little and Millham, 1993; Sinclair, Garnett and Berridge, 1995). By sensitive consultation, observation and inquiry, it is possible to come to a judgement about the relevance of the plan to the current needs of, and long term objectives for, the child. The assessment should then be able to suggest options for decision making and to support a reasoned and cogent set of decisions.

If the assessment made by the social worker is to contribute to an integrated planning process it is crucial that the professionals in other agencies are enabled to work on parallel lines. For example, it is no use collecting data about a child's height or educational attainments if these are not put in any meaningful context, or do not help to shape thinking about the next stage in the child's development. Cooperative working around the Assessment and Action Records offers a structured path for this kind of multidisciplinary planning.

> *Key point*: A planning process forms part of a developing sequence in which the objectives of the plan and the current needs of the child are reconsidered on the basis of changing circumstances and fresh experience.

Reviewing

There should be a new statement about the functions of plans and reviews which unambiguously challenges the view that planning can be separated from reviewing. Though the Guidance defines a planning process, it is less clear about the review process. Yet the two processes should be consistent. As was stated at the beginning of the chapter, it is necessary to clarify the constituent parts of a review, particularly meetings with different titles (Volume 3, Ch. 8.3) and different functions, such as case conferences (Ch. 8.4). If meetings form parts of a review, then the review is a process. But in other statements, the review is treated as an event. For example, the Guidance seems to use the terms 'review' and 'review meeting' interchangeably at times.

> If the need arises for substantial changes to the plan, then **the date of the next review** should be brought forward. (emphasis added) (para. 8.6)

> Before the **review** is arranged the field social worker responsible for the case, in discussion with his line manager, should identify who should be **invited**. (emphases added) (para. 8.10)

Hence, there is a subtle contradiction in the Guidance between the idea that different meetings can be part of a review and the idea that a meeting on a given date constitutes the review. It may have given some credence to the notion persisting in local authority circles that planning and reviewing are separate activities and are events, rather than processes.

The current Guidance on reviews is heavily focused on the arrangements for the holding of a meeting. Though the Guidance allows for a number of meetings, there is a temptation for practitioners to concentrate as much as possible on a single meeting. Indeed they may wish to do so because they are aware of the expectation in the Guidance that children and parents should normally attend the 'whole of the review'. This expectation is complemented by the idea that a core group consisting of the child, parents, social worker and carer(s) should be identified. However, if the meeting is to be largely confined to a 'core group', it is difficult to see how all the business of the review can be completed without a thorough preparation beforehand, which may involve subsidiary contacts and meetings with a range of providers and decision makers. If this preparatory process is to be meaningful it needs to be fully acknowledged and recorded. The message that the review is a process, and not just a meeting, has to be reinforced.

If there is to be continuity in the planning of children's care it is vital that the definition of a review is consistent with the definition of a plan. The first task of a review is of course to look back at the progress of the plan; this fulfils one of the monitoring functions of reviews. But once these lessons have been identified the process of reviewing is very close indeed to the process of planning. If the planning process has focused accurately on objectives that serve to meet the developing needs of the child, then any adjustments to the plan are likely to be technical. However, if consultations and inquiries lead to the identification of new needs, then a redefinition of planning objectives must be contemplated.

Reviewing is therefore *planning* informed by *monitoring* – not a separate activity in its own right but a periodic continuation of planning assisted by the wisdom of hindsight. It is itself a process combining the distinct components of planning added to the monitoring of the current plan. The review cannot be reduced to a particular component, such as monitoring or decision making. It is never simply about reading a case report, checking the file or holding a meeting. These should be regarded as aspects of a process which involves carrying forward the planning of a child's care.

> *Key point*: Reviewing is a planning process that starts from a monitoring of the existing plan.

Participation

Although the Guidance talks about 'participation', it is not clear how participation is to be defined. In a previous chapter, the concept of participation was analysed into stages or levels, using the idea of a ladder. This analysis should prompt us to look more closely at such notions as 'consultation' and 'partnership'. We can then go on to look at more concrete suggestions for improvements in participation.

In relation to children, the use of the term 'consultation' derives from a basic principle of the Children Act, that decisions should take into account their wishes and feelings. In relation to parents, consultation is supported by the principles of parental responsibility and partnership. However, the concept of participation is rather more broad than consultation, on its own, might suggest. It is possible to identify levels of participation which, in the case of children, should reflect their knowledge and understanding. For example, consultation, by itself, may not signify very much unless it is accompanied by a process through which a child or parent absorbs information. A participant, in the truest sense of the word, takes an active role, having learnt about the topic and become familiar with the conventions of discussion and decision making. A partnership takes the process further, defining shared goals.

If participation is to be advanced, we might envisage the development of 'participation plans', especially for children. These should set objectives for increasing and deepening the participation of children and parents. These educational tasks can be taken forward in individual or group settings, by carers or by social workers.

The Guidance should specify more clearly that if children prefer not to attend meetings then alternative arrangements should be put on record (Ch. 8.16).

Though the Guidance states that children and parents may ask for a review and any such request should be taken seriously, there is no mechanism for enabling them to keep abreast of current events. Children and parents should normally be kept informed about external decision-making processes and consultative meetings with other professionals, so that they can give their views and say whether or not they wish to ask for a full review. These discussions should be noted and attached to the next review record.

A more participatory approach to health care planning would be encouraged by a change in the Regulations concerning 'medicals'. The Regulation stipulating that a regular medical examination take place should be revised so as to allow for a health assessment supervised by a medical practitioner and to contain provision for the making of a health plan agreed with a young person of sufficient understanding (RCC 6).

Above all, a forward-looking approach, increasing participation over time, should replace a static conception, going through a similar repetitive routine each time.

> *Key point*: Practitioners should understand that participation is a general concept, with various possible levels: 'consultation' is a first stage in participation; a 'participant' makes an active and informed contribution to decision making; 'partnership' implies shared goals.

Reviewing timescales

A clarification of what is meant by a care plan should focus attention towards fundamental objectives and away from the particulars of executive arrangements. Events which challenge the fundamental objectives of a plan will always trigger an immediate and full review. Other changes will need to be assessed and considered on their merits.

Taking account of planning timescales is not straightforward. There may well be some overlapping timescales as different aspects of a plan are put into practice and monitored. For example, if one of the educational objectives is to improve a child's reading, the various steps to achieve this and to monitor progress may involve a very different timescale from steps to safeguard the child, such as seeking an emergency protection order or instigating care proceedings.

It is possible that the timescales for such different objectives will bring tensions. For example, if a child protection assessment questions the child's current living situation, the educational placement might also need to be reviewed sooner than expected. There will be an understandable temptation in these circumstances to look for a pragmatic solution and to foreshorten or compress the planning process. Calling a meeting to settle all decisions about this plan may, on its own, mean that some of the strands have not been tied up. Maintaining the educational aspects of the plan can involve additional planning activity in consultation with the young person, the parents, teachers or educational managers. It will be necessary to decide whether the overall plan is under threat and thus whether an immediate statutory review is appropriate.

Key point: The timescales for reviewing should reflect the objectives of the plan and take account of their diversity.

The statutory review

Once the care plan is defined it becomes possible to identify more clearly the business of a statutory review under the Regulations, compared with any other consideration of arrangements. But if we think of the review as a process, where does this leave the statutory review? In terms of a meeting held at fixed intervals, the review, as we have seen, can appear artificial. However, the Regulations do not speak of fixed periods but of time limits. There is no reason why the review process should not vary in its format or frequency within these limits provided that certain fundamental standards are borne in mind throughout.

If a number of meetings have to be organised in order to define the plan or clarify the executive arrangements, then so be it. It is understandable that different objectives in the plan will involve a range of timescales. This may mean holding a series of meetings with different people in attendance.

The key requirement is that the main functions of the system are kept at the forefront – participation, structure, coordination, monitoring and so on.

The business of coordinating the review involves more than chairing a meeting; above all, it means monitoring and guiding the planning process, ensuring that it makes good sense not simply for the benefit of professionals but for children and parents too. Clear records of planning prior to the final statutory review meeting should be available.

A final statutory review meeting must be seen as a culmination of the reviewing process in which the complete care plan is clearly examined and the executive arrangements are discussed with the child and the parents.

Guidance on the timescales for reviews should therefore insist that these are minimum intervals and that the actual intervals should always reflect the objectives of the plan and the significance of the decisions to be taken, as they affect the whole care plan (RCC 3). Once the care plan has stabilised it is still advisable to look for natural landmarks in the child's life which might anchor the holding of a statutory review.

> *Key point*: A statutory review is a process of considering the whole care plan, concluded by a final child-centred meeting and the completion of all the pertaining records.

Implications for local authorities

In the previous section the discussion has focused on fundamental issues that clearly fall within the regulatory framework. However, there are other problems identified by the study which seem less attributable to the framework's imperfections. Local authorities have the responsibility and power to address such problems.

The general responsibilities of local authorities in relation to plans and reviews seem to be more weakly reflected in practice than in procedure documents. The Regulations make clear that local authorities must coordinate reviews, monitor them, and set in place arrangements for implementing decisions. Yet the Guidance refers to these comparatively briefly (Ch. 8.9; 8.24; 8.26). There is a good case for policy initiatives which help local authorities to appraise the state of their current arrangements and identify effective models of oversight.

Four specific issues should be the subject of attention: the status of care planning within the broader decision-making environment of local authorities; ensuring greater participation; multidisciplinary working; and monitoring of reviews.

The status of care planning

At any point in time, it should be possible to identify a care plan that represents the local authority's best judgement of the arrangements appropriate for an individual child. It is usually better for the plan to be formulated as a set of positive steps rather than as recommendations to a higher body.

Care planning is affected by the decisions of a variety of bodies with specific responsibilities – reviews for child protection or secure accommodation, panels for special education, care placement or adoption, and the courts. If the decisions of a particular body are likely to affect the care plan it is important that the plan is presented formally to that body before its deliberations are complete. Otherwise there is a risk of discontinuity in the process. Any substantial decision affecting the overall plan must prompt an immediate resumption of the planning process.

Local authorities should be reminded that all meetings at which aspects of the care plan are considered form subsidiary parts of the review; records of those meetings should be attached to the next review record. They should be reminded of their obligations to maintain accurate and continuous records (APC(G) 8(2); Ch. 2.81–3).

However, there will be no progress in this direction unless local authorities define very clearly the decision-making purpose of the statutory review, and, in particular, the remit of the chair or coordinator. Clear definitions at local level will help to focus attention on the review as a major forum, rather than a bureaucratic monitoring exercise.

A key problem emerging from the interviews with senior managers was the inconsistent supervision of reviews at this level: there seemed to be no formal mechanism by which senior managers were drawn to look closely at reviews. Part of the reason may be the confusion over which should be supervised – planning or reviewing? But a more significant reason may be the failure to define the decision-making remit of review chairs. Their role in decision making was not only problematic in the fieldwork study; the national survey of chairing arrangements identified it as a bone of contention within a number of systems leading to some conflicts between independent chairs and supervising team managers.

In some systems, the coordinator of a statutory review possesses the delegated authority of the principal officer responsible for the area (Kendrick and Mapstone, 1989). This may not be sufficient to prevent questioning of the chair's decisions. But it represents an advantage if it means the review is clearly seen as the executive planning process for the child rather than just a monitoring exercise which other decision makers can safely ignore. It also encourages principal area managers to take a close interest in review decisions, rather than seeing themselves as 'holding the ring' among various units competing for resources. However, if attitudes to delegation are too cautious, this may lead to undue delays while principal area managers ratify individual decisions made in their name.

> *Key point*: Local authorities should clarify the decision-making role of reviews in relation to other decision-making bodies and to the responsibilities of senior management.

Participation

Local authorities should be reminded of their specific duties to ensure the full participation of children and parents, in particular:

- to provide information for users and to help them understand it (Volume 3, Ch. 2.10, 2.47);
- to ensure that efforts are made to communicate with young children (Ch. 2.47);
- to give the same attention to the wishes and feelings of parents, regardless of whether the child is in care or accommodated under S.20 (Ch. 2.5, 2.12, 2.19);
- to notify children and parents of the results of reviews (RCC 7(3)).

Multidisciplinary working

In order to create structured and coordinated planning systems, local authorities should be made more keenly aware of their obligation to co-ordinate assessment and planning in conjunction with other agencies (Ch. 2.51–2, 2.54–5). Children's Services Plans offer an opportunity to bring greater clarity to local arrangements, as suggested by the relevant Guidance (Department of Health/DFEE, 1996).

The objective of improving educational achievements represents a good example of the challenge ahead. In 1994, a joint departmental circular on the education of children looked after by local authorities was issued, in order to promote higher standards of achievement. Recent joint work by Ofsted and SSI has identified some of the factors behind the current problems. It was noted that teachers received no training in the needs of looked-after children or multidisciplinary working (Ofsted/SSI, 1995). Moreover, the responsibilities of carers towards children's education were poorly defined. To address such difficulties, LEAs and local authorities will have to commit themselves to a new level of cooperation and investment in shared ways of working.

Key point: National policies on joint inter-agency working have to be translated into concrete initiatives at a local level.

Monitoring of reviews

The monitoring of reviews by local authorities is a more general task than the monitoring of previous decisions in an individual case. It also involves more than the supervision of individual reviews. Information about reviews must be collected which enables the local authority to identify shortfalls in the fulfilment of standard requirements. Apart from determining how frequently children's cases are reviewed, the monitoring process can help to provide data about the ways in which children and parents are consulted, the frequency with which they attend planning meetings, and so on. Once it is clear that reviews make major decisions, it is possible for data about the aggregate numbers of such decisions to be noted and classified. Using the LAC system, the outcomes of such decisions can also be traced. In addition to helping guarantee a standard of service to individuals, monitoring assists the local authority to identify trends which have general implications for the management of services for children. The significance of monitoring reviews will only be enhanced once local authorities are convinced that reviews represent the centrepiece of individual child care planning, with considerable implications for the management of services.

> *Key point*: The monitoring of reviews is intended to show whether children are receiving certain standards of service from the local authority as a whole and not simply from the individuals responsible for a child's care.

In the preceding discussion, a number of redefinitions have been suggested which are intended to bring planning and reviewing more closely together. Once the definition of planning is incorporated inside the review, it becomes less appropriate to speak of a 'planning and reviewing' system, just as it would now seem odd to refer to an 'assessment and planning' system. Perhaps we should be seeking another more all-encompassing term than 'review'. Certainly, the terms that we use have significant implications for our practice in dealing with the care of children. This is why a new statement of fundamentals would help to re-orient practice and, we hope, give fresh impetus to positive developments at a local level.

Bibliography

Ahmed, S, Cheetham, J and Small, J (1986) *Social Work with Black Children and their Families*. Batsford, in association with British Agencies for Adoption and Fostering

Arnstein, S (1969) 'A ladder of citizen participation', *Journal of American Institute of Planners*, 35, 4, 216–224

Bamford, F N and Wolkind, S N (1988) *The Physical and Mental Health of Children in Care: Research Needs*. ESRC. Two discussion papers

Batty, D and Robson, J. eds (1992) *Statutory Reviews in Practice. A Workbook*. British Agencies for Adoption and Fostering

Bebbington, A and Miles, J (1989) 'The background of children who enter local authority care', *British Journal of Social Work*, 19, 5

Birmingham City Council Social Services Department (1994) *The Language of the Children Act 1989. A Glossary for Interpreters and Translators*

Black, R (1992) *Orkney – A Place of Safety? The Story of the Orkney Child Abuse Case*. Canongate Press

Blaug, R (1995) 'Distortion of the face-to-face: communicative reason and social work practice', *British Journal of Social Work* 25, 423–439

Boddy, M and others (1995) *Socio-demographic Change and the Inner City*. HMSO

Booth, T (1988) *Developing Policy Research*. Gower

British Agencies for Adoption and Fostering (1995) *Statutory Reviews in Practice: A Scottish Supplement*

British Association of Social Workers (1983) *Evidence to House of Commons Social Services Committee Inquiry into Children in Care*. BASW

Bryman, A (1988) *Quantity and Quality in Social Research*. Unwin Hyman

Bullock, R, Little, M and Millham, S (1993) *Going Home. The Return of Children Separated from their Families*. Dartmouth

Bullock, R, Little, M and Millham, S (1994) 'The care careers of young people in youth treatment centres', *Social Services Research*, 2, 28–33

Cadman, M (1988) 'Patterns, policies and issues in child care reviews' *in* Freeman, I and Montgomery, S *(eds) Child Care: Monitoring practice. Research Highlights in Social Work, 17.* Jessica Kingsley

Challis, L (1991) 'Quality assurance in Social Services Departments – new wine in old bottles?', *Research, Policy and Planning*, 9, 1, 17–19

Cheetham, J, Fuller, R, McIvor, G and Petch, A (1992) *Evaluating Social Work Effectiveness.* Open University Press

The Children's Legal Centre (1984) *'It's my life not theirs'*

Cloke, P, Milbourne, P and Thomas, C (1994) *Lifestyles in Rural England.* Rural Development Commission

Cloke, P, Milbourne, P and Thomas, C (1995) 'Poverty in the countryside: out of sight and out of mind' *in* Philo, C *ed. Off the Map: The social geography of poverty in the UK.* Child Poverty Action Group

Cooper, P, Smith, C and Upton, G (1994) *Emotional and Behavioural Difficulties: Theory to Practice.* Routledge

Courtney, M (1993) 'Standardised outcome evaluation of child welfare services out-of-home care: problems and possibilities', *Children and Youth Services Review*, 15, 5, 349–371

Cullen, J and Hills, D (1996) *The role of random controlled trials in assessing effectiveness of services: a critical review.* Draft discussion document. Tavistock Institute

Department for Education (1994) *Pupils with Problems.* Circulars 8/94–13/94

Department of Health (1989) *The Care of Children: Principles and Practice in Regulations and Guidance.* HMSO

Department of Health (1990) *Consultation Paper No. 10. Reviews of Children's Cases. Arrangements for Placement of Children. Guidance and Regulations.* HMSO

Department of Health (1991a) *Patterns and Outcomes in Child Placement.* HMSO

Department of Health (1991b) *The Children Act 1989 Guidance and Regulations. Volume 3. Family Placements.* HMSO

Department of Health (1991c) *The Children Act 1989 Guidance and Regulations. Volume 4. Residential Care.* HMSO

Department of Health (1994) *Children Act Report 1993.* Cm 2584. HMSO

Department of Health (1995a) *Looking After Children: Good Parenting, Good Outcomes.* A set of materials. HMSO

Department of Health (1995b) *Respite Care: Series of short-term placements of children.* Local Authority Circular LAC (95) 14

Department of Health/Department of Education and Employment (1996) *Children's Services Planning: Guidance*

Department of Health and Social Security (1985) *Social Work Decisions in Child Care: Recent Research Findings and their Implications.* HMSO

Department of Health and Social Security/Welsh Office (1988) *Working Together: A guide to arrangements for inter-agency co-operation for the protection of children from abuse.* HMSO

Dewar, J (1995) 'The courts and local authority autonomy', *Child and Family Law Quarterly*, 7, 2, 15–25

Dingwall, R, Eekelaar, J and Murray, T (1995) *The Protection of Children.* Avebury

Doig, B and Littlewood, J. eds (1992) *Policy Evaluation. The Role of Social Research.* HMSO

Dolphin Project (1993) *Answering Back: A report by young people being looked after on the Children Act 1989.* Department of Social Work Studies, University of Southampton

Family Rights Group (1985) *Statutory Reviews of Children in Local Authority Care*

Farmer, E and Owen, M (1995) *Child Protection Practice: Private Risks and Public Remedies.* HMSO

Finch, J (1986) *Research and Policy: The uses of qualitative methods in social and educational research.* Falmer

Fisher, M and others (1986) *In and Out of Care: The experiences of children, parents and social workers.* Batsford, in association with British Agencies for Adoption and Fostering

Fitches, R (1994) 'Disability in the Bengali community', *Children UK*, 1, 12–13

Fletcher, B (1993) *Not Just A Name. The Views of Young People in Foster and Residential Care.* National Consumer Council/Who Cares? Trust

Fox, W (1988) *Parental participation in child care planning.* Social Work Monographs, University of East Anglia

Frost, N and Stein, M (1989) *The Politics of Child Welfare: Inequality, power and change.* Harvester Wheatsheaf

Gardner, R (1985) *Child Care Reviews.* National Children's Bureau

Gardner, R (1987a) 'Children's participation in care decisions', *Adoption and Fostering*, 11, 2, 12–14

Gardner, R (1987b) *Who Says? Choice and Control in Care.* National Children's Bureau

Gibbons, J and Bell, C (1994) 'Variation in operation of English child protection registers', *British Journal of Social Work*, 24, 701–714

Gibbons, J, Conroy, S and Bell, C (1995) *Operating the Child Protection System.* HMSO

Hallett, C (1995) *Interagency Coordination in Child Protection.* HMSO

Hallett, C and Birchall, E (1992) *Coordination and Child Protection: A review of the literature.* HMSO

Hamill, H (1996) *Family Group Conferences in Child Care Practice.* Social Work Monographs, University of East Anglia

Herman, J L, Morris, L L, and FitzGibbon, C T (1987) *Evaluator's Handbook*. Sage Publications

Hodgson, D (1988) 'Participation, not principles', *Social Services Insight*, 3, 30, 20–21

Hoinville, G, Jowell, R and others (1977) *Survey Research Practice*. Heinemann Educational Books

House of Commons (1984) *Second Report from the Social Services Committee. Children in Care, Volume 1*. HMSO

Howe, D (1992) 'Child abuse and the bureaucratisation of social work', *Sociological Review*, 40.3, 491–508

Howe, G (1983) 'The ecological approach to permanency planning: an interactionist perspective', *Child Welfare*, 57, 4, July/August, 291–301

Hughes, S (1992) 'Centre of attention', *Social Work Today*, 13 August

Jackson, S (1987) *The Education of Children in Care*. Bristol Papers in Applied Studies No. 1. The School of Applied Social Studies, University of Bristol

Jamieson, S (1995) 'The reviews of children in care: A Scottish perspective on policy and practice' *in Statutory Reviews in Practice: A Scottish Supplement*. British Agencies for Adoption and Fostering

Kelly, A (1996) *Introduction to the Scottish Children's Panel*. Waterside

Kelly, D and Warr, B. eds (1992) *Quality Counts. Achieving Quality in Social Care Services*. Whiting and Birch

Kelly, N and Milner, J (1996) 'Child protection decision-making', *Child Abuse Review,* 5, 2, 91–102

Kendrick, A and Mapstone, E (1989) 'The chairperson of child care reviews in Scotland. Implications for the role of reviews in the decision making process', *British Journal of Social Work*, 19, 277–289

Kendrick, A and Mapstone, E (1991) 'Who decides? Child care reviews in two social work departments', *Children and Society*, 5, 2, 165–181

Kohar, S 'Improving services for black families in Warwickshire' *in* Tunnard, J ed. (1994) *Family Group Conferences. A report commissioned by the Department of Health*. Family Rights Group

Krueger, R (1994) *Focus Groups: A Practical Guide for Applied Research* (Second edition). Sage

Levy, P and Goldstein, H (1984) *Tests in Education: A book of critical reviews*. Academic Press

Lewis, A (1992) 'An overview of research into participation in child protection work' *in* Thoburn, J ed. *Participation in Practice*. University of East Anglia

Lewis, A (1994) *Chairing Child Protection Conferences. An Exploration of Attitudes and Roles*. Avebury

Little, M and Gibbons, J (1993) 'Predicting the rate of children on the Child Protection Register', *Research Policy and Planning*, 10, 2, 15–18

London Borough of Brent (1985) *Report of the Panel of Inquiry into the circumstances surrounding the death of Jasmine Beckford: A Child in Trust*

Lupton, C, Barnard, S and Swall-Yarrington, M (1995) *Family Planning?: An evaluation of the Family Group Conference model.* University of Portsmouth

Macadam, M and Robinson, C (1995) *Balancing the Act: The impact of the Children Act 1989 on family link services for children with disabilities.* National Children's Bureau

Mallucio, A, Fein, E and Olmstead, K (1986) *Permanency Planning for Children. Concepts and methods.* Tavistock

Marsh, P (1994) 'Partnership, child protection and family group conferences – the New Zealand Children, Young Persons and their Families Act 1989', *Journal of Child Law*, 6, 3, 109–115

Marsh, P (1996) 'The development of FGCs in the UK – an overview' *in* Morris, K and Tunnard, J eds *Family Group Conferences: Messages from UK practice and research.* Family Rights Group

McDonnell, P and Aldgate, J (1984a) 'Review procedures for children in care', *Adoption and Fostering*, 8, 3, 47–51

McDonnell, P and Aldgate, J (1984b) 'An alternative approach to reviews', *Adoption and Fostering*, 8, 4, 47–51

McDonnell, P and Aldgate, J (1984c) *Reviews of Children in Care.* Department of Social and Administrative Studies, University of Oxford

Millham, S, Bullock, R, Hosie, K and Little, M (1986) *Lost in Care: The problems of maintaining links between children in care and their families.* Gower

Mohan, J (1995) 'Missing the Boat: poverty, debt and unemployment in the South East' *in* Philo, C ed. *Off the map: The social geography of poverty in the UK.* Child Poverty Action Group

Morris, K (1996) 'An introduction to Family Group Conferences' *in* Morris, K and Tunnard, J eds *Family Group Conferences: Messages from UK practice and research.* Family Rights Group

Morris, K and Tunnard, J eds (1996) *Family Group Conferences: Messages from UK practice and research.* Family Rights Group

Newell, P (1993) *The UN Convention and Children's Rights in the UK* (Second revised edition). National Children's Bureau

Ofsted/SSI (1995) *The Education of Children who are Looked After by Local Authorities.* Ofsted

Omond, P (1995) 'Involving young people – a positive choice' *in Statutory Reviews in Practice: A Scottish Supplement.* British Agencies for Adoption and Fostering

Owen, D (1994) 'Spatial variations in ethnic minority group populations in Great Britain', *Population Trends*, 78, Winter, 23–33

Owen, M (1992) *Social Justice and Children in Care.* Avebury

Packman, J and Jordan, B (1991) 'The Children Act: looking forward, looking back', *British Journal of Social Work*, 21, 4, 315–327

Packman, J, Randall, J and Jacques, N (1986) *Who Needs Care? Social Work Decisions About Children*. Blackwell

Parker, R, Ward, H, Jackson, S, Aldgate, J and Wedge, P eds (1991) *Looking After Children: Assessing Outcomes in Child Care*. HMSO

Parkinson, L (1992) 'Shared parental responsibility' *in* Batty, D and Robson, J eds *Statutory Reviews in Practice. A workbook*. British Agencies for Adoption and Fostering

Parton, N (1991) *Governing the Family: Child Care, Child Protection and the State*. Macmillan Education

Patton, M Q (1986) *Utilisation-focused Evaluation (Second edition)*. Sage Publications

Phillips, C, Palfrey, C and Thomas, P (1994) *Evaluating Health and Social Care*. Macmillan

Robbins, D (1990) *Child Care Policy: Putting it in Writing*. Social Services Inspectorate

Robinson, C, Minkes, J and Weston, C (1993) 'Room for improvement', *Community Care*, 974, 26–27

Rowe, J and Lambert, L (1973) *Children Who Wait: A study of children needing substitute families*. Association of British Adoption Agencies

Rowe, J, Hundleby, M and Garnett, L (1989) *Child Care Now: A survey of placement patterns*. BAAF Research Series 6

Shah, R (1995) *The Silent Minority. Children with Disabilities in Asian Families* (Second edition). National Children's Bureau

Sinclair, R (1984) *Decision-making in Statutory Reviews on Children in Care*. Gower

Sinclair, R and Grimshaw, R (1995) *Planning and Reviewing Under the Children Act: Shaping a framework for practice*. An interim report. National Children's Bureau

Sinclair, R and Grimshaw, R (1996) *Planning and Reviewing Under the Children Act*. Final research report for the Department of Health. National Children's Bureau (unpublished)

Sinclair, R, Garnett, L and Berridge, D (1995) *Social Work and Assessment with Adolescents*. National Children's Bureau

Smith, G and May, D (1980) 'Executing "decisions" in the children's hearings', *Sociology*, 14, 4, 581–601

Social Services Inspectorate (1989) *A Sense of Direction: Planning in Social Work with Children*. HMSO

Stein, M and Carey, K (1986) *Leaving Care*. Basil Blackwell

Stein, M and Ellis, S (1983a) *'Gizza say': Reviews and Young People in Care*. NAYPIC

Stein, M and Ellis, S (1983b) 'Wallflowers at their own reviews?', *Community Care*, 8 September

Swain, D (1995) 'Family group conferences in child care and protection and in youth justice in Aotearoa/New Zealand', *International Journal of Law and the Family*, 9, 155–207

Thoburn, J, Lewis, A and Shemmings, D (1995) *Paternalism or Partnership? Family Involvement in the Child Protection Process.* HMSO

Thorpe, D (1988) 'Career patterns in child care – implications for service', *British Journal of Social Work*, 18, 2, 137–153

Valentine, M (1994) 'The social worker as "bad object"', *British Journal of Social Work*, 24, 1, 71–86

Veitch, W (1995) 'Rights and the children's hearings system: the perceptions of five participant groups', *Children and Society*, 9, 3, 99–120

Vernon, J and Fruin, D (1986) *In Care: A study of social work decision making.* National Children's Bureau

Walton, M (1993) 'Regulation in child protection – policy failure?', *British Journal of Social Work*, 23, 2, 139–156

Ward, H ed. (1995) *Looking After Children: Research into Practice.* HMSO

Wassell, S and Wilson, D (1992) 'Preparing children and young people for reviews' *in* Batty, D and Robson, J eds *Statutory Reviews in Practice. A Workbook.* British Agencies for Adoption and Fostering

West, R (1994) *After the Deluge – Changing Roles and Responsibilities in the Primary School.* ATL Publications

Wheal, A and Sinclair, R (1995) *It's Your Meeting. A guide to help young people get the most from their reviews.* National Children's Bureau

Yin, R (1989) *Case Study Research. Design and Methods* (Revised edition). Sage

Index

Entries are arranged in letter-by-letter order (hyphens and spaces between words are ignored).